Studies in Church History

VOLUME I

Studies in Church History

VOLUME I

Papers read
at the first winter and summer meetings
of the
Ecclesiastical History Society

Edited by

C. W. DUGMORE D.D.
Professor of Ecclesiastical History in the
University of London

and

CHARLES DUGGAN B.A. Ph.D.
Reader in History, University of London
King's College

NELSON

THOMAS NELSON AND SONS LTD
36 Park Street London W1
Parkside Works Edinburgh 9
10 Warehouse Road Apapa Lagos
P.O. Box 25012 Nairobi

THOMAS NELSON (AUSTRALIA) LTD
597 Little Collins Street Melbourne

THOMAS NELSON AND SONS (AFRICA) (Pty) LTD
P.O. Box 9881 Johannesburg

THOMAS NELSON AND SONS (CANADA) LTD
81 Curlew Drive Don Mills Ontario

THOMAS NELSON AND SONS
Copewood and Davis Streets Camden 3, N.J.

SOCIÉTÉ FRANÇAISE D'ÉDITIONS NELSON
97 rue Monge Paris 5

———

First published 1964

Printed in Great Britain by
Thomas Nelson (Printers) Ltd, London and Edinburgh

Preface

This book contains the main papers (with two exceptions) and the shorter communications read by members of The Ecclesiastical History Society at its first winter and summer meetings in January and July 1962. The Society, founded in 1961 at a meeting at University of London King's College, whose objects are 'the furtherance of the study of Ecclesiastical History and the maintenance of relations between British ecclesiastical historians and scholars abroad,' includes members of all communions and of most of the British Universities. Its first President was Dom David Knowles, whose Presidential Address delivered at Peterhouse, Cambridge, in July 1962, on 'Recent Work on the Benedictine Rule' is here printed for the first time. Le Révérend Père Paul Grosjean, S.J., Bollandiste, had promised to read a paper on 'The origins of Irish Christianity—some problems and opinions,' but was prevented by illness and his place was taken at rather short notice by Fr Aubrey Gwynn, S.J., whose paper is included in this volume. Professor Dimitri Obolensky's paper on 'The Principles and Methods of Byzantine Foreign Policy' and the Reverend Professor W. O. Chadwick's paper on 'The Victorian Church and Public Money' had already been earmarked for publication elsewhere. It should perhaps be stressed that the authors of the studies in this volume had not originally prepared their work for publication and as a result of quite unexpected delays in the preparation of the book several authors have, in the meantime, developed their contributions further elsewhere. The editors wish to thank Dr Patrick Collinson of University of London King's College for his help in preparing the typescript for press. In view of the diversity of subjects dealt with in this book, it was decided that an index would serve no useful purpose.

A second volume containing the papers read at the winter and summer meetings of 1963 is in an advanced stage of preparation.

C. W. D.
C. D.

Abbreviations

AHR   *American Historical Review*, New York 1895–

CSEL   *Corpus Scriptorum Ecclesiasticorum Latinorum*, Vienna 1866–

DDC   *Dictionnaire de Droit Canonique*, ed. R. Naz, Paris 1935–

DNB   *Dictionary of National Biography*

DTC   *Dictionnaire de Théologie Catholique*, ed. A. Vacant, E. Mangenot and E. Amann, Paris 1903–1950

EHR   *English Historical Review*, London 1886–

HBS   Henry Bradshaw Society, 1891–

HMC   Historical Manuscripts Commission

JBL   *Journal of Biblical Literature*

JEH   *Journal of Ecclesiastical History*, London 1950–

MGH   *Monumenta Germaniae Historica*

PG   *Patrologia Graeca*, ed. J. P. Migne, Paris 1857–1866

PL   *Patrologia Latina*, ed. J. P. Migne, Paris 1844–1864

PRO   Public Record Office

RHE   *Revue d'Histoire Ecclésiastique*, Louvain 1900–

RS   Rolls Series

TLZ   *Theologische Literaturzeitung*, Leipzig 1876–

TRHS   *Transactions of the Royal Historical Society*

VCH   *Victoria County History*

ZRG   *Zeitschrift der Savigny-Stiftung für Rechtsgeschichte. Kanonistische Abteilung*, Weimar 1880–

Contents

Problems of the Church Historian   1
C. N. L. BROOKE

Arminianism and Laudianism in Seventeenth-Century England   20
T. M. PARKER

Some Recent Work on Early Benedictine History   35
M. D. KNOWLES, O.S.B.

The Irish Missal of Corpus Christi College, Oxford   47
AUBREY GWYNN, S.J.

Jews and Christians in the Constantinian Empire   69
JAMES PARKES

Reflections upon the study of the General Councils in the
Fifteenth Century   80
E. F. JACOB

The Gospel of Philip   98
R. MCL. WILSON

Augustine's Visit to Caesarea in 418   104
GERALD BONNER

What is *Mediana* Week?   114
GEOFFREY G. WILLIS

Donatism: the Last Phase   118
R. A. MARKUS

Birinus and the Church at Wing   127
ERIC FLETCHER, M.P.

Primitive Decretal Collections in the British Museum   132
CHARLES DUGGAN

The Archbishopric of Lichfield   145
C. J. GODFREY

Contents

The Letters of Pope Innocent III to Ireland 154
P. J. DUNNING, C.M.

Mixed Marriages in Byzantium in the Thirteenth Century 160
D. M. NICOL

Archbishop Pecham's Register 173
DECIMA L. DOUIE

Ely Diocesan Records 176
DOROTHY M. OWEN

Correspondence between England and the Council of
 Constance, 1414-18 184
C. M. D. CROWDER

The Beginnings of English Sabbatarianism 207
PATRICK COLLINSON

Peter Gunning, 1613-84: Scholar, Churchman, Controversialist 222
H. A. LLOYD JUKES

Oxford and the Origins of Liberal Catholicism in the
 Church of England 233
W. R. WARD

The Theology of Graduation: an Experiment in
 Training Colonial Clergy 253
PETER HINCHLIFF

Problems of the Church Historian

C. N. L. BROOKE

Professor of Mediaeval History, University of Liverpool

THE members of some newly formed academic societies peer forward into the future with a nice mixture of enthusiasm and uncertainty: enthusiasm for a subject in which they are so fanatically interested that they have dared to found yet another society; uncertainty whether the world at large will admit that the subject exists, whether it will be accorded proper academic respectability.[1] We share, I hope, this enthusiasm; but we have no grounds for uncertainty. It was the study of the Church's history, from within, which did more than anything else to lay the foundations for the critical study of historical sources, most notably in the work of Mabillon and the Maurists. The study of the Church's history, and most particularly the history of its founder, rocked the world in the nineteenth century, and played a large part in providing the intellectual grounds both for modern belief and for modern disbelief. The Church's history has, in the past, provided the *locus classicus* of

---

[1] This lecture was written for an occasion, and I have made no attempt to alter its character or to provide it with more than a skeleton of footnotes. Some historians dedicate almost the whole of their scholarly effort to the study of the Church; but I do not wish to confine the label 'Church historian' to these, nor would I count myself among them. By 'Church historian' I simply mean a historian who has more than a passing interest in the problems raised by the history of the Church. To some of these my selection of problems will appear arbitrary. I have certainly made no attempt to catalogue problems; and there are many scarcely touched on here, such as the problems of miracles and of the supernatural, on which large books can be (and have been) written.

Among recent general discussions, I have found special interest in the late Norman Sykes's *Man as Churchman*, Cambridge 1960, ch. 1.

I am grateful to A. & C. Black for permission to quote from Albert Schweitzer's *Quest of the Historical Jesus*, translated by W. Montgomery, and to Messrs Hodder & Stoughton for a similar permission to quote from Paul Sabatier's *Life of St Francis*, translated by L. S. Houghton.

My wife and Dr R. A. Markus kindly read this lecture at various stages, but neither is to be held responsible for its errors and idiosyncrasies.

I

the problem of historical bias: is it possible, the question has been asked times out of number, for historians of different persuasions to agree in the study of the early Church, or of the Reformation? The question is a real one; we cannot confidently say more than that they can, without much difficulty, talk the same language; that true scholars nowadays will not think of not talking the same language. And this fact reveals the extraordinary power of reconciliation which the study of the Church's history has had. It does not always reconcile; the common pursuit of truth did little to foster good relations between Coulton and Gasquet. But this spirit of reconciliation is clearly a feature of our age. It is part of a much larger movement, of which we are all witnesses. I have seen with my own eyes a Jesuit father give a public lecture in Winchester College; I have not seen, but millions of my fellow-countrymen have, Catholic and Anglican metropolitans sitting side by side in cosy amity in a television studio. We all know how limited, in terms of visible reunion, is the significance of these events; but the movement towards reunion among Protestant churches and towards better relations among all the sane branches of the Christian family is one of the striking historical phenomena of our age; and a movement (if I may strike a personal note) of hope and joy. Beyond doubt the study of the Church's history and the dominance of the historical outlook over the last century and a half have much to do with this.

The Church historian, then, works in a great tradition, inherits a discipline which has profoundly influenced the intellectual world in which we live, has proved itself capable of wielding both the axe and the olive branch. It is an old subject; and for this reason there are not wanting those who feel that it has had its day, and is ripe for Christian burial. There has been a reaction—in some circles a violent reaction—against the dominance of history over the study of theology. In this room and on this occasion, the study of the Church's history needs no defence, and I shall not waste your time proving what we all already know. We view the future of this subject with no uncertainty about its status and its value; yet I hope not without anxiety, self-questioning and surmise—for without these an academic subject is indeed dead, and scarcely deserves maimed rites, let alone a requiem. My purpose is to ask myself a few questions in your presence this morning; my hope, that you will help me at the end to answer them.

I wish to start by reading brief extracts from two of the most influential historical studies published in the generation before I was born—from Albert Schweitzer's *Quest of the Historical Jesus*, published in 1906, and from Paul Sabatier's *Life of St Francis of Assisi*, published, according to the title page of the first edition, in 1894, according to the bibliographers, in 1893. Schweitzer wrote:

It was not only each epoch that found its reflection in Jesus; each individual created Him in accordance with his own character. There is no historical task which so reveals a man's true self as the writing of a Life of Jesus. No vital force comes into the figure unless a man breathes into it all the hate or all the love of which he is capable. The stronger the love, or the stronger the hate, the more life-like is the figure which is produced. For hate as well as love can write a Life of Jesus, and the greatest of them are written with hate: that of Reimarus, the Wolfenbüttel Fragmentist, and that of David Friedrich Strauss. It was not so much hate of the Person of Jesus as of the supernatural nimbus with which it was so easy to surround Him, and with which He had in fact been surrounded. They were eager to picture Him as truly and purely human, to strip from Him the robes of splendour with which He had been apparelled, and clothe Him once more with the coarse garments in which He had walked in Galilee.

And their hate sharpened their historical insight. They advanced the study of the subject more than all the others put together.[1]

Schweitzer was born in Alsace, a German subject because of the Franco-Prussian war. Sabatier became a pastor in Strasbourg, and so an Alsatian by adoption; but his refusal to assume German nationality compelled him to spend most of his earlier career in his native Cevennes. In his Introduction he wrote:

When I began this page the sun was disappearing behind the ruins of the Castle of Crussol and the splendours of the sunset gave it a shining aureola; the light flooded everything, and you no longer saw anywhere the damage which wars had inflicted upon the old feudal manor. I looked, almost thinking I could perceive at the window the figure of the chatelaine. . . . Twilight has come, and now there is nothing up there but crumbling walls, a discrowned tower, nothing but ruins and rubbish, which seem to beg for pity.

It is the same with the landscapes of history. Narrow minds cannot accommodate themselves to these perpetual transformations: they want an objective history in which the author will study the people as a chemist studies a body.

Objective history is . . . a utopia. We create God in our own image, and

---

[1] English translation by W. Montgomery, 2nd ed., London 1911, 4f.

3

we impress the mark of our personality in places where we least expect to find it again.

But by dint of talking of the tribunal of history we have made most authors think that they owe to themselves and their readers definitive and irrevocable judgements.

But perhaps below the Areopagites, obliged by their functions to pronounce sentence, there is place at the famous tribunal for a simple spectator who has come in by accident. He has put together a *dossier*, and would like very simply to tell his neighbours his opinion. This . . . is not a history *ad probandum.* . . .

Francis's official historians . . . in general have done him ill-service. Their embellishments have hidden the real St Francis, who was, in fact, infinitely nobler than they have made him out to be. Ecclesiastical writers appear to make a great mistake in thus adorning the lives of their heroes, and only mentioning their edifying features. . . .

By such means the saints, perhaps, gain something in the respect of the superstitious; but their lives lose something of virtue and of communicable strength. Forgetting that they were men like ourselves, we no longer hear in our conscience the command 'Go and do likewise.'

It is, then, a work of piety to seek behind the legend for the history. Is it presumptuous to ask our readers to try to understand the thirteenth century and love St Francis? They will be amply rewarded for the effort, and will soon find an unexpected charm in these too meagre landscapes, these souls without bodies, these sick imaginations which will pass before their eyes. Love is the true key of history.[1]

We shall not, now, agree wholeheartedly with either statement; but in three ways these passages will help to introduce us to our theme. They remind us that the study of history is not something we can divorce from our own concerns and personalities; they remind us, none the less, of how much we may have in common in the study of history which is independent of our religious differences; and they remind us that not all historians brought up in the late-nineteenth century agreed with Acton and Bury that the historian is a judge or history a science, no less and no more.

If we ask, what is it which sets the Church historian's field apart from that of other historians; and further, what is it which separates history from all other branches of knowledge; what is the nature of the walls this society can build round its world?—then the first, the strict answer to these questions is a very simple one: nothing. History is not a separate compartment in the intellectual mansion,

[1] English translation by L. S. Houghton, London, 1926 edn., xxxi-xxxiv (slightly adapted).

4

nor an independent constellation in the academic firmament; nor is it a form of experience divorced from all others. Nor can we build any walls round our own particular province. The history of the Church is somehow related to the history of the Christian religion; but it is a religion which repudiates water-tight compartments, which claims to be concerned in all fields of human life, and in the world as a whole. Mr Christopher Hill has taught us that we cannot understand the English Church in the sixteenth and seventeenth centuries unless we study feoffees and impropriators.[1] St Francis not only insisted on poverty in his Order, but forbade his friars to handle coins, except in extreme emergency. How can we hope to understand this unless we know what money meant to a merchant's son in thirteenth-century Italy? The early heresies have their counterpart in the economic, social and political history of their time. All this is well known; so well known that we have seen a reaction, that we have in recent years been forcibly (and needfully) reminded that heresy is also an intellectual thing. Franciscan poverty is as unintelligible without the Gospels as it is without twelfth-century heresies and thirteenth-century trade; even the Anglican Church in the seventeenth century thought of other things than tithes and the road to promotion.

There are, then, no compartments in the study of Church history; and this raises the first of my problems. Church historians have a good record for avoiding parochialism, anyway parochialism in time; and this good record many of them still sustain. To take one example from many, the ease with which Professor Owen Chadwick passes from Cassian, via Bossuet, to Newman is a constant source of astonishment to me, and an example to us all. It is growing increasingly difficult: the periods of history and its various aspects grow increasingly specialised, and specialisation is to be welcomed as the condition of growth. Yet it must remain possible for the different specialities to fertilise one another. We cannot hope to be specialists in many fields, but we must at least be able to have a sympathetic understanding of what they are at, and what we may hope to learn from them.

This problem, acute enough in itself, is closely related to the wider problem of the relation of Church history to the whole world

[1] C. Hill, *Economic Problems of the Church from Archbishop Whitgift to the Long Parliament*, Oxford 1956.

of academic disciplines, above all to theology, and to the personal beliefs of Church historians. On this issue both Sabatier and Schweitzer were quite specific: the historian cannot be divorced from his personal beliefs; the true interest, the true value of his work, will be lost if he is. This is not a *carte blanche* for prejudice and bias. In Sabatier the critical spirit mingled with the romantic, as in his master Renan; in Strauss the critical and scientific spirit mingled with the philosophy of Hegel. A passionate desire to strip Our Lord or St Francis of the fog of conventional hagiography was a vital inspiration, which helped them both to be so drastic and so effective, and sustained Strauss in the pursuit of truth as he saw it, through a lifetime of bitterness and persecution. Sabatier lived in happier times. His book was put upon the Index, indeed; but he lived to enjoy in some measure the fruits of his own desire for reconciliation; he lived to proclaim that the originality of St Francis lay in his catholicism—not perhaps quite the catholicism of the pope who canonised him, but the word was not thoughtlessly used[1]; he lived to have friends and disciples of many communions and of none. I cherish the story told by A. G. Little of how he visited Sabatier in his parish in the Cevennes, and found him with the material symbols of his attempt to heal the religious feuds of the village in the form of two loaves; Sabatier had bought one from each of the bakers of the village—'pain protestant,' 'pain catholique.' [2] It is wrong, and useless, to divorce our work as historians from our beliefs; if we try to do so, we deceive ourselves.

This leads us at once to the central paradox of our Ecclesiastical History Society. The study of Church history depends for its success on men and women of widely different personality and belief finding in it a common interest, a sense of common purpose. It is not only that our Society is open to the Catholic, the Protestant, the Jew and the Agnostic—but the study of the Church's history would be less respectable, less valuable, less fruitful than it has been if it had not been so diverse in the past. Sabatier's love expresses very forcibly the need for the historian to sympathise with the subject he is studying; Strauss's hate the need for him not to swallow it whole. That measure of scepticism which is the condition

[1] P. Sabatier, 'L'originalité de S. François d'Assise', in *Franciscan Essays*, British Society of Franciscan Studies, I (1912), 1-17.
[2] A. G. Little, *Franciscan Papers, Lists and Documents*, Manchester 1943, 179f.

of all scientific enquiry must be mingled with other more human qualities, of love and hate, of like and dislike, before a balanced view of the past can be produced. All this sounds very personal, very subjective; yet it is this mingling of attitudes which is needed to give a cutting edge to our judgements, to enable us to penetrate to the heart of the problems we study. And it is the dialectic set up by this mingling of qualities and attitudes which has provided historians of widely different outlook with a sense that there is a common language which they can talk, common ground on which they can meet. In this sense the study of history, and of the Church's history, are distinct slices of human experience; not because they are separated from other kinds of experience by impenetrable barriers, but because they provide a meeting place, a space within which it is possible for scholars of very different outlooks—not to reconstruct a certain and irrefutable account of the past—but, quite simply, to agree.

This area of agreement is by no means a confined space; we meet in a large room. We meet in perfect security in it, sure that however our biases and prejudices may pull us (and, even more, our private quirks and vanities) we are safe from interference. We do not fear that the Protestant Truth Society may bring some of us to heel, or that the minions of the Rationalist Press Association or the Holy Inquisition will be spying on us. We trust one another. The common pursuit of historical truth gives us an instinctive respect and interest in each other's work, however specialised or obscure it may be.

Yet we do not live our lives wholly in this room; and for most of us the true significance of what we do here lies in its relation to our wider beliefs. The original charter of the University of Liverpool laid it down 'that no Theological teaching shall be given by or under the authority of the University but nothing contained in this Clause . . . shall in any way affect the power of the University to give teaching in the Semitic Languages Hellenistic Greek and Ecclesiastical History. . . .' Happily this clause became of no effect on 1 October 1961, and so it is no longer heretical to question whether the distinction between Theology and Ecclesiastical History is or can be a very precise one. The historian's field is the whole of the past; nothing in it is alien to him. Yet what he sees as significant in it, what he chooses to study, must depend on his present interests. It is these which often give direction, actuality to his studies; it is often a sense of relation between past and present which gives history its constant, chronic excitement. I say 'often' because it is quite false to confine interest in the past into any single channel; and the only quality which we should regard as wholly necessary is the pursuit of historical truth. Without that, history as we understand the term could not exist at all; without a lively sense of its present actuality, of its relevance, as the cant phrase has it, it would, for most of us, be only partly living.

We are sometimes told that all historians in the late-nineteenth century believed history to be a science, a fact-grubbing empirical science, with objective criteria, aiming to eliminate bias and diversity of view. It is true that notions akin to this were widely held; true too, that in their naive form they no longer command wide assent. Yet one pillar of this doctrine is still very widely accepted; and this bland generalisation about nineteenth-century historians is itself an example of it. Historians still feel a deep urge, an inescapable urge, to generalise; they feel it their duty, even in circumstances which are hardly congenial to generalisation. Is it or is it not true that religious changes and the rise of capitalism were closely connected? Was the fourteenth or the fifteenth or the eighteenth century less religious than those which had gone before? Do we ourselves live in a materialistic age? It is no doubt true that in this crude form most scholars have lost the temptation to generalise; that the discussion of the relations between religion and the rise of capitalism has passed out of this realm. But in less crude forms the idea that our main business is to make general statements is still very powerful. A generalisation is normally a judgement of quantity; it is obviously appropriate to certain aspects of social and economic history, where we have something like statistical information, and where quantitative analysis is valuable and interesting. Even in economic history, generalisation alone can never be the aim; in Church history its place must commonly be peripheral. Questions like the ones I asked just now are quite devoid of meaning.

Sabatier and Schweitzer may serve to remind us, then, that not all nineteenth-century historians believed history to be an objective science. They managed to be both profound students of advanced critical method and profoundly personal in their approach. And the same can be said of some of the greatest scholars of the age. A medievalist may be forgiven for citing the names of Maitland and Edmund Bishop.[1] Both were fascinated by the technical achievements, especially of German scholarship. But Maitland's scholarship was intensely personal, constantly inspired by a vision of the human mind, the concrete situation in which the absurdities of English law had lived and moved and had their being. Bishop was a great technician; one might even call him the Housman of medieval liturgical texts—and that analogy will serve to remind us that just as the editor of Manilius was also the author of the *Shropshire Lad*, so the religious quest of Edmund Bishop, often frustrated and always tortuous, lay behind the precise language and the rare technical subtlety of the great studies collected in *Liturgica Historica*.[2] Bishop had his faults; yet he remains one of the immortals; and it is his capacity to penetrate a religious situation, to see liturgical texts as the expression of a whole civilisation, without fog and without sentimentality, as much as his technical skill, which earned him this immortality.

The Church historian of the future, studying the roots of good feeling between the Christians of different communions, and especially among Christian intellectuals in the mid-twentieth century, will find the study of these four scholars of absorbing interest. He will see how the work of agnostics like Maitland, of liberal Protestants like Schweitzer and Sabatier, and Catholics like Bishop, combined to create the atmosphere of mid-twentieth century scholarship; and he will see that Bishop's theological views, and his insistence that Catholic liturgical scholars must not ignore non-Catholic liturgies, and, even more specifically, Sabatier's passionate desire to subdue Protestant and Catholic feuds, were not irrelevant to their place in this movement (even if he has also to recall that Bishop was an *eminence grise* in the condemnation of Anglican orders). It is the historian's task to generalise where he can; but he is often more concerned to analyse trends and ideas; especially the possible range of ideas. The fourteenth-century *Modus Tenendi Parliamentum*[3] propounded a view of the function of

---

[1] Maitland was not, of course, a Church historian in any narrow sense of the term, but clearly falls within my definition, above, p. 4.

[2] Oxford 1918; cf. N. Abercrombie, *The life and work of Edmund Bishop*, London 1959 (with a Foreword by Professor Knowles).

[3] See V. H. Galbraith, *Journal of the Warburg and Courtauld Institutes*, XVI (1953), 81-99.

2

the Commons in Parliament which would have been thought quite daring in the early seventeenth century. On this account some historians have written it off as hopelessly eccentric and of no significance. What is significant is that such views could be held in the fourteenth century. How widely they were held we have no means of knowing. Their practical influence was small. But the historian can too easily be enslaved by practical consequences: he only knows what happened, not what might have happened; and it is this enslavement which makes the range of opinion held by thinking men in any age so interesting. We are sometimes told that agnosticism and atheism (in the modern sense) were unknown in the Middle Ages; that all men believed, even if their beliefs were not orthodox. But Wolfram von Eschenbach in the early-thirteenth century wrote a large poem, the *Parzifal*, one of whose central themes is loss of faith—and his poem was widely read. He went on, furthermore, to write his *Willehalm*, in which he analysed, in trenchant fashion, the problem of the good heathen, his place in God's providence and his chances of salvation. He made it abundantly clear that the good heathen (in his view) has his place in God's providence. He never finished the poem, probably because his story had got to the point where one of his best heathen, Rennewart, was in danger of baptism. Wolfram was a Christian, and would have liked to see Rennewart baptised—but his baptism would have weakened the force of the problem: what difference would baptism make to a good heathen?[1] The attitudes here revealed were not perhaps common ones, but they are none the less interesting for that. They serve to remind us how wide intellectual horizons can be; how much more interesting it often is to analyse the variety of human thought and opinion than to amass generalisations of dubious validity.

Sabatier and Schweitzer introduced us to a variety of problems and difficulties on which the Church historian needs constantly to reflect. They have now, I think, served their turn, and I propose to make these problems somewhat more concrete by an exercise in historical fiction. State the case that a historian has it in mind to

---

[1] My knowledge of Wolfram I owe to Mr Hugh Sacker of University College, London, and to his unpublished doctoral thesis, 'The Tolerance Idea in Wolfram's Willehalm', Frankfurt-am-Main 1955. [See now also his *Introduction to Wolfram's Parzival*, Cambridge 1963.]

write a history of Christian marriage. He would find that he had many predecessors in the field, and that much important work had been done on many aspects of it[1]; yet he would also find that he had started a project of profound interest and relevance, and of almost insurmountable difficulty. The interest and the relevance need no underlining. In no age has the ideal of Christian marriage been so widely studied, or—within countries once Christian—so widely attacked. The Churches have asserted their views with much firmness, diversity and heat; and sometimes with charity too. There can be no doubt, to my mind, that charity is what is needed above all—charity towards one another's differences, and towards the non-Christian point of view. Nor can the study of the history of Christian marriage fail to arouse in the theologian or the lawyer a sense of humility, a realisation of the Church's failings and inadequacies. We need not take this too seriously: the Churches are young. Two thousand years may seem a long time in relation to recorded human history, but as a slice of the world's history, and of human experience, it is extremely short. None the less it is sufficiently long for us to learn many lessons from it, and not least the difficulty, the prevarication, the constant ambiguity of the Church's attitude to marriage. And if this teaches our theologians that the problems are not so easy as some of them think, it will have done good.

Study of the history of marriage is exceedingly difficult. It can never be divorced from current prejudice; it cannot, it should not be written without love or hate; it is no task for the Laodicean. Yet it is a task of extreme delicacy. The sacrament is performed by the parties themselves; in what it consists has never been clearly defined —and a theologian who tries to do so is guilty of interfering in matters which are not his concern. 'Those whom God hath joined

---

[1] The literature on the theology and law of marriage is especially copious; for the period with which I am here particularly concerned, see especially A. Esmein, *Le mariage en droit canonique*, 2 vols, revised ed. by R. Génestal, Paris 1929-35; J. Dauvillier, *Le mariage dans le droit classique de l'Eglise*, Paris 1933; and, more generally, A. L. Smith, *Church and State in the Middle Ages*, Oxford 1913, 57-100; provisional bibliographies may be found in the ecclesiastical and theological dictionaries. The only general survey of the whole subject in English known to me is G. H. Joyce, *Christian Marriage*, London 1933. From the point of view of social history, a particularly interesting example of recent studies is L. Stone's investigation of marriage in the English upper classes in the sixteenth and seventeenth centuries: 'Marriage among the English Nobility in the sixteenth and seventeenth centuries', in *Comparative Studies in Society and History*, III (1961), 182-206.

together let no man put asunder' is a proposition to which most Christians would say heartily, Amen; but no Church has ever claimed to know, when man had witnessed a ceremony of marriage, whether in every case God had joined the couple. This may seem at first sight mere casuistry, but a little reading in the case-law of the medieval Church (to take no other example) quickly shows that it is not. More important, no Christian has ever been able to evade St Paul's elaborate insistence that the union of husband and wife was the symbol of the union of Christ and his Church; an inspiration and a terror to those for whom the doctrine of Christian marriage lies near the centre of their faith. But that is not all that St Paul said on the subject. In the same passage in Ephesians he gave the husband Christ's role in the union, which has been taken by male commentators to imply male superiority; and in 1 Corinthians ch. 7 he shows a more ambiguous attitude to marriage, twisting and turning between a lofty view and one not so lofty in an attempt (if I have understood recent commentators aright) to save the institution in a chaos of conflicting opinions in the Corinthian church.

The historian of marriage would have to understand what biblical scholarship has to say about these and many other passages, and in every epoch which he studied the current interpretation of the Bible would have to be one of the starting points of his enquiry. Church history divorced from the Bible is meaningless. We all know, to give only one example, how the New Testament has ambushed the Churches time and time again—and broken the even flow of historical development—and in the history of marriage it is St Paul, in both moods, who has been particularly influential in directing the Church's course.

There is indeed a sense in which the history could be written as a commentary on 1 Corinthians ch. 7 and Ephesians ch. 5. But there is always a danger, if this is attempted, that the historian will discover the link between his own views and St Paul's, and assume that their common ground existed throughout the story. These passages have been open to the inspection of every Christian since the Epistles first circulated in the Church. But ideas on marriage have been as much influenced by the social background of the people and peoples who have been converted to Christianity as by St Paul, or Our Lord himself. Here we must return to our paradox. A living interest in the subject is vital if the history of marriage is to be a living work. But the historian will have from time to time quite self-consciously to un-think the present and to un-think St Paul. To help him, he has the copious literature on the Roman law of marriage, on Jewish ideas of marriage, and the more conjectural, but no less important, Germanic marriage customs. This context, indeed, should be widened by comparative study of the rich, almost fantastic, diversity of marriage customs and notions revealed by the social anthropologists. In his earlier passages, this will be primarily of comparative value to him, to stir his imagination and fertilise his ideas; but, later on, as the Christian churches expand over the whole known world, it becomes directly relevant. In a word, our historian has passed from being a biblical critic and expert in the history of exegesis to being an anthropologist. Nor is there any visible limit to the number of disciplines he must encounter. Marriage is related to theology and canon law, and he will need to use patristic scholarship, to understand the techniques of the scholastics, to capture the thought of the reformers, and so forth—and all this without becoming buried under the mountain of their works, or drowned in the rivers of ink which have flowed in their interpretation. When that is done, he will have some understanding of the idea of marriage; and history without ideas is a twilight subject. But marriage does not live wholly in the realm of theory; it is lived out in practice, in the dialectic of daily life, as some would say, in the Armageddon of daily life. And it is here that the problem of method becomes most acute; and to lend some precision to what I wish to say, I propose to concentrate now on a period about which I have myself some information, from the eleventh to the thirteenth centuries.

First of all, there is, needless to say, no sharp division between theory and practice; one of the most interesting realms is that which lies poised between—the realm of common assumptions, of ordinary attitudes, and of gossip; for this provides the link between the two. Here, then, is Walter Map, the late-twelfth-century satirist:

Pacuvius, weeping, said to his neighbour Arrius: 'Friend, I have a disastrous tree in my garden: my first wife hung herself on it, so did my second later on, and now my third has done the same.' Said Arrius: 'I wonder that after so many strokes of luck you find it in you to weep.' And again: 'Good gods, what expenses has that tree suspended for you!' And a third time: 'Friend, give me some cuttings of that tree to plant.'[1]

[1] *De nugis curialium*, IV, 3, trans. M. R. James, Cymmrodorion Record Series 1923, 166.

Map was a man of great learning, and this little story is a pastiche from Cicero, Quintilian and Aulus Gellius—improved, be it said, by a brilliant story-teller. He was writing in a well-worn tradition; his little tract, which pretends to dissuade a benighted friend who is engaged to be married from taking the fatal step, was very popular, and so skilful is its anti-feminine satire that in due course it was attributed to St Jerome.

This satire is still in the world of learned humour, and it reminds us how difficult it is to get in touch with the notions of married folk in an age when the majority of those who have left us a memorial, the educated clergy, were celibate, and the majority of the married laity illiterate. To make contact with the lady's point of view is even more difficult, if not impossible. We must start, as must every medievalist, with a confession of ignorance: the acreage of our ignorance enormously exceeds, and will always exceed, the area of possible knowledge.

What we can do, first of all, is to study the practice of marriage in high society from narratives in the chronicles, from the case-law, by constructing genealogies; and, so far as high society is concerned, we are comparatively well served by the evidence, because the pursuit of good marriages for their children was a favourite sport for the lay upper classes of Europe—perhaps after hunting and hawking, the most favoured sport of all. Kings like our own Henry II were well aware that a well-planned marriage conquered territory more effectively than armies, and the marriage game was played for the highest stakes. Children unborn were married off in imagination, babies betrothed in fact; and widows sometimes paid heavy fines to stay single or have a say in their own disposal. The one thing which seems rarely to have been considered was the happiness of the partners.

We should be wrong, however, to take this evidence entirely at its face value, just as we should be wrong to assume from the strictness of the law that marriage was a more stable institution in that age than in ours. The law of marriage was, indeed, in a somewhat chaotic state, though rapidly being developed in the twelfth century; annulment was common, death even commoner. Since the men's occupation was war, which was not without its dangers even then, it was no uncommon thing for an eligible lady to have three husbands. Since the lady's occupation was bearing children, which was not much less dangerous than war, it was no uncommon thing for a man to have two wives.[1] Few men were quite so ruthless in disposing of their wives as Henry VIII was later to be, but eleventh-century Celts and Vikings were still unused to monogamy; and the Church had the greatest difficulty in restricting divorce.

Yet we should be quite wrong to think that the upper classes of Europe in this age viewed marriage cynically. Great men might often be unfaithful to the marriage bed, but inheritance, in most legal systems, was strictly confined to legitimate heirs. William the Conqueror was a bastard; one of the very few to win a duchy, let alone a kingdom; he knew what bastardy meant, and was faithful to his wife. Among Henry I's comparatively few known acts of generosity was the acknowledgement of upwards of twenty illegitimate children—but it was his nephew who succeeded him.

If we wish to go further than this in penetrating the lay view, we can observe something of the detailed practices by reconstructing genealogical trees and tables of succession; above all, we can observe the close lien between marriage and property in every class. We can occasionally tell the story of a marriage in some detail. What we lack entirely is the sort of intimate picture of married life which sources from the seventeenth century onwards provide so copiously. I do not know of any case history which is really revealing, save that of Heloise and Abelard, between the ancient world and the fourteenth century.

In the down-to-earth letters of the Merchant of Prato and his wife we see a fourteenth-century marriage revealed with something of the subtlety and ambivalence of Shakespeare and the actuality of Tolstoy.[2] The marriage was not a happy one, though it grew warmer in later years; but that makes it all the more revealing of the strains and dangerous assumptions and ultimate strength of medieval marriage; and one would give much to have more such case

[1] As a sample, a rough count of the twelfth-century marriages recorded in vols. X, XI, XII (pts 1 and 2) of the revised ed. of the *Complete Peerage* produced the following figures: cases in which husband and wife are only known to have married once, 63; cases in which husband or wife or both are known to have married more than once, 55. In these 55 cases 18 husbands had two wives each, and one three; 31 wives had two husbands, 4 wives had three husbands and one four. The information relates solely to the baronial class; and even so, it is based on scanty indications, so that the number of second and third marriages may be seriously under-estimated.

[2] See Iris Origo, *The Merchant of Prato*, London 1957.

histories for earlier centuries. In their absence one has to rely, for the atmosphere of marriage, on the stray comments of chroniclers and letter writers and the gossip of satirists; and, above all, on the assumptions, ideals and aspirations revealed in secular literature. The twelfth century saw the rise of the romantic ideal, of the cult of courtly love. Whatever its origins it had from the first a religious and an irreligious element in it, just as it had a moral and an immoral face. It sanctified adultery; it also did much to humanise marriage. There is no world of experience in this period in which it is more dangerous to generalise, more necessary to analyse. It is a very delicate matter, inevitably, to decide how much relation there was between the world of courtly ideal and the world of courtly practice.[1] The difficulty is made substantially worse by the difficulty of interpreting the vernacular French literature of the twelfth century. There has been a singular reluctance among the literary critics until quite recently to treat the romances as serious works of literature.[2] This is especially true of the French critics. The Germans have served us better. We can at least be sure that Wolfram's fierce attack on courtly love as currently understood, his elaborate analysis of many kinds of love and friendship, and his idealisation of married love were meant to be taken seriously. How seriously they were taken by others we can never hope to know. But we shall be wise, on the one hand, not to wax too romantic about the code of chivalry, and, on the other hand, to take the vernacular literature of this age seriously: it is our one real contact with the minds of laymen.

The Church succeeded, by and large, in retaining control over the law of marriage and even extended the area of its control. Its law was ambiguous. In the Church's eyes marriage was tossed between the two traditions which had inspired the eleventh-century reformers—the development of sacramental doctrine, which enhanced the religious prestige of marriage, and the development of the ascetic

[1] It is, indeed, difficult to see any substantial effect of the romantic ideal on marriage customs before the nineteenth century, and on this ground it has been denied that marriage was affected at all by it in the Middle Ages. This is unduly sceptical, just as it is unduly sceptical to deny that medieval romances have something to teach us about medieval marriage. They have much to tell us, so long as we do not erect general theories out of them, and so long as we do not read them in the light of twentieth-century notions of romance; just as *Romeo and Juliet* has much to tell us of sixteenth-century notions of love and marriage, so long as we remember the same provisos.

[2] Cf. H. Sacker, *Germanic Review*, XXXVI (1961), 25f.

and celibate ideal, which made the married life seem to many fervent churchmen a second best, the life suitable for weaker vessels, the view expressed in 1 Corinthians: 'It is better to marry than to burn.' The ascetic ideal was in tune with many of the strongest forces in the Church of the time and made the twelfth century a golden age in the history of medieval monasticism. But it also provided fertile soil for one of the most dramatic developments of the age: the rise of the Cathar heresy in the mid- and late-twelfth century. With a suddenness very difficult to explain, the Cathar Churches, with an organised episcopate in France and Northern Italy, were able to challenge the monopoly of the Catholic Church in the west[1]; and it was the first time that the challenge had been really dangerous since the barbarian tribes had abandoned Arianism. The Cathars were dualists; they repudiated the world; they abominated procreation, which imprisoned more spirit in the evil world of matter. The Cathar *perfecti* maintained (on the whole) a very high standard of asceticism; their adherents lived more normal lives. But there is some evidence (though this has been disputed) that the Cathars preferred casual liaisons to marriage, which they regarded as organised vice.

But the Church did not forget its sacramental teaching. Already in the early twelfth century one voice had been raised to show the woman's point of view. It was a very personal, very striking viewpoint: but it was Heloise's own view of the secret and illegal match which had united her, fleetingly, to Abelard, which elicited from the warm heart and the courtly pen of Peter the Venerable of Cluny one of the very few descriptions of marriage from this age which seem to measure up to the standard set in Ephesians v.[2] The Church responded to the challenge of the Cathars by Crusade and Inquisition. But it was not persecution alone which destroyed the Cathar Church. The Catholic Church was recovering from the repudiation of man and the world which had threatened its doctrine in earlier centuries; its theology was becoming more humane; St Francis himself combined an extreme personal asceticism with a passionate delight in the world as God's world. It has been said that Francis's

[1] See A. Borst, *Die Katharer*, Stuttgart 1953, especially 208-13, 231-9 (on the organisation of the Cathar bishoprics).

[2] Peter the Venerable, *Ep.* 4:21 (PL, CLXXXIX, 346-53, esp. 352); on the marriage, cf. *Cambridge Historical Journal*, XII (1956), 4 and *n*.

interest in animals was derived from the Cathar doctrine that animals had souls.[1] The connection is the exact reverse: to the Cathars the material world was the symbol of Satan; to Francis it was the symbol of God. His delight in the world was not due to nature mysticism; he preached to the birds and called the sun, moon, fire, water and even death his brothers and sisters, to emphasise to his hearers that all these things were of God's making, and in their nature good. To the history of marriage Francis contributed little directly, but his notions could not fail to fertilise the soil for the growth of an ideal which incorporated the idea of two human beings dedicating themselves to one another in perfect obedience, and in the hope (if they are so fortunate) that they may be able to share in God's creative work.

Between the eleventh and thirteenth centuries our material forbids us to make generalisations.[2] But it allows us to observe something of the range of ideas, and of the range of practices—not to produce average ages of marriage, or to deduce shifts in size of family, but examples to illustrate and illuminate the forces at work. There is much analysis that remains to be done; and from it the historian of society would learn a great deal of which he is profoundly ignorant at present; the historian of politics, of kings and courts, would learn something, too, of the forces at work behind the marriage game. The historian of marriage cuts as it were a section through the other historical approaches and reveals much that is familiar in an unfamiliar light. He proceeds by analysis, not by generalisation; he never ceases to confess his ignorance; but in these two ways he is only doing what every medievalist must do. His worst headache is that he must make some acquaintance with every historical discipline, and with some which are not normally thought of as historical. He cannot be an expert, a specialist, in all; what he needs is imaginative sympathy and understanding of what each can do, and a friend in each who is an expert to help him on his way. This is the essential nature of historical collaboration. Some tasks can be done by teams and seminars; many can not. We need to devise a type of co-operation in which we understand each others'

[1] Sir Steven Runciman, *The Medieval Manichee*, London 1947, 129, 174.

[2] L. Stone, art.cit., is an interesting example of what can be done in a period for which some generalisation is beginning to be possible, i.e. the sixteenth and seventeenth centuries.

problems and can help in them, while remaining specialists in our own particular fields. That is the special justification for this kind of society: not to sanctify a schism, to divide 'Church historians' from 'secular historians'; but to provide a meeting place in which historians of every feather may meet to exchange ideas about the themes and interests which are involved in studying the history of the Christian Church.

Arminianism and Laudianism
in Seventeenth-Century England

T. M. PARKER

*Fellow, Chaplain and Praelector in Theology and Modern History,
University College, Oxford*

I T is, I suppose, an indication of the general bewilderment caused
by the apparently abrupt appearance of a new and strangely
named religious party in the England of James I, the Arminian,
which makes one's pupils occasionally describe the High Churchmen of those days as 'Armenians'. It is a pardonable mistake. They
are vaguely aware that many have regarded Arminianism as a
theological heresy. They have no doubt also heard rumours that the
Armenians are regarded by most of the rest of Christendom as
heretical. Hence the natural confusion.

The error, however, raises once more in one's mind the haunting
question of just how much substance there was in the labelling as
Arminian of those later to be called Laudians. Clearly the name was
not self-chosen, any more than the terms Puritan or Lollard were
willingly adopted by those to whom they were applied. 'I am no
more an Arminian,' said Richard Montagu in *Appello Caesarem*,
'than my traducers are Gomarian.' [1] Not only did he refuse the
name; he declared flatly that he had never read an Arminian book.
Such a disclaimer does not of itself disprove the aptness of the label,
but it does at least show that Montagu and his friends were not
prepared to accept the identification. If so, why not?

In order to approach the problem let us first remind ourselves
briefly of the history of the Arminian controversy. Its eponymous
hero, Jakob Hermandszoon, was born in 1560 at Oudewater, on the
Yssel in South Holland, the son of a cutler, Hermand Jakobszoon.
Apparently in this part of the world a custom akin to the Welsh
system of patronymics was usual, for the young Jakob, named

[1] Quoted by A. W. Harrison, *Arminianism*, London 1937, 130.

presumably after his grandfather, was known as 'Hermandszoon'. It is this name, Latinised in accordance with continental humanist practice, which gives 'Arminius'. (There seems to be no conscious association of the name with that of the Teutonic patriot leader who had destroyed the legions of Augustus, Arminius the Cheruschan.) Left early an orphan, the young Arminius was adopted by Peter Bertius, Calvinist pastor of Rotterdam. After education at Geneva under Beza (with an interval at Basle) he was ordained a minister in Amsterdam in 1588, the year of the Spanish Armada. His ordination perhaps took place during that August, the very month in which the Armada was being defeated.[1]

A call to ministry in critical days is perhaps symbolical of the whole career of Arminius, who up to his death in 1609 was *signum cui contradicetur* and, like Cornelius Jansen, even more of a name of discord posthumously. Already at Amsterdam he had fallen under suspicion, in his exposition of the Epistle to the Romans, of drifting away from the strict Calvinist supralapsarian tradition, which held that God's decrees of election and reprobation were formed without regard to the subsequent decree that Adam should fall, and indeed were logically prior to the decision to create man. Arminius was in fact turning against this view, although he did not publish his opinions. It was his appointment in 1602 to a chair of theology at Leyden which started more open controversy.[2] Already the senior professor there, Francis Gomar (usually known as Gomarus), and others suspected him, and the civil authorities of Amsterdam agreed to release him from his ministerial charge only if he could satisfy Gomarus of his orthodoxy. This he did, to the extent of clearing himself from imputations of Pelagianism or Socinianism, and so was able to take up his chair in 1603, the year of James I's accession in England. But nevertheless trouble at once developed between the

[1] Harrison (op. cit. 15) gives the date of Arminius's ordination as 11 August 1588, 'the day before Communion Sunday,' a date repeated from his earlier book, *The Beginnings of Arminianism to the Synod of Dort*, London 1926, 11. But 11 August was not a Saturday in 1588, either according to Old Style or New Style, so this is impossible. He has in fact misunderstood the clear statement of Arminius's biographer, Brandt, who says that Arminius was invited by the consistory of Amsterdam to accept ordination on 11 August, but was ordained later *die quodam Saturni pridieque ante coenae dominicae celebrationem.* (*Historia vitae Jacobi Arminii auctore Casparo Brantio,* ed. I. L. Moshemius, Brunswick 1725, 19. The passage is quite correctly translated by John Guthrie, A. M., *The Life of James Arminius, D.D., trs. from the Latin of Caspar Brandt,* London 1854, 31.)

[2] Harrison, *Arminianism,* 84.

two professors—a not unusual academic situation and, also characteristically, caused not solely by high matters of doctrine, but because Gomarus regarded the New Testament as his peculiar province and objected to Arminius's citing it in his lectures; he ought not to stray outside the Old Covenant. With time the dispute became less a university squabble than an issue which divided the whole Dutch Reformed Church and so led to a demand for a national synod for its settlement. Before this could meet Arminius was dead. The Synod of Dort did not take place until 1618, by which time the widening ripples of the quarrel in the Netherlands had disturbed the whole Calvinist world and Dort became in fact a Calvinist General Council. In addition to the eighteen lay deputies, thirty-seven ministers, nineteen elders and five professors from the United Provinces, there were present twenty-six foreign divines, making up a total membership of one hundred and five. From England came George Carleton, bishop of Llandaff; Joseph Hall, dean of Worcester; John Davenant, Lady Margaret professor of divinity at Cambridge; and Samuel Ward, archdeacon of Taunton; in addition, John Hales, chaplain to the English ambassador at the Hague, later to be professor of Greek at Oxford, held a watching brief and reported the proceedings to his master. Geneva, the Calvinist Rome, was represented, as were the German Calvinists. From France, the chosen delegates were not permitted by the king (oddly identified by J. T. McNeill[1] as Louis XIV, who did not come to the throne until 1643) to attend, but Scotland had an equivocal representative in Walter Balcanquhall the younger, King James's personal choice and apparently no great friend to rigid Calvinism.[2]

[1] J. T. McNeill, *The History and Character of Calvinism*, New York 1954, 265.

[2] He was the son of Walter Balcanquhall (1548-1616), the presbyterian minister, who was one of the most prominent opponents of James VI on the question of episcopacy and was publicly rebuked by the king in St Giles, Edinburgh, in 1586. Walter the younger was born about that year and died in 1645. After taking his M.A. at Edinburgh in 1609, he significantly migrated to Oxford, where he proceeded B.D. and became a fellow of Pembroke in 1611. Before the Synod of Dort the university conferred on him the D.D. degree. He was a royal chaplain, became master of the Savoy in 1617, dean of Rochester in 1625 and dean of Durham in 1639. In 1638 he returned to Scotland as chaplain to the marquis of Hamilton, Charles I's royal commissioner, and aroused great hatred as a prominent supporter of Charles's ecclesiastical policy which had led to the Bishops War; in 1641 he was among those denounced by the Scottish Parliament as 'incendiaries'. He suffered much in the royalist cause and died in Wales. So he was very much an Anglicanised Scot.

Once again let us notice coincidences of dates. In 1617 James VI had revisited his northern kingdom for the first time since he became also James I of England in 1603. In the interval he had been busily completing the policy, begun before his accession to England, of reintroducing episcopacy into the Scottish Kirk and now was beginning to assimilate it to the English Church liturgically as well. After his return to England and about a month before the meeting of the Synod of Dort, the Privy Council ratified the acts of the General Assembly of Perth, held that August, and so made compulsory the observance of Christmas, Easter and other festivals, private baptism when necessary, confirmation, private communion of the sick and kneeling at communion. James, therefore, was not likely just then to favour the association of Scots with their fellow-Calvinists abroad and, whatever his dislike of Arminianism, preferred to be represented at Dort by Anglican divines. Nor are other coincidences that year without significance. On 23 May 1618 occurred the 'Defenestration of Prague,' the throwing from the windows of the Hradschin Palace of the two Catholic members of the Estates, Martinek and Slavata, an action which precipitated the Bohemian revolt against the Empire and so the outbreak of the Thirty Years War. On 29 October, less than a month before the Synod opened, James I executed Sir Walter Raleigh, a sacrifice to the friendship with Spain which he was cultivating. So the Synod of Dort was held at a time regarded by Continental Protestants and English Puritans alike as fateful for the protestant cause in Europe.

It might be concluded from what has just been said of James I that he would be found upon the Arminian side in the Synod. Nothing could be further from the truth. In 1610 he had indeed advised silence upon the points at issue, with the characteristic remark that he himself, although he had studied the matter deeply, could not make up his mind about it. 'My Lords the States would therefore do well to order their doctors and teachers to be silent upon this topic.' [1] Where the author of the *Basilikon Doron* was brought to a standstill, how could mere professional theologians go further? But James was none the less active in Dutch theological controversies. Vorstius (Konrad von der Vorst), the Rhineland convert from Catholicism, had published in 1610 his treatise on God

[1] D. Harris Wilson, *King James VI and I*, London 1958, 399 f.

which was alleged to diminish the divine attributes. James, who had once declared that, just as it was impious to dispute what God could do, so it was impious to discuss the limits of royal power,[1] could not look with indifference upon this reputed constitutionalising of his divine ally. So he demanded nothing less than the stake for Vorstius, who was being proposed as a successor to the recently deceased Arminius at Leyden. In the end a curious compromise was reached in 1612 between the States of Holland and West Friesland by which Vorstius received the chair and its emoluments, but was debarred from actually lecturing. So he remained, compelled to live at Gouda, away from Leyden, until after the Synod of Dort when he was dismissed from his chair and expelled. James had pressed for his dismissal earlier and in 1612 published the correspondence with the Netherlands in which he had repeatedly attacked the heretic, as he considered him.[2] And from 1617 onwards James was constantly urging the States-General, through his ambassador, Carleton, to call a Synod.[3] He was in fact one of its chief begetters and afterwards approved its condemnation of the Arminians.

It is not altogether easy, however, to believe that James's sympathies were wholly controlled by theological considerations, or that he, who had revolted so far against the Calvinist church polity he had known and fought in Scotland, was deeply attached to Calvinist views of predestination because of their origin. One possible source of his zeal has already been mentioned, namely the view that divine and royal prerogatives were closely connected. 'No bishop, no king' was a maxim which largely determined James's attitude to episcopacy; 'no absolute God, no absolute king' might well be his understanding of the Arminian dispute. But there were even more immediate political considerations at stake. For the theological schism in the Netherlands coincided with a political schism between the republican John of Oldenbarnevelt, advocate of Holland since 1586, and Maurice, count of Nassau and second son of William the Silent, stadtholder of Holland and Zealand since 1585, and of Utrecht, Overysel and Gelderland since 1590. From 1600 onwards Oldenbarnevelt, in opposition to Maurice, who was also captain general and admiral of the United Provinces, began to work for peace with Spain, with whom he concluded a truce in 1609,

---

[1] J. R. Tanner, *Constitutional Documents of the Reign of James I*, Cambridge 1930, 17.
[2] Harrison, op. cit. 54 ff., Wilson, op. cit. 240. [3] Harrison, op. cit. 73 f.

so ending, in effect, the War of Dutch Independence. Since in the theological quarrel the advocate took the side of Arminius, it was not too difficult to represent both him and his Arminian friends as crypto-papists, watering down pure Calvinism and seeking friendship with the Spanish Antichrist. On the eve of the synod the quarrel between advocate and stadtholder had reached the verge of civil war. On 5 August 1617 Oldenbarnevelt persuaded the States of Holland to pass the 'Sharp Resolution,' by which towns might raise a local militia which should take an oath of allegiance to the States, instead of to Prince Maurice. This naturally aroused the prince's opposition. He gained support, militarily and politically, and by July 1618, in addition to moving against the Arminian or 'Remonstrant' party, he had managed to suppress the new militia, which was dissolved by the States-General. Next month he had Oldenbarnevelt and others arrested and, in May 1619, after the conclusion of the Synod of Dort, the advocate was sentenced to death.

Like many other theological disputes, such as, for example, Iconoclasm, Arminianism was therefore bound up with political issues, constitutional questions and matters of foreign policy and, like them, its fate was determined as much by political events as by weight of argument. Indeed, it may be claimed, as by the distinguished Dutch historian, Pieter Geyl, that:

Pursued to their logical extremes, the two principles led to two completely different worlds of ideas. On the one side there were those who sacrificed all humanity to the dizzy edifice erected by Calvin to the honour of God. With these nothing counted save the eternal decree whereby God had lifted them, unworthy as they were, from out the universal perdition of the human race. In the face of haters and seducers they clung to the conviction that, no matter what they did, they could not fall lastingly from grace, nor anything deprive them of salvation. For them and for the Reformed Church alone Christ had died and the Republic of the Seven Netherlands been delivered out of Spanish chains, for so it had pleased God to decree for all eternity. As against that, the others were unwilling to ascribe that certain power for good, which they too felt within themselves, so exclusively to an arbitrary working of God's will; and the smallest encroachment which they ('contrary to Christ's honour') allowed themselves in that direction was like a door wide open to the whole world of mankind outside the little community of their little Church, to love joy and beauty.[1]

[1] Pieter Geyl, *The Netherlands in the Seventeenth Century, Part I, 1609-1648*, London 1961, 43 f.

With all this in mind let us turn back to England and pursue our search for the relationship between Arminianism and Laudianism. Here one preliminary point stands out beyond dispute, namely that the major issues in the Arminian dispute had been fought out in England before the name of Arminius was known and long before the Arminian controversy became acute. The point was noticed by Principal A. W. Harrison, writing in 1937:

Hooker at Oxford, Andrewes and Overall at Cambridge, must be regarded as the representatives of the new school of thought that was alive in England before Arminius began to lecture at Leyden.[1]

More recently Dr H. C. Porter of Cambridge, in his *Reformation and Reaction in Tudor Cambridge*, has brought this out very clearly in his detailed analysis of the disputes about the Calvinist doctrine of grace which began in Cambridge as early as the 1580s. Of Bishop Overall's struggle against Calvinism when regius professor at Cambridge, Dr Porter writes interestingly:

The Synod of Dort (on the left bank of the Old Meuse, about fifteen miles south-east of Rotterdam) began in November 1618. The canons were promulgated in the following May; the month in which Bishop Overall died at Norwich. Of the six Englishmen who attended the synod officially, four were Cambridge men: Joseph Hall, Dean of Worcester and sometime Fellow of Emmanuel, who retired after a short time because of ill health; Dr Thomas Goad, sometime Fellow of King's, chaplain to Archbishop Abbot, and son of the Provost Roger Goad who had crossed swords with Baro and Overall: he replaced Joseph Hall; Dr Sam Ward, Master of Sidney Sussex, who had once confided to his undergraduate diary his sorrow at the deaths first of Whitaker, then of Perkins; and Dr John Davenant, President of Queens', who had succeeded Playfere as Lady Margaret Professor in 1609, and whose Cambridge lectures 'in which he clearly confuted the blasphemies of Arminius, Bertius, and the rest of the rabble of Jesuited Anabaptists', had been greatly admired in 1618 by the young Symonds D'Ewes of St John's. The four men must have been quite at home in Dordrecht. The issues there discussed were those which had been debated in Cambridge in the later 1590's and which had been causing argument in the Church of England since the early 1580's.[2]

[1] Harrison, op. cit. 123.
[2] H. C. Porter, *Reformation and Reaction in Tudor Cambridge*, Cambridge 1958, 409.

It is interesting to notice that Overall, who lived to see the Arminian controversy, regarded the Church of England as being neither Arminian nor Gomarist but as holding the *via media* between them, and he claimed to base his arguments upon the Prayer Book and Articles.[1] His view was that the controversy within the Church of England had not even been set within the precise lines followed in Holland. His opinion is borne out by the fact, well established by Dr Porter, that Whitgift's notorious Lambeth Articles of 1595, resulting from the conference he held at his palace that November, were in fact mediatory. They used to be thought of as a High Calvinist manifesto. Indeed they were unwelcome to many anti-Calvinists, and, when Dr Reynolds, at the Hampton Court Conference of 1604, wanted them to be added to the Thirty-nine Articles, the proposal was defeated largely by the influence of Bancroft and Overall.[2] But really to understand their bearing one must read them side by side with the propositions of Dr William Whitaker, master of St John's, Cambridge, and regius professor of Divinity, of which the Lambeth Articles are an amended version, revised by Whitgift himself and, as Dr Porter says:

All the changes are in the direction of making the original draft less uncompromising and more scriptural.[3]

When we remember that the controversy leading up to the Lambeth Articles had been begun by a sermon of William Barrett, chaplain of Gonville and Caius, which denied the Calvinist doctrine of assurance, asserted that the decree of reprobation was caused by God's foreknowledge of sin, and made a direct attack upon Calvin, this is the more remarkable.[4] Yet Whitgift, before he became archbishop, had made it clear that he regarded Calvin as fallible, in fact sometimes a misinterpreter of Scripture and, in connection with Barrett's case, Whitgift, then archbishop, declared that he knew of no article of religion which forbade criticism of Calvin, Beza or Peter Martyr. 'Much less,' he went on, 'do I know any cause why men should be so violently dealt with withal for it, or termed ungodly, popish, impudent: for the doctrine of the Church of

[1] Ibid. 411 f.
[2] Ibid. 405 f.
[3] Ibid. 367.
[4] Ibid. 344.

England doth in no respect depend upon them.'[1] Even in Elizabeth's day what might be termed Arminianism by anticipation was not regarded by all in authority as wholly heterodox.

Indeed, we shall never understand this issue if our viewpoint is too narrow either in time or space. It is extraordinary how few seem to reflect that on the issues of grace and predestination in the sixteenth and seventeenth centuries the ordinary denominational boundaries, as they were then being established, were crossed. Thus, despite the predestinarianism of Luther and his doctrine of the servile will, the Lutheran Formula of Concord of 1577 affirmed that God willed all men to be saved, taught that God's foresight of our unbelief is the cause of reprobation and stigmatised the view that reprobation is arbitrary as 'false, horrid and blasphemous'; to some Puritans, the Lutherans were more than suspect on this very point.[2] Moreover, side by side with the controversies on grace in the Protestant camp, were disputes no less heated within the Catholic fold on the same topic. The later sixteenth century saw the growth and condemnation of Baianism at Louvain and with the turn of the century came the long drawn out disputes between Dominican and Jesuit theologies discussed at Rome in the Congregation *de auxiliis*. Just round the corner in the wings waited the still more formidable figure of Jansenism.

It would indeed be difficult to find a time, from the days of St Augustine onwards, when grace, freewill and predestination were *not* matters of dispute in Western Christendom. The names of the Semi-Pelagians, Gottschalk and St Bernard recall arguments in the Dark and earlier Middle Ages. The fourteenth century saw endless debates on these subjects, which indeed occupied a disproportionate amount of attention in the minds of later medieval theologians; the only difference between these controversies and those of the Reformation age lies in the fact that they were mainly confined to the academic schools, to which in fact many Anglican divines of the sixteenth and seventeenth centuries maintained that they would be better restricted.[3]

---

[1] Ibid. 350 f.

[2] 'Formula Concordiae, Epitome xi,' in *Die Bekenntnisschriften der evangelisch-lutherischen Kirche*, 3, verbesserte Aufl., Göttingen 1956, 821. Cf. Porter, op. cit. 282 f.

[3] Porter, op. cit. 387 f.

It is interesting to find even the Calvinist Whitaker appealing both to medieval schoolmen and to St John of Damascus when he writes to Whitgift about the Barrett case. Peter Baro, the French-born Lady Margaret professor at Cambridge from 1574 to 1596, distinguished his own view of predestination both from those of Calvin, Beza and the mature Augustine (namely absolute pre-destination) and from those of Zanchius, St Augustine in his middle period and Bellarmine (the sublapsarian view), holding instead, with Melanchthon, the early Fathers and the young Augustine, predestination *ex praevisis meritis*. It can be seen at once how little his distinctions either follow the denominational lines of his own day or show an indiscriminate following of the Fathers.[1] In no dissimilar way, during the Arminian dispute, Francis Junius of Leyden, corresponding with Arminius himself, divided Predestinarians into Calvinist supralapsarians, Aquinas and the Thomist school (who hold that the divine decrees relate to man as created) and Augustine and his followers, who consider that the decrees relate to fallen man.[2] These controversialists are well aware that they are taking part in perennial arguments.

It is, therefore, unnecessary to look for an Arminian invasion of England, or indeed for any foreign influence, in order to explain the theology of grace characteristic of the anti-Puritan Jacobean and Caroline Anglicans, in so far even as they agree—and they are not all of one mind. One may easily believe Montagu's assertion that he had never read the Arminians. At most the word 'Arminian', when applied to such men, can mean that they recognised in Arminius an ally. On one man, indeed, he did have a converting effect. John Hales, the English ambassador's observer at Dort, went there a Calvinist and returned otherwise-minded. As he said, whilst listening to Episcopius's defence of the universality of the salvific will of God, he changed his views and 'bade John Calvin good-night.'[3]

It would be fascinating, did time permit, to follow out many lines of thought suggested by all this. It is noteworthy, for example, that much of the reaction to doctrinaire Calvinism can be traced to

---

[1] Harrison, op. cit. 20.
[2] On the English disputes see Mark H. Curtis, *Oxford and Cambridge in Transition, 1558-1642*, Oxford 1959, 211 ff.
[3] Harrison, op. cit. 90.

the spread of patristic studies in England, and the consequent move away from the forensic approach to grace and salvation which had characterised most Reformation teaching. Harrison rightly draws attention to the patristic learning of Andrewes, exemplified in his seventeen Christmas sermons at court, so like those of St Leo in the emphasis on the redemption of our nature by the Incarnation.[1] The influence of Christology is no less obvious in Hooker. It is fair, too, to say that Calvin himself set predestination in a Christological context, a fact which was too easily forgotten by some of his admirers. It is significant that Andrewes, in his comment upon Article II of the Lambeth Articles, thought that the words 'in Christ' should be added to the assertion that God's will is the cause of predestination, for, as he pointed out, the moderns concentrated upon God's absolute act and almost ignored the work of Christ.[2] What was happening—and the Arminian protest was but one symptom of a general trend—was that the hypnotic influence of the greater reformers was waning as many came to see them less as giants than as individual Christian theologians among many others, and so were disposed to appeal to the whole of Christian tradition instead of to the affirmations of a particular age. English 'Arminianism' was parallel to Arminianism proper, not its product; it was not created by Arminius nor did it follow him in detail.

How then are we to see the Laudians? First and foremost we must remember that to them grace and freewill were not the centre of Christian theology, as they seemed to be to many Puritans. A proof of this is the small number of works on these subjects that they produced. It was their predecessors, culminating in Andrewes and Overall, who had fought that battle; the Laudians for the most part were content to accept their positions without further analysis or development. Their interests were centred on other matters, the relation of Church and nation, the conduct of worship and the development of personal piety. It has, indeed, been pointed out that not all seventeenth-century High Churchmen were, even in the broad sense, Arminian—Harrison instances Hammond and Sanderson—whilst some Puritans were Arminian.[3]

Equally it is a mistake to assume that all non-Puritans, especially

[1] Ibid. 128 ff.
[2] Porter, op. cit. 368 f.
[3] Harrison, op. cit. 141 f.

in James I's reign, can be described as 'Laudians.' As a matter of historical fact, it was not until after the Synod of Dort that James, reluctantly, agreed to the episcopal promotion of Laud himself. Whatever his dislike of Puritans, however much he suspected them of presbyterian sympathies and intentions, James did not close the door of preferment to them; he even chose Abbot as Bancroft's successor. Geoffrey Soden's interesting, if ill-written, life of Bishop Godfrey Goodman[1] makes the point that Goodman, quite as extreme in doctrine as Montagu, who was suspected like him of crypto-papism, was always on bad terms with Laud and was persecuted by him. More surprisingly, Goodman was popular among his puritan ecclesiastical subjects at Gloucester. He was, as his biographer points out, a survival of the more tolerant type of episcopacy of Jacobean days, when thought was more free and conformity less pressed. There is much truth in Professor Trevor-Roper's characterisation of the Jacobean episcopate as 'indifferent, negligent, secular,'[2] although it might be fairer to say rather that they were not fanatical, without being irreligious. As he goes on to say, 'there was a Puritanism of the "right" also, a Puritanism of Archbishop Laud as well as of Oliver Cromwell.'[3] Speaking of the early Caroline period, the same author tells of the harrying of the surviving Jacobean prelates and their replacement:

And, as each old bishop died, his place was taken by a new 'Laudian' bishop, of a very different kind: a Piers, a Wren, a Montague, vigorous administrators of their sees, tenacious stewards of their property, firm asserters of their rights, formidable harriers of Dissent: men with little time or inclination for poetry or satire, court-history, *convensazioni* or the philosopher's stone.[4]

That, however, is not the whole truth. For the basis on which the Laudians proper erected their theory of 'Thorough' in church administration was one which they had inherited from the anti-puritan Jacobeans and, further back still, from the school of Hooker, namely a profound conviction of the unity of Church and nation

[1] Geoffrey I. Soden, *Godfrey Goodman: Bishop of Gloucester, 1583-1656*, London 1953.

[2] H. R. Trevor-Roper, *Historical Essays*, London 1957, 136.

[3] Ibid. 143.

[4] Ibid. 144 f.

and, therewith, of the royal supremacy. It was a view which was not fully Erastian because, as J. W. Allen has pointed out, they believed strongly in the right of the clergy to make ecclesiastical law under the King. Allen calls attention to the fact that both Bishop George Carleton (one of James I's delegates at Dort) and his friend Field assert the right of the Church to control its own affairs, to decide its own controversies; royal supremacy comes in only to give coercive effect to these decisions.[1] Equally, Allen shows that it is dangerous to assume that to High Churchmen royal divine right was synonymous with absolutism.[2]

Here the Laudians were at one with their predecessors. Allen says of Laud:

> But the main question that had been raised under James I was whether power to define and determine doctrine and ritual lay essentially with the clergy or with Parliament. On that strictly practical and constitutional question Laud's language is confused and ambiguous. 'The determining power for the truth and falsehood of the doctrine, heresy or no heresy,' he says, 'is in the Church.' Who, then, or what is it that represents and speaks for the Church? Carleton had declared that Church and State are fundamentally distinct. Laud, in describing the union of Church and State, used almost the phrases of Hooker. But, clearly he did not accept Hooker's conclusion. Hooker had argued that if 'with us one society is both Church and commonwealth' it follows necessarily that 'to define of our Church's regiment, the Parliament of England hath competent authority.' Laud admitted that 'the King and his High Court of Parliament may make any law what they please,' and 'by their absolute power' might legally disestablish Christianity and establish Mohammedanism. Yet he declared roundly that Parliament 'cannot determine the truth of doctrine without the assent of the Church in Convocation.' Parliament, that is, can make it punishable to deny this or that; but it can do no more. No one is morally bound to accept its determinations.[3]

With this position the actions of the Laudians fit in well. The Canons of 1640, carried through in the teeth of Parliament, form one illustration. Still more is their attitude shown by their use of the church courts, although here they were not so consistent, for they

[1] J. W. Allen, *English Political Thought, 1603-1660*, I [1603-1644], London 1938, 131 ff.

[2] 'But none, or, if any, certainly very few of them, were believers in royal absolutism.' Allen, op. cit. 185.

[3] Allen, op. cit. 187 f.

were willing to make use of Star Chamber as well as of the High Commission in ecclesiastical causes. The fact is, no doubt, that, like those closest to them in attitude, the Gallicans, they were not too clear in mind. To preach divine right of kings, royal supremacy and the divine right of the Church all at once is to make questions of frontier delimitation in jurisdiction difficult.

What is clear is that it was the Laudians' disciplinary activity, the policy of 'Thorough' in ecclesiastical matters, already referred to, which most distinguished the Laudians proper from their Jacobean predecessors. The difference is well brought out in Dr Marchant's book on *The Puritans and the Church Courts in the Diocese of York, 1560-1642*. He demonstrates the increase of repression which came to York with the Laudian Archbishop Neile, after a long regime of relative tolerance, and part of his conclusion merits quotation, where, after speaking of the toleration and preferment given to moderate Puritans by earlier archbishops, in contrast to Neile's boycott of them, he says:

Even so, there remained in other places in the Church persons of authority who still retained much of the beliefs and policies of the Elizabethan prelates. These latter had performed a signal service to England by marrying Reformed theology to the traditional ecclesiastical order of the country, and the tradition which they established was by no means obliterated by the rise of the Arminian party whose piety was more akin to that of the Counter-Reformation and whose general attitude owed more to the Renaissance. Neile's church polity, while ostensibly setting out to re-establish Anglican principles, was in fact ecclesiastical conservatism, lacking the spirit or the theology which had animated those who had originally penned the Elizabethan injunctions and orders which lay behind the canons of 1603. That spirit and that theology were maintained in the face both of Arminianism and of radical Puritanism though, because it tried to accommodate itself to the latter, it is easily confused with it. The royalist Puritans who have been encountered in these pages—and they doubtless represent a large number—were faithful exponents of a tradition which they had inherited from their teachers.[1]

Marchant's categories, and especially his use of the term Arminianism, are not precisely those which I have tried to use, but his point is valid. It was not so much doctrine as discipline which was the distinguishing mark of the Laudian; Arminian he may have

[1] Ronald A. Marchant, *The Puritans and the Church Courts in the Diocese of York, 1560-1642*, London 1960, 204 f.

been in the broad sense, but he was an Arminian with a belief in a 'godly discipline' as rigid as that of any presbyterian Puritan. And, therein, he differed perhaps most of all from both the authentic Arminian of Holland or his English predecessor who, even in the sixteenth century, had rejected Calvin's God. Both of them were champions of human free-will; the Laudians substituted for an arbitrary and all powerful God the arbitrary and absolute prelate.

Some Recent Work on Early Benedictine History

DAVID KNOWLES

Emeritus Regius Professor of Modern History,
University of Cambridge

THIRTY years ago a phase of monastic historical scholarship was drawing towards its close. For some forty years previously a group of scholars, who may fitly be considered the founders of critical monastic history of our century, had been actively at work. Almost all belonged to, or were connected with, three Benedictine abbeys: Maredsous in Belgium, Farnborough and Downside in England, belonging respectively to the Congregations of Beuron, France and England. Among them stood out Ursmer Berlière of Maredsous, creator and for long editor of the *Revue Bénédictine* and historian of medieval monasticism; his colleague Germain Morin, equally distinguished in the patristic and monastic fields; André Wilmart of Farnborough, unrivalled in our age in his knowledge of monastic literature and spirituality, and his colleagues Ferdinand Cabrol and Henri Leclercq; and at Downside Edmund Bishop and Cuthbert Butler. To these may be added John Chapman, originally of Maredsous and later of Downside who, though primarily a patristic and New Testament scholar, turned in his last years to the age of St Benedict; and Abbot Delatte of Solesmes who, though not an historian, distilled and presented to modern monks the wisdom of innumerable commentators of the past on the Rule of St Benedict. Taken as a group, these men had surveyed the history and literature of the Benedictine order between 540 and 1350, while Butler had produced a sound critical edition of the Rule and, together with others, had analysed the legislation and spiritual doctrine of Benedictine monasticism with a fulness that had not been achieved for any other medieval order, save perhaps that of St Francis.

Thirty years ago all these scholars were either dead or approaching the term of their active lives, and in the decade before the Second

World War very little new work appeared; only Dom Wilmart continued from time to time to discuss a problem or edit a text, while Dom Philibert Schmitz was beginning his great survey of the order's history.

Then, suddenly and unexpectedly, a burning topic appeared which was to occupy the attention of monastic scholars for a quarter of a century, and which helped to revive their interest in the whole field of early monastic history and to give direction to the studies of a new and able generation. This was the controversy over the so-called *Regula Magistri* which has continued to the present day without final resolution, and which was to arouse a new interest in the whole field of monastic history during the sixth and seventh centuries. Conducted in at least seven languages and twenty learned journals, it has given birth to more than a hundred articles, monographs and books, and has been called the Homeric question of our day.[1]

Here no more than the briefest outline can be given. The *Regula Magistri* [*RM*] was no new discovery; it had existed in manuscript since the days of Louis the Pious in several monastic libraries of France and Germany, and had been in print in several editions for three hundred years. It is a long, diffuse and at first sight confused directory of monastic life and spirituality. The prologue and first ten chapters are almost identical with the prologue and first seven chapters of the Rule [*RB*], and there are many subsequent similarities. It is thrice as long as the Rule, but lacks almost entirely the firm and comprehensive framework of the monastic life which the Rule displays, and even in its own day must have been an unpractical document read in isolation from an established community. For these reasons and others it had been assumed universally that *RM* was the work of a clumsy legislator who made liberal use of *RB*. Now at last, in 1938, Dom Augustin Génestout, a monk of Solesmes, proposed to reverse this judgment. The long and confused controversy that ensued owed much of its confusion and sense of frustration to two circumstances. The first was that it went off at half-cock. Before Génestout had prepared his case for publication a Spanish acquaintance, who had heard some of his arguments and conclusions

---

[1] As this paper is in large part based on a longer account, with full references, of the *Regula Magistri* controversy, now published in *Great Historical Enterprises*, Nelson, Edinburgh 1963, I have felt it unnecessary to burden these pages with detailed notation.

in conversation, used them to implement his case in a controversy of his own with a confrere who was studying the *Regula Magistri* in another context. His article sparked off a series of replies, counter-replies and novel theories before Génestout was able to present his thesis in all its amplitude. The second adverse circumstance was the almost contemporary outbreak of the war followed by the Fall of France. This prevented consultation of manuscripts, circulation of journals and private exchange of views; and in consequence almost every scholar for several years was a jump or two behind the leader of the race for the time being, and no one was able to get a clear view of the whole field.

Naturally, the first announcement of Génestout's thesis produced a violent reaction. Morin, Schmitz, Herwegen, Capelle and McCann, the leading Benedictine historians of the day, came out strongly against it. When at long last Génestout produced his case in full,[1] in 1940, Europe was in a state of chaos. Moreover, his suggestions regarding the authorship and date of *RM* were at once found unacceptable and are held by no one to-day. Nor did he answer the objections to his view that had already been made by the conservatives. Nevertheless, his main arguments were strong: the primitive character of the monasticism portrayed by the Master, visible alike in observance, claustral customs and liturgy; the integrity of *RM* as a document taken as a whole; and the textual and other difficulties in the way of explaining the differences in the passages common to both, if *RB* were the prior document. But on the crucial point of MS anteriority there was still uncertainty. Génestout loyally admitted that the two earliest (and only principal) MSS of *RM* appeared to be at least fifty years later than the date of *RB*. Meanwhile industrious and ingenious scholars in Belgium, France and Germany continued to put forward various counter-theories. One of the most distinguished, Abbot Capelle of Mont-César (Louvain), adopted the old and reputable hypothesis of a double redaction of *RB* to suggest that the Master had made use of *RB* 1, while St Benedict in his turn used the Master's work in *RB* 2. This suggestion, which could be used to explain almost all textual difficulties, proved attractive to many in the sequel.

[1] A. Génestout, 'La Règle du Maître et la Règle de saint Benoît,' *Revue d'Ascétique et de Mystique*, XXI (1940), 51-117: this article must always remain the cornerstone of the controversy.

To summarize the controversy in a few pages would be impossible. It may be better to analyze the various phases of the discussion.

When the mutual relationship of two texts is in question, scholars naturally try first to discover what palaeography and criticism have to say of the priority and dependence of MSS. In both these fields the evidence turned out to be either ambiguous or insufficient for clear proof. As we have seen, Génestout had acknowledged that the extant MSS of *RM* were of a later date than the accepted date (525-50) for the composition of *RB*. Clearly this was a crucial point, and two Belgian scholars, Dom Hubert Vanderhoven of St André and M. François Masai, then Keeper of MSS at the Royal Library of Brussels, undertook to make a fully critical examination of the MSS. They completed this difficult task with remarkable speed, and published their findings in 1953.[1] As only one complete independent MS existed, they decided that a critical edition would be impossible, and presented instead a luxurious diplomatic edition of the complete MS and of an incomplete early MS of a different tradition. Though they were themselves persuaded of the priority of *RM*, they made it clear that these two MSS dated from about 600, though the differences between them argued a long manuscript tradition. In other words, palaeography could give no certain solution to the problem. Meanwhile, others had been examining the texts of *RB* and *RM in vacuo*, in an endeavour to discover in this way evidence of priority for one or the other. Here again, however, opinion was divided, and though individual scholars and their readers may and do express themselves convinced, the spectator from without must pronounce that certainty has not yet been attained. It was necessary, therefore, to cast the net of criticism more widely, and endeavours were made to discover, from an examination of the sources of each document, which of the two was the earlier. This again proved inconclusive on the essential point of priority, but established with a fair degree of certainty that both could have been written between 525 and 550, and that, of the two, *RM* appeared to be the earlier in general character. Finally the net was thrown wider still to discover which of the two seemed to

---

[1] H. Vanderhoven and F. Masai, *Aux sources du monachisme bénédictine: I. La Règle du Maître*, in Publications de Scriptorium, Brussels-Paris, III (1953).

represent the older tradition on liturgy, discipline and observance. Again the evidence was strongly in favour of the priority of *RM*, though it could always be argued that old traditions and practices might linger in remote or conservative circles around the coast of the Mediterranean.

While the general drift of thought had followed the course just described, there had not been wanting scholars to put forward ingenious hypotheses as to the authorship of *RM* and its relation to *RB*. Dom Capelle, as we have seen, had used the hypothesis of the double redaction of *RB* to explain the contrary conclusions of textual scholarship. Others adopted his opinion to frame other theories, often of extreme elaboration, while others still searched for an original text that might lie behind both *RM* and *RB*. More revolutionary solutions were also forthcoming. Dom Odo Zimmermann, actually a monk in Mexico City, maintained that both *RM* and *RB* were the work of St Benedict, being earlier and later versions of his Rule. Dom Louis Brou of Quarr suggested that *RM* was the work of St Benedict and *RB* a much later document based upon it, while Dom Jacques Froger of Solesmes came out with the still more extreme opinion that *RM* was the work of the Master, and that Benedict of Monte Cassino wrote no rule at all, the present *RB* being the work of an unknown abbot of the same name c. 650. These three suggestions, though causing much searching of heart at the time, were ultimately exploded by sober criticism. The two rules differ far too widely to be the work of a single mind, at whatever interval of time, while on the other hand the internal and external evidence for the Benedictine authorship and the traditional date of the Rule is too strong, as we shall see, to be set aside.

During the past ten years or so the efforts of scholars have been devoted principally to presenting the evidence from style and usage, and from the nature of the liturgy and observance seen in the two rules. Dom Génestout, Dom François Vandenbroucke of Mont César and M. François Masai have succeeded in showing, in different contexts, that, if the passages common to *RM* and *RB* are ignored, the two rules show very great differences of style and vocabulary, while, if the common matter is then compared with each, the similarity to *RM* is remarkable. Masai, for example, showed that the common introductory word *autem* is used eighty-one times in the portions of *RB* peculiar to St Benedict, whereas the

Master never uses the word, and in the passages common to both rules it occurs only in scriptural quotations. Similarly, though *magister*, *schola*, *discipulus* and *Dominus* are common in *RM* they are rare or unknown in *RB*, while the opposite is the case with *monachus* and *Deus*. Still more recently, a younger generation has turned its attention to the liturgical and disciplinary regulations of the two rules and has shown conclusively that *RM* represents an earlier tradition—the initial *Deus in adjutorium*, the use of *Kyrie eleison* and hymns, the hour of Prime, are all found only in *RB*, whence they became common form. The debate is not yet closed, and when the long-awaited critical edition of *RB* appeared at the end of 1960 the editor was found to support, but on textual grounds alone, the priority of *RB* over *RM*. Nevertheless, a large majority of scholars and students, among them the present writer, feel that Génestout's opinion of the priority of *RM* must be pronounced very probable, if not reasonably certain. The existence of two versions of the Rule, or of a common document behind both rules, which are essential ingredients of several of the divergent opinions, must be pronounced wholly hypothetical, whereas the solid literary and historical arguments, to say nothing of the palaeographical and textual evidence, are strongly in favour of the anteriority of the Master. This conclusion must necessarily be unpalatable to Benedictine monks, but it is far from reducing the saint of Monte Cassino to a nonentity. The code which by its intrinsic excellence imposed itself upon Western Europe is not the *RM*, which was never, so far as is known, followed anywhere after the early seventh century. It is the *RB* which, while making considerable use of the spiritual directions of the Master, supplied what was lacking in the *RM*, namely, the administrative and practical framework of a fully conventual monastic life.

The controversy over *RM* has had the valuable effect of stimulating research over the whole field of early monastic history. One example of this must suffice. As we have seen, Dom Froger proposed the view that *RB* was the work of an unknown abbot *c*.630-60. This was not as absurd a view as might appear at first sight. The Rule has only one literary mention in the abundant source material of the period before *c*.630, while Benedict is likewise mentioned only once in connection with a rule before 680. Monte Cassino was destroyed by the Lombards in 570, and there is no certain evidence of the subsequent existence of the community. The one reference is indeed of quite unique excellence, namely, the second book of the *Dialogues* of St Gregory, with its celebrated tribute to Benedict *qui scripsit regulam discretione perspicua et sermone luculenta.* This, however, did not deter the hardy Dom Froger, who did not hesitate to suggest either that the rule referred to was the *RM* or that the Benedict of the *Dialogues* was not the author of *RB* but of another rule now lost. This suggestion fluttered Benedictine dovecots for a time, and cautious historians (including even Dom Jean Leclercq) accustomed themselves to referring to 'the author of the Rule *Obsculta.*' Then Christine Mohrmann, writing with another opponent in view, showed that the language of *RB* exactly suited the requirements of a central Italian document of *c.*550, while shortly after Dom Anskario Mundó of Montserrat assembled indications of every kind[1] to show that the Rule dated from *c.*530-50 and showed also that a passage in the *Dialogues* recorded an observance in the Rule, followed at Monte Cassino, which was in agreement with *RB* and contrary to the practice of *RM*. The date of *RB* and its identification with the rule mentioned by St Gregory as written by Abbot Benedict may thus be taken as established.

Nevertheless, what the traditionalists had gained on the swings they were soon to lose on the roundabouts. The number of *Studia Anselmiana* containing Dom Mundó's article contained a still longer one by his sometime confrere at Sant' Anselmo, Dom Kassius Hallinger.[2] In this, with an immense weight of learning and ponderous hammerblows of argument, Dom Hallinger set about demolishing the traditional opinion that St Gregory the Great was a Benedictine monk, trained and training others in the discipline of *RB*, and that in consequence the monks of his monastery, Augustine and his contemporaries, were themselves 'Benedictines,' and took *RB* with them to England. This, the primeval tradition of the 'Benedictine centuries,' had been attacked by the great Baronius in 1596. He had gone beyond the evidence of his documents, and was himself at once attacked by Dom Augustine Baker and other English Benedictine scholars, and eighty years later Mabillon

[1] A. Mundó, 'L'Authenticité de la Regula Sancti Benedicti,' *Studia Anselmiana,* XLII (1957), 105-58.

[2] K. Hallinger, 'Papst Gregor der Grosse und der hl. Benedikt,' *Studia Anselmiana,* XLII (1957), 231-319.

provided what all contemporaries accepted as the complete and final refutation of Baronius. Since then, Mabillon's conclusions have remained as accepted doctrine, though individuals have hinted dissatisfaction. The corollary that St Gregory is the supreme representative and expounder of Benedictine spirituality has naturally become axiomatic with all Benedictine writers and modern historians of religious sentiment. Bit by bit, however, silently and imperceptibly as by an encroaching ocean, the bases of Mabillon's position have been eroded as scholars in fields other than that of monastic history have shown the documents on which he and all his contemporaries relied to be unauthentic. At the same time, historians of the sixth and seventh centuries have gradually built up a new picture of the monastic life of the age very different from that of Benedictine tradition. According to this, Benedictine monachism grew rapidly into a forest from the mustard seed of Monte Cassino. Nowadays it is clear that for more than a century after St Benedict's death his Rule remained almost unknown, and that it was only in the late seventh century, and in Gaul and Northumbrian Britain rather than in Anglo-Saxon England, that it was adopted, at first along with other rules, and then finally in the complete isolation of victory.

All this left St Gregory as an isolated rock, apparently firmly based, but in fact resting largely on water. Dom Hallinger now attacked him from all sides. Gregory himself had not been trained in the Rule; his monastery did not follow *RB*, but held to a regime differing in many important respects from it. Gregory never mentions *RB* explicitly save in the book of the *Dialogues* devoted to St Benedict, and the resemblances in his writings, hitherto regarded as hidden quotations, may well be derived from the great fund of monastic regulations from which all writers of the sixth century drew. So far from Gregory being the typical representative of Benedictine spirituality, his conception of contemplation and his insistence upon it as the crown of the spiritual life is in direct contrast to that of Benedict, as is also his conception of the *Opus Dei* and other features of the monastic life. There is no evidence whatsoever that Gregory as pope favoured the spread of the *RB* or of the Benedictine ideals. As his own monastery on the Coelian was not Benedictine, so Augustine and his companions were not Benedictines, and there is no evidence or likelihood that any of the group departing for the English mission took *RB* with them. The great days of the diffusion of specifically Benedictine ideas and practices came with Wilfrid and Benedict Biscop. The second book of the *Dialogues* and the celebrated reference to the Rule are themselves further evidence that St Benedict was in no sense the familiar patron of Gregory's monastery, and there is no direct evidence of the presence of Cassinese monks on the Coelian.

Dr Hallinger certainly does not pull his punches, and he sometimes gives an impression of partisanship which is probably no more than a scholar's excitement in putting a strong case. Reacting with reason against the over-optimistic picture drawn by Mundó, he himself probably exaggerates when portraying St Gregory as all but ignorant of *RB*. The second book of the *Dialogues* surely implies a very great interest and respect for St Benedict and his Rule, and for myself I would be ready to see a direct or hidden reference in passages where Hallinger speaks of monastic commonplaces. Nevertheless, the concept of Gregory as a representative Benedictine monk, and of his mystical teaching as an extension of that of St Benedict, together with the popular picture of St Augustine as a Benedictine missionary, must probably be abandoned in the future, though we must not forget that both Gregory and Augustine, even if not Benedictines, were certainly monks.

Meanwhile, another cyclone had blown up from Germany. This, though not directly connected with the *RM* affair, helped to clear the air and improve visibility. It is a remarkable fact that until very recently no attempt had been made to present a fully critical text of the Rule. The *textus receptus* or vulgate version, current in Benedictine monasteries throughout Europe for at least seven or eight centuries, had no warranty in detail and was the outcome of endeavours to provide a smooth and intelligible text for monks to use in daily life. Late nineteenth century attempts to give a critical text were faulted by Ludwig Traube in an essay that became a classic, in which he traced the history of MS 914 in the library of the abbey of St Gall, and upheld its claim to be a copy by two German monks in the early ninth century of the codex sent to Charlemagne from Rome in 787, purporting to be itself a careful copy of the autograph of St Benedict preserved first at Monte Cassino and later in the papal archives. Traube in consequence held that Sangallensis 914 was a unique and supreme witness to the authentic text of the Rule. He did not live to produce the edition for the Vienna Corpus, but Dom Morin published a superb diplomatic edition of the St Gall MS, and this was followed by Cuthbert Butler's semi-critical edition of 1912, which was based on Sangallensis 914 but retained a number of the conventional modifications made in the interests of classical usage and intelligibility. Some years later Dom Benno Linderbauer published an edition of greater philological accuracy. But these were in a sense interim works, for Plenkers had been commissioned to take up Traube's task, with other rules added to the Benedictine. In the event, Plenkers lived long and achieved nothing. Then, in the midst of the *Regula Magistri* disturbances, Dom P. Paringer, an elderly monk of Weltenburg, submitted to the *Revue Bénédictine* a long and crabbed article[1] written to prove that Sangallensis 914, so far from being a near autograph, was to be considered a barbarous text, probably the work of an uncouth Anglo-Saxon. Paringer, who was in his mid-seventies, died within a few months of the appearance of his article, which might have caused a great expense of wasted energy had it not been shot down within a year by Miss Christine Mohrmann of Nijmegen, who demonstrated convincingly that the St Gall MS, in regard to grammar, vocabulary and spelling, represented exactly the style of central Italy in the mid-sixth century. Nevertheless, Paringer's study was an ill-informed example of a two-fold tendency among recent textual critics of the Rule who on the one hand, while accepting the importance of Sangallensis 914, are ready to find at both ends of the process of transmission opportunities for copyists' changes, and on the other hand wish to re-examine the family of so-called 'interpolated' texts, of which the earliest extant example is the Worcester book of *c*.700, now Bodleian MS Hatton 48.

Since the war several new, if somewhat conventional, editions of the text have appeared. That of Dom Philibert Schmitz, based on Sangallensis 914, is valuable for its French translation and for the essay by Miss Mohrmann on St Benedict's language. That of the Cassinese Dom A. Lentini divided the chapters into verses, a useful practice since adopted by others. Those of B. Steidle of Beuron, G. Colombas of Montserrat and G. Penco of Finalpia (particularly the last) are all valuable in one way or another for introductory matter. Finally, in the last weeks of 1960 there appeared the long-

---

[1] B. Paringer, 'Le MS. de Saint-Gall 914 représente-t-il le latin original de la règle de s. Benoît?', *Revue Bénédictine*, LXI (1951), 81-140.

awaited text in the Vienna Corpus by Professor G. Hanslik, preceded by a number of articles on textual topics by its editor, and accompanied by a supporting essay by his pupil, Miss Theresa Payer.[1] The reception of this has not been enthusiastic. All readers and reviewers have felt or expressed gratitude to the editor for his rich apparatus and his remarkably ample indices, one of which amounts in fact to a concordance, but experts are agreed that Hanslik has not said the last word on the principles to be followed in constituting the text. Hanslik followed the St Gall MS with some reservations, but failed to integrate the 'interpolated' family satisfactorily into his account. Above all, critics and readers alike suffered a shock of disappointment at Hanslik's attitude to *RM*. At a moment when an overwhelming weight of critical opinion lay on the side of those who maintained the priority of *RM*, Hanslik pronounced roundly for the anteriority of *RB*, but without giving any other arguments save a textual one drawn from a handful of selected passages. More unfortunately still, he allowed this judgment to have its logical consequence in his edition. The readings of *RM* do not appear among the sources; and, though the principal passages of agreement are noted and often printed at the foot of the page, many passages of less complete resemblance are omitted, and it is in practice impossible to find all the resemblances of *RM* either to the printed text of *RB* or to the variant readings of the 'interpolated' family of MSS.

All these controversies have stimulated research on every aspect of the Rule, and several passages, regarded as difficult or inexplicable in the past, have received new and sometimes definitive elucidation. Of these perhaps the most interesting is the interpretation proposed by Dom Mundó[2] for the passage in the Rule which lays down that at the beginning of Lent all are to receive books from the library (*codices de bibliotheca*) which they are to read *per ordinem ex integro*—straight through without omissions. Ever since the Carolingian revival monks and commentators alike have understood *bibliotheca* in the sense just given. In the early medieval period books, not necessarily of a devotional kind, were dealt out for the

---

[1] R. Hanslik, *Benedicti Regula, CSEL*, LXXV (1960).

[2] Mundó, ' "Bibliotheca": Bible et Lecture du Carême d'après saint Benoît', *Revue Bénédictine*, LX (1950), 65-92.

year's reading; in modern times it has been the custom for a book to be assigned for Lenten spiritual reading. The passage has nevertheless often troubled readers and commentators. Few books would suffice as reading matter for a year, and opinions were divided between the allocation of a particularly massive work and a smaller book for Lenten use. Dom Mundó took the simple way out by proposing to understand *bibliotheca* in its secondary but not uncommon sense of Bible. He showed that in the early medieval period it was customary to divide the OT and the NT into nine volumes or *codices* with conventional names, of which seven are in fact found in the Rule. The direction that the book should be read straight through without omissions was to contrast this reading with public reading of various kinds, when only portions were read and some books were omitted as over-exciting. The long gap between 570 and 800, when there was no single and constant tradition in monasteries using the Rule, would sufficiently explain the loss of all memory of the original meaning of the passage. In short, there would seem little doubt that Dom Mundó has supplied the true meaning of the passage, thereby providing an interesting example of the success of critical acumen applied to a text which had been universally misunderstood for more than a thousand years.

As regards a broad view of early monastic history, the controversy over *RM* has resulted in a clearer knowledge in a number of ways. *RB* emerges as a text more indebted than was thought to contemporary literature and competitive rules, but still an epoch-making document in its clear and comprehensive legislation and spiritual doctrine. It seems, however, that when Monte Cassino was destroyed by the Lombards a long period ensued in which many and various rules found favour here and there. *RB* made its way slowly, and first of all in Gaul, whence it was carried to north Italy and by visiting or exiled Englishmen back to England. It had not returned to Cassino till the end of the seventh century, and it was not till Cluniac influence entered Rome under Alberic that the Rule came to be a code in use in the Roman monasteries.

The Irish Missal
of Corpus Christi College, Oxford

AUBREY GWYNN, S.J.

Emeritus Professor of Medieval History, University College, Dublin

EIGHTY years have gone by since F. E. Warren published his work on *The Liturgy and Ritual of the Celtic Church*.[1] Two years before that date Warren had published the full text of a very puzzling Irish missal which had been in the library of Corpus Christi College, Oxford, probably for some three hundred years.[2] Since Warren wrote, the manuscript has been transferred from the library of Corpus Christi College to the Bodleian Library, where it is kept in a box which contains the missal and its satchel of leather. Its class-number is C.C.C. 282. In 1892 an English Jesuit scholar, H. Lucas, made a careful collation of Warren's readings with the manuscript text; a note in his handwriting, which records a few minor errors, is preserved in the box with the manuscript.

Nothing seems to be known of the missal's history. In his introduction[3] Warren says that 'there is no record of the past history of this Missal, which has lain for a long time past in the Library of Corpus Christi College, Oxford.' He adds that 'there is a tradition in the College that it [the MS] was discovered in an Irish bog.' There seems to be no better foundation for this tradition than the assumption commonly made by many Oxford scholars that everything Irish must have come from a bog. It is true that the first twenty leaves and the last sixty leaves of the vellum manuscript are badly stained with damp; but, apart from this blemish, the book is in exceedingly good condition, and cannot possibly have been

---

[1] Oxford 1881.

[2] *The Manuscript Irish Missal belonging to the President and Fellows of Corpus Christi College, Oxford*, ed. F. E. Warren, London 1879. For a brief summary of Warren's conclusions see J. F. Kenney, *Sources for the Early History of Ireland, I: Ecclesiastical*, New York 1929, 706.

[3] Warren, ed. cit., intro. 49.

exposed to the moisture of an Irish bog for any length of time. Warren found a few 'very minute earthy particles deposited between some of the later leaves,' and had these particles analysed in the British Museum; but the test failed to give any definite proof that the book had once lain in a bog. Unless we are prepared to postulate some miraculous intervention by some unknown Irish saint in an unknown locality, we may dismiss the whole tradition as absurd. By good fortune the elaborately decorated initial letters on ff. 1ʳ, 51ʳ and 114ᵛ (at the beginning of the Canon of the Mass, and the Mass for Christmas and for Easter), and the many coloured initial letters which occur on almost every page of the book, together with the rubricated titles, are as a rule in excellent condition and show no trace of damp.

Since Warren's day very little attention has been paid to this manuscript. Kenney, writing in 1929, does not list a single bibliographical item since the date of Warren's edition in 1879. Here Kenney is at fault. The earliest printed notice of this book is in Coxe's *Catalogue* of 1852.[1] In 1897 John Wickham Legg examined this missal in connection with his study of the Sarum group of English missals, and wrote as follows:

> To them (the Sarum group) may be added the Irish missals, the Drummond and Rosslyn missals, and the missal belonging to Corpus Christi College, Oxford; but these three books do not contain masses for every day in the Christian year, but only a selection of masses, so that the comparison with the English books is necessarily imperfect, and uncertain. The Rosslyn and Corpus missals may with some hesitation be assigned to the fourteenth century, and the Drummond missal perhaps to a century earlier.[2]

The surprisingly late date which Legg assigns to the Rosslyn and Corpus missals is also apparent in a comment which he makes elsewhere in the same introduction:

> The Irish manuscripts should perhaps be excluded from consideration, akin as they are to Sarum, and though English rites were ordered at the Synod of Cashel in 1172; as it is not possible to be sure that no influence from England was brought to bear in the thirteenth or even fourteenth century.[3]

[1] H. O. Coxe, *Catalogus Codicum Manuscriptorum qui in Collegiis aulisque Oxoniensibus hodie adservantur*, Oxford 1852, II, 121.

[2] *Missale ad Usum ecclesie Westmonasteriensis*, ed. John Wickham Legg, (HBS XII), III (1897), 1409-10.

[3] Ibid., 1423.

Warren's own estimate of the date of the Corpus missal is very different. He was, of course, writing eighty years ago, when very little scientific work had been done on the history of Irish handwriting; and he prudently warns his readers that 'it is generally admitted among experts that there is no class of MSS the date of which it is so difficult to ascertain with precision on purely palaeographical grounds as the Irish.' Warren had not the benefit of Dr Best's admirable introduction to the facsimile edition of the Annals of Inisfallen[1]; but he compared the script of the Corpus missal with the script of the Annals of Tigernach (so-called) in Rawlinson B 502, and also with the script of the fragment of the Irish *Liber Hymnorum*, now preserved in the Franciscan house of studies at Dún Mhuire, Killiney, County Dublin, but then (1879) in the library of the Franciscan Fathers at Merchants' Quay, Dublin. Arguing from this admittedly slight evidence, Warren 'ventured on purely palaeographical considerations, to assign A.D. 1150-1250 as the extreme limits within which it [the Corpus missal] must have been written, and to incline towards the earlier rather than the later limit on other grounds to be forthwith mentioned.' [2]

Quite recently two exceedingly competent French scholars, Dr Françoise Henry and Madame G. L. Marsh-Micheli, have examined the initials and illuminated pages of this missal as part of their study of a group of Irish manuscripts which can be dated, some of them precisely, to the twelfth century.[3] They have examined eighteen manuscripts which they date within these limits, on the ground of a very careful study of the artistic and technical development that can be seen in the work of the illuminators of these books. Their final conclusion may be quoted for the light it throws on the nature of their study and the validity of their joint conclusions:

If we look back on that collection of manuscripts spread out over a century they will appear as a very coherent series, in spite of several

[1] *The Annals of Inisfallen, reproduced in Facsimile . . . with a descriptive Introduction by R. I. Best and Eoin MacNeill*, Royal Irish Academy 1933.

[2] Warren, ed. cit., intro., 43. Ibid., 49, arguing from what he believed to be the historical background of the missal, Warren narrowed these limits to the years 1152-7.

[3] Françoise Henry, M.R.I.A., and G. L. Marsh-Micheli, 'A Century of Irish Illumination (1070-1170)', *Proceedings of the Royal Irish Academy*, LXII, Sect. C, no 5 (1962), 101-64, with 44 Plates.

variations. Their dominant feature is the way in which old methods of Irish illumination survive, ready to absorb new patterns, whether the Scandinavian foliage or beast or the continental vegetable designs. Everything is merged into an original version of the various sources of inspiration, so much so that they are sometimes difficult to detect exactly. Though no figure scenes have survived, the sense of composition and cohesion of the decoration makes several of these manuscripts outstanding works of art. What they tell us of Irish decoration in the eleventh and twelfth centuries is very closely parallel to the evolution of Irish metalwork of the same period, whilst the carvings, with their strange mixture of Romanesque motifs and of old Irish patterns, belong to a very different atmosphere. Apart from the artistic and archaeological point of view the study of these manuscripts has the added interest of enabling us to get a very vivid picture of the life of the Irish monasteries at home and abroad in the century before the Norman invasion.

Of the twenty manuscripts examined by these two French scholars, five can be dated and located with fair accuracy. The Book of the Dun Cow, now MS 23.E.25 in the library of the Royal Irish Academy, was written at Clonmacnois before the death of Mael Muire mac Célechair in 1107. The copy of the Epistles of St Paul, now in the National Library of Austria at Vienna as MS Lat. 1247 (Theol. 287), was written by Muiredach (Marianus Scotus) of Ratisbon in 1078. The Chronicle of Mael Brigte (the second Marianus Scotus of Mainz) was written at Mainz in the year 1072-3. The Gospel-book, now in the British Museum Library as MS Harley 1802, was written by another Mael Brigte (Ua Maelunaigh) at Armagh in 1138. And the main body of the text of the great vellum miscellany, commonly known as the Book of Leinster, but now known to be more properly called the Book of Noughaval, was written by Colm mac Crimthainn, most probably at Terryglass in North Tipperary, soon after the year 1150.[1] These dates give us five fixed points which justify the two French scholars in their claim that the twenty manuscripts which they have examined can be roughly dated to the century 1070-1170. The authors of this very learned and stimulating paper have gone further, and have sought to group these twenty manuscripts by their known or supposed place of origin. Here there is room for criticism, since the evidence for many of the identifications is very slight. For the

[1] For the correct identification, see R. I. Best's introduction to *The Book of Leinster*, edd. Best, Osborn Bergin and M. A. O'Brien, (Dublin Institute for Advanced Studies), I (1954), xi-xvii.

purpose of the present paper it is perhaps sufficient to note that the Corpus missal is tentatively assigned by the two French scholars to the decade 1120-1130; and a western origin is thought probable.[1]

Since the argument for this date depends in part on the artistic and stylistic evidence, it is only right to quote here one or two sentences from their description of the MS. The authors begin by noting that the book 'has a very peculiar decoration based chiefly on combinations of a beast, often of elongated body, and snakes with their heads seen from above.' They add that, whilst this decoration has probably a good deal in common with the Scandinavian 'Great Beast' style and one of its aspects, the 'Urnes style,' they have purposely refrained from classing the group to which they assign this missal as 'The Urnes Group,' 'for fear of taking for granted what is to be demonstrated and also because, striking as the resemblance may be, there are great differences which a too sweeping identity of names might obscure.' In a later paragraph they say that the elaborate capital letters which appear on practically every page of the book 'are made all the more striking by the intensity of the colour scheme—bright blue, deep reddish purple and golden yellow on a background of sealing wax red.' 'They are,' so the two authors summarise their judgment, 'obviously the work of a painter of strong individuality who deals with all patterns, whether traditional or foreign-inspired, in his own way and is able to remodel them into a rather fierce but extremely effective decoration. . . . All the chief elements of the Urnes style are there; the emphasis given to the large ribbon bodies of the beasts in contrast to the thin network of snakes, and the general rhythm of the composition based on sinuous lines. But the heads of the beasts are not the flattened, disquieting heads of the Scandinavian monsters. They are the sturdy, active, barking and biting heads of the Irish initials turned to a new purpose.'

If we accept, even with a fairly large margin for error, the date proposed by these two very competent French scholars for the decoration of this missal, it is plain that Wickham Legg was far astray in his suggestion that it was written in the fourteenth century; and we shall see that there are also very definite reasons of a purely historical character for questioning so late a date. Warren suggested a date soon after the Synod of Kells (1152); but he was taking it for

[1] Art. cit., 137-40. Excellent illustrations are found in Plates XVII-XXI.

granted that the Corpus missal was a Roman missal, and that a book of Roman rite was not likely to have been used in Ireland before the middle of the twelfth century. Wickham Legg was undoubtedly right in his judgment that the Drummond, Rosslyn and Corpus missals form a distinct group, which is not Roman in origin, but has marked affinities with early missals of the Sarum rite. The date 1152 is thus irrelevant, and the contents of the Corpus missal may be older than the probable date of the book itself, which we may take as having been written and decorated in Ireland at some date in the twelfth century, very probably in the first half of that century.

Two names occur in marginal entries which afford some slight evidence as to previous owners before this missal came to Corpus Christi College. On f. 157 a list, partially obscured, of five or six Irish names has been entered in the outer margin. The first of these names is Macrobius, followed by an obscured mac Cor .... Warren very rashly sought to identify this name as that of an abbot of Clones, whose name is given by the Four Masters as Mac Robias, who died in 1257. Apart from the obvious difference in spelling, the Latin form Macrobius was commonly used in medieval Ireland as an equivalent for more than one Old Irish name, and it is not possible to take this isolated use as evidence for any identification of this kind. Very much more suggestive is the name Tomas O Sínachan, which is enclosed in a formal square bracket at the top of f. 2^v. The name is almost certainly that of a former owner, and (since the book is a sacred book) may well be the name of an owner to whose family the book had been entrusted according to Old Irish custom. Warren confused this name with Sinach, which has been anglicised in modern times as Fox.[1] But the names are distinct, and an entry in the Annals of the Four Masters, for 1052, records the death of Muireadhach Ua Sinnacháin, steward of Patrick (*maor Pátraicc*) in Munster.[2] The office of *maor Pádraig* occurs commonly

[1] Warren, ed. cit., intro. 50. He adds that this allegedly Irish form of thename later anglicised as Fox 'may suggest some connection of the volume with the family of the founder of the College, Richard Fox, Bishop of Winchester, A.D. 1516.'

[2] The name O Sínachan is plainly written with the mark of a long syllable over the letter *i* on f. 2^v of the Corpus missal. The Four Masters are known to have been somewhat careless in their transcription of earlier names from the Old Irish texts which they used when compiling their annals in the early seventeenth century; and they seem to have read this name as having the long stroke over the letter *n*, thus reading the name as O Sinnachain.

in the eleventh century, and seems to have been an institution created at that time to ensure the payment of tribute to Patrick's church in Armagh, more especially in the kingdom of Munster.[1] From the evidence of this name, formally recorded on the second folio of the missal, the book would seem to be most probably of Munster origin, though a connection with the church of Armagh is also probable.

Some other details may be noticed before we begin the description of the missal's liturgical character. The book has been preserved together with its leather satchel and part at least of its original wooden covers. Warren's description may be cited in full: 'It is a volume of small dimensions, being about six and a half inches in length by five in breadth, but of great thickness in proportion to its height, owing partly to the solid character of the tough dark vellum on which it is written, and partly to the large handwriting with which its pages are filled. Its outer pages are blackened with age. It was originally bound in strong wooden covers, portions of which remain, polished by long wear. It is preserved in its ancient leather satchel, the back of which is ornamented with diagonally-impressed lines and circles now nearly obliterated by constant use. At the upper angles strong leather straps are affixed, fastened with leather ties to a broader central strap which passed over the shoulders, from which it was suspended.'

At this point Warren breaks off his description of the book to suggest that these leather straps were used 'by itinerant Irish priests, visiting distant villages and outlying hamlets on foot or horseback.' These imaginative and romantic details are not supported by any solid evidence. The straps were probably used simply to bind the book securely in its satchel. It has been suggested that the wooden binding is the oldest extant binding of any Irish book. This may perhaps be true, but the French authors of the paper dealing with this missal note that the binding 'has a good deal in common with that of Add. MS 40,618 in the British Museum.' [2]

Warren continues his description as follows: 'The MS itself in its present condition consists of 212 leaves, which have been

[1] For a discussion of the origin of this office see Aubrey Gwynn, S.J., and Dermot F. Gleeson, *History of the Diocese of Killaloe*, Dublin 1962, 92.

[2] See F. Henry, *Journal of the Royal Society of Antiquaries of Ireland*, 1957, 147ff.

numbered consecutively, but nine leaves are missing between fol. 117b and fol. 118a, containing the *missae* for Rogation Days and for Ascension Day; one leaf between fol. 202b and fol. 203a, containing a portion of the baptismal office; and one leaf or more (probably six leaves) at the end of the book, which accounts for the "Ordo commendationis animae" ending somewhat abruptly on fol. 212b.' Warren states that the gatherings were of twelve leaves, and were signed in the middle of the lower margin of the last page of each gathering with Roman numerals, enclosed within square brackets. This signing in Roman numerals ceases at the end of the fifteenth gathering, but Warren's examination of the back of the volume, which has not suffered in re-binding, convinced him that there were originally nineteen gatherings of twelve leaves each, the loss of sixteen leaves being accounted for as stated above. The two French scholars give a slightly more detailed and accurate account of these matters: 'The first quire has now eleven folios, but one folio is missing in the beginning. The sixth had originally ten folios; two have been excised. The eleventh has at present only three folios, but there are nine stubs, so there were twelve folios originally. The nineteenth is a bifolium. The twentieth has eight folios (probably four bifolia). All the others are quires of twelve folios.'

Warren devoted a great deal of attention to the script of this missal, and has printed in his introduction a very full account of the abbreviations and other peculiarities of the scribe.[1] In his view the main body of the text, ff. 1-170, was written by a single scribe. From f. 171 onwards some slight differences occur, which suggest the appearance of a second scribe, whose work began with the *sanctorale*. The last section of the missal, ff. 191-212, beginning with the *ordo baptismi*, seems to have been written by a third scribe. But all three sections may have been written by one scribe. The script is described by the two French scholars as 'a slightly irregular, very large Irish minuscule'; there are usually eighteen lines to a page, but seventeen or nineteen lines also occur.

The book begins with the text of the canon of the mass, opening with the words: *Per omnia secula seculorum. Amen. Dominus vobiscum. Et cum spiritu tuo. Sursum corda*, etc. The text of the canon corresponds closely with the text of the Roman canon as it is

---

[1] Warren, op. cit., intro. 22-36.

said to-day, with one significant exception. The *Memento* for the living (f. 2ᵛ) is continued with the words: *et omnium circumstantium quorum tibi fides cognita est et nota devotio qui tibi offerunt hoc sacrificium laudis*. In the Roman rite, from at least the tenth century onwards, this formula has been altered so as to draw a sharp distinction between the priests at the altar and the people who share his offering, but who do not stand at the altar: *pro quibus tibi offerimus vel qui tibi offerunt*.[1] Warren was puzzled by this peculiarity since he dated the missal to the middle of the twelfth century and assumed that it was a missal of the Roman rite. But the Corpus missal is not a Roman missal, and this retention of an older formula is but one of the many signs of difference between the rite preserved in this missal, and in the Drummond and Rosslyn missals, as compared with the Roman rite of the twelfth century.

The text of the *canon missae* is followed in the Corpus missal by a series of votive masses: in honour of the Holy Trinity, the Holy Ghost, the Holy Cross; three votive masses of Our Lady, one for the season of Advent and another for the time between Christmas and the feast of the Purification; a votive mass of the Resurrection; of SS Peter and Paul; of the saints of the church in which mass was offered (*de sanctis presentis ecclesie*); for the bishop; for the king; for peace; for local peace (*pro pace in loco*); for travellers; for friends and kindred; against temptations of the flesh; for fine weather; for the gift of tears; for the safety of the monastery and those who dwell in it; three forms of a general mass (*missa communis*) for all saints; and a mass for benefactors who give alms. There follow the usual requiem masses, with special masses for a dead bishop, abbot, priests, deacons, brethren of the congregation, and so forth. Finally, there is a *missa communis* for all intentions.

This long series of votive masses is followed by an *ordo nuptiarum* in which Warren has noted certain minor peculiarities which need not detain us here. The *ordo nuptiarum* is followed by a *temporale*, which gives masses for the principal feasts of the Church's year from the first Sunday in Advent to Whitsunday. There is only one mass for Advent; the traditional three masses for Christmas night and morning are given, and are followed by masses of St Stephen, St John and the Holy Innocents. There is a mass of the Epiphany,

[1] Josef A. Jungmann, S.J., *Missarum Sollemnia: eine genetische Erklärung der römischen Messe*, Vienna 1948, II, 204.

but no mass of the Circumcision; a mass for Septuagesima, but not for Sexagesima or Quinquagesima; a mass for Ash Wednesday (*in capite ieiunii*) with a blessing of the ashes; but there is only one mass for the Sundays in Lent. The blessing of the palms is given for Palm Sunday, with a mass for the day and the Passion according to St Matthew. There is a short mass for Wednesday in Holy Week, and a mass *in cena domini* for Holy Thursday, with a special absolution of a bishop or priest as in the Roman *Pontificale*. The mass for Good Friday includes the Passion according to St John, with the ceremony of the adoration of the Cross as we have it to-day.

The office for Easter Eve includes the blessing of the fire and the full text of the *Exultet*, but with one notable addition. After the Roman prayer for the reigning pope and bishop a prayer is given for the reigning king and his children: *et gloriossimo rege nostro N. eiusque nobilissima prole N.* This double prayer is not found in the Roman rite nor in the Sarum rite, with which the rite of this Corpus missal has so many close resemblances. We shall see that a prayer for 'the glorious king of the Irish' is also inserted in the litany of Holy Saturday, and again in the litany which occurs in the baptismal service. The office for Holy Saturday includes a litany of saints, which is somewhat shorter than the litany which is sung in the Roman rite. The litany begins with a double invocation of Our Lady: *sancta Maria, sancta dei genetrix*. There follow the first three only of the twelve apostles, SS Peter, Paul and Andrew; the martyrs SS Stephen, Laurence and Vincent; the confessors SS Martin, Patrick and Benedict; SS Mary Magdalen, Felicitas, Margaret, Petronilla and Brigid. There are thus only two Irish saints in this Easter litany; but we shall see that several other Irish saints are invoked in the less solemn litany of the baptismal service. The prayers which follow these invocations resemble the prayers which are still said in the Roman rite as part of the Litany of Saints. But there is one notable divergence. Instead of the Roman prayer (*ut regibus et principibus christianis pacem et veram concordiam donare digneris*) the litany in the Corpus missal has the two following prayers: *ut regem hibernensium et exercitum eius conservare digneris; ut eis vitam et sanitatem atque victoriam dones.* Warren saw that the form of this prayer points to a date at which it was still possible to offer public prayer for a king of the Irish: *árdrí Érenn*, to use the traditional Irish title. For that reason he put forward a date soon after the Synod of Kells

(1152), when Turlough O Conor was still alive and recognised as *árdrí*, with Rory as his son and heir. We shall return to this question.

The *temporale* of the Corpus missal is followed by a *sanctorale*. The number of saints commemorated in this *sanctorale* is small: the conversion of St Paul; St Brigid; the Purification B.V.M. with an office for the blessing of candles; St Patrick; the Annunciation; the Finding of the True Cross; the vigil and feast of St John the Baptist; the vigil and feast of SS Peter and Paul; St Mary Magdalen; the vigil and feast of St Laurence; the vigil and feast of the Assumption B.V.M.; the Beheading of St John the Baptist; the Nativity B.V.M.; the Exaltation of the True Cross; St Michael the Archangel; the vigil and feast of All Saints. It will be noted that there are only four feasts of Our Lady, as in the contemporary Roman rite: the Purification, Annunciation, Assumption and Nativity B.V.M.

These masses for feast-days are followed by a short *commune missarum*, with masses for the vigil and feast of an apostle and of several apostles; the vigil and feast of a martyr and of several martyrs, for paschal time as well as for the rest of the year; a mass for simple confessors, and for confessors who are bishops; a mass for a virgin and martyr, for a simple virgin and for several virgins.

The Corpus missal ends with an *ordo baptismi*; the form for blessing holy water; the blessing of a house, and of a house where someone lies sick; the visitation of the sick; the form for administration of extreme unction and of Holy Communion for the sick; and, at the end of the volume, the *ordo commendationis anime*. This last *ordo* ends abruptly with the first invocations of yet another litany of the saints, which includes several apostles and martyrs not included in the litany for the baptismal service; but it breaks off before the invocation of confessors and virgins, so that we cannot compare its list of Irish saints with the list of the *ordo baptismi*.

Warren draws attention to certain minor peculiarities in both the nuptial and the baptismal services; and Mr D. H. Turner has very kindly called my attention to several other peculiarities of this missal at various points in its contents.[1] I prefer to leave the discussion of these minor points to scholars who are more familiar with

---

[1] I am very much indebted both to Mr Turner (in a letter dated 14 July 1958) and to Mr Christopher Hohler for information on the liturgical character and contents of this missal.

the niceties of liturgical observances than I can claim to be. It will be sufficient for my purpose to note that the Irish saints included in the litany of the baptismal service are SS Patrick, Columba, Brendan, Finian, Ciaran and Fursee among the confessors, with St Brigid as the only Irish virgin here commemorated. There is also a slightly different form of the prayer for the king and his army: *ut dominum illum regem et exercitum christianorum in perpetua pace et prosperitate (conservare) digneris.* There is also a rubric that the bishop, if he is present, is to administer the sacrament of confirmation immediately after baptism. This rubric is found in some other early missals, and is of special interest in an Irish missal since neglect of the sacrament of confirmation is one of the charges brought against the Irish church by St Bernard in his *Vita S. Malachiae.*[1]

Warren notes certain obvious peculiarities in the order of contents of the Corpus missal. The canon of the mass occurs at the beginning of the missal, not in its customary place after the office of Easter Eve and before the mass of Easter Sunday. The various prefaces, proper to each feast, are not given one after the other at the beginning of the canon, as in a Roman missal, but each preface is given under the feast to which it belongs. Both the *temporale* and *sanctorale* omit several well known masses, whilst the *commune sanctorum* is ample, and there is an unusually long list of votive masses. Finally, the absence of a calendar (which may perhaps have been given at the end of the volume) is most regrettable.

In the absence of a liturgical calendar it is not easy to determine the church for which this missal was compiled, nor the date at which it was compiled for Irish use. Warren was writing at a time when it was assumed that the introduction of the full Roman rite into the Irish Church was the work of St Malachy, who was papal legate in Ireland for eight decisive years in the history of the Irish Church (1140-48). But it is now known that the reforming movement which brought the Irish Church more closely in touch with contemporary Roman policies and observances was active throughout Ireland from the first years of the twelfth century; and the very fact that the rite

[1] H. J. Lawlor, trans. and ed., *St Bernard's Life of St Malachy of Armagh*, S.P.C.K. 1920, 18; see Lawlor's note, ibid., 162. There is an excellent discussion of the whole problem, in the light of fuller evidence, by Margaret W. Pepperdene in *Irish Theological Quarterly*, XXII (1955), 110-23.

which appears in the Corpus missal is not a Roman rite is in itself an argument for an earlier date. Two important reforming synods were held in Ireland in the first decade of the twelfth century: the first synod of Cashel, which met at Cashel in 1101, over which an Irish bishop (Maol Muire Ua Dunáin) presided as papal legate, with authority from Paschal II; and the synod of Rath Breasail, which met in Tipperary in the early weeks of 1111, and which for the first time established a purely diocesan hierarchy for the churches of Ireland. The legate who presided over this synod was Gilbert or Gille Easpuig, bishop of Limerick, who wrote a treatise *De usu ecclesiastico* for the instruction of the Irish clergy.[1] In this treatise, which seems to have been written expressly for the use of the synod which met in 1111, Bishop Gilbert says that he has endeavoured to set down in writing the canonical custom of saying the hours and performing the office of the whole ecclesiastical order (*canonicalem consuetudinem in dicendis horis et peragendo totius ecclesiastici ordinis officio scribere conatus sum*). He then states the immediate purpose of his reform in the clearest terms: 'that those diverse and schismatical orders with which nearly all Ireland has been deluded may give place to one catholic and Roman office' (*ut diversi et schismatici illi ordines quibus Hibernia pene tota delusa est uni catholico et Romano cedant officio*). Plainly the missals, breviaries and other service-books introduced by Bishop Gilbert in the course of his work as papal legate (1111-40) would have been books of purely Roman usage.

The Corpus missal contains masses which follow a rite that is not Roman, but seems to be closely akin to an early Sarum rite. Can we date the introduction of this rite into Ireland? Can we suggest a church that is likely to have been the centre of such liturgical observance? These questions are, of course, distinct from the question which we have already discussed: the probable date of the manuscript which is now preserved in the Bodleian Library.

Warren is certainly correct in his view that the missal was originally compiled for use in a monastic church. There are votive masses *pro custodia monasterii et habitatorum eius, pro abbate* and *pro fratribus nostre congregationis*. The rubric for the blessing of candles

---

[1] Gilbert's treatise was first printed by J. Ussher from Cambridge Univ. MS Ff. i, 27 in *Veterum Epistolarum Hibernicarum Sylloge*, Dublin 1632; and has been reprinted by C. R. Elrington in *The Whole Works of... J. Ussher*, 1847, IV. 500-10.

begins with the words: *postquam fratres exierint a capitulo.* A rubric for the prayers for the dying bids the brethren assemble as follows: *cum anima sit in exitu (et) sui dissolutione corporis visa fuerit laborare, tunc omnes fratres cum summa velocitate occurrant canendo moderata uoce: Credo in unum deum.* The litany of the baptismal service includes a prayer for the whole community: *ut istam congregationem in sancta relegione conseruare digneris.*

Warren seeks to identify the church for which this missal was compiled as the monastic church of SS Peter and Paul at Clones, in what is now county Monaghan. Here he has almost certainly gone astray. Arguing from the appearance of a votive mass of SS Peter and Paul in the missal, as well as masses for the vigil and feast of the two apostles and for the conversion of St Paul, he believes that the missal was compiled for use in a monastic church dedicated to the two patrons of the Roman Church. The argument is weak if we assume (as Warren did, and as the two French authors of the recent paper in which this missal is described also assume) that the rite followed in this missal is a Roman rite. Warren's argument gains in strength from the fact that the rite of this missal is not a Roman rite, but the evidence he has adduced is too slender to justify his conclusion. Nonetheless, it is at least probable that the church for which this missal was compiled had a special devotion to the two apostolic patrons of the Roman Church.

For reasons that are not very plain to-day, Warren convinced himself that the most likely monastic church in Ireland for which this missal was compiled was the monastic church of Clones. His argument is singularly weak. There was an ancient monastic church at Clones, founded by St Tigernach, whose death is recorded in the Annals of Ulster under the year 549 or 550. But there is no record of a church dedicated to SS Peter and Paul at Clones before the early fifteenth century, when a papal indulgence was granted for the benefit of the church and cloister of the monastery of SS Peter and Paul at Clones.[1] An old Irish monastery was burnt by Hugh de Lacy II at Clones in 1207, and the monastery was rebuilt by the Normans five years after that date.[2] Church dedications before the coming of the Normans were rare in Ireland, and the dedication

[1] *Calendar of Papal Letters*, VI. 421.

[2] M. Archdall, *Monasticon Hibernicum*, Dublin 1786, 583.

mentioned in the papal grant of 1414 may perhaps be due to this Norman refoundation. Other monastic churches dedicated to SS Peter and Paul were as a rule of Norman origin, such as the Augustinian priory at Selsker near Wexford, and the Augustinian priory of Newton near Trim in Meath. The monastery founded by Domnall O Briain near Ennis was dedicated to the two Roman saints, but its foundation is not much earlier than 1189; whilst the Augustinian abbey founded by Donnchad O Cearbhail at Knock near Louth belongs to the years 1140-48.[1]

By far the most famous of the Irish monastic churches dedicated to SS Peter and Paul was the church which Cellach (Celsus), archbishop of Armagh, consecrated at Armagh in 1126. Devotion to the two Roman apostles was an old tradition at Armagh, for relics of SS Peter and Paul are mentioned there in the Annals of Ulster under the year 734.[2] If we are to look for an old monastic church of this dedication, Armagh must be counted the most probable church. But proof positive is lacking.

A very much more fruitful line of investigation can be found in the bidding prayer for the king of the Irish and his army, which occurs in the litany of saints for Easter Saturday. Warren noted the importance of these petitions as having a special historical significance, and as perhaps yielding a clue to the date of the book. But he went no further than a brief list of the Irish kings of the twelfth century, one of whom might perhaps be the king mentioned in this prayer. He was unaware of the abundant evidence for petitions of this kind in Frankish books of the Carolingian, and even of the Merovingian age. In 1886 Leopold Delisle published an important paper on ancient sacramentaries of this type[3]; and in this paper he

---

[1] For these dates I have made use of unpublished notes by F. Neville Hadcock, who has been at work for several years, with my assistance, on an Irish companion volume to that on the *Medieval Religious Houses of England and Wales*, London 1953, in which he collaborated with Professor David Knowles.

[2] The entry, which is plainly very old, reads as follows: 'Commotatio martirum Petir ocus Phoil ocus Phatraicc ad legem perficiendam.' W. Reeves, in his edition of Adamnan's *Life of St Columba*, Dublin 1857, 313, n. *c*, interprets the phrase *commotatio martirum* as meaning the disinterring and enshrining of the relics.

[3] L. Delisle in *Mémoires de l'Académie des Inscriptions et Belles-Lettres*, XXXII (1886), 57-423. I owe my knowledge of this important paper to the kindness of Rev. Paul Grosjean, S.J., whom I had consulted on the general problem of this bidding prayer for the king of the Irish and his army. It should be noted that the pronoun *illum* or *illam* is commonly used in texts of this kind where the modern usage is to print *N.* as a substitute for the name of a king or queen.

cites an extract from ancient *Orationes et preces pro regibus* (Vat. MS Reg. Lat. 257), which is dated by its script to the late seventh or early eighth century.[1] The following petitions occur among these prayers:

f. 89 Ut regni Francorum nomenis secura libertas in tua devotione semper exultet.

f. 90 Et Francorum regni adesto principibus.

f. 91 Et Francorum regnum tibi subditum protege principatum.

A sacramentary of the church of Senlis, written *c*. 880 and now preserved in the Bibliothèque S. Geneviève as MS Lat. BB. 20, has a litany which includes the following petitions:

f. 23ᵛ Ut *illum* apostolicum in sancta religione conservare digneris.

Ut Hludouvicum regem perpetua prosperitate conservare d.

Ut ei vitam et sanitatem atque victoriam donare d.

Ut *illam* reginam conservare d.

Ut ei vitam et sanitatem donare d.

Ut Hadebertum episcopum et cunctam congregationem sibi commissam conservare d.

Ut exercitum Francorum conservare d.

Ut eis vitam et sanitatem atque victoriam donare d.

A breviary and missal of the abbey of Corbie, which had many links with English monastic churches, has been preserved at Paris in the Bibliothèque Nationale as MS Lat. 11522.[2] Canon Victor Leroquais, who has published two separate notices of this manuscript, dates it either to the end of the eleventh or the beginning of the twelfth century.[3] The litany of saints occurs on f. 90, and includes the following petitions:

Ut *illum* regem et exercitum Francorum conservare d.

Ut eis vitam et sanitatem atque victoriam dones.

Ut sanitatem nobis dones.

It is thus plain that there was a traditional form of petition for the king and his army in the Frankish lands. A more complete study of the available evidence might well be of assistance in tracing the

---

[1] Art. cit., 71-2.

[2] M. Vernet of the Ecole des Chartes has very kindly sent me some notes concerning the history of this manuscript.

[3] V. Leroquais, *Les sacramentaires et les missels manuscrits des Bibliothèques publiques de France*, Paris 1924, I, 192-4, n. 85; and also in *Les bréviaires manuscrits des Bibliothèques publiques de France*, Paris 1934, III, 222-3, n. 604.

development of these petitions from the ninth century onwards. I owe to the kindness of Mr D. H. Turner a suggestion which has led me to a text which comes nearer than any other text known to me, when compared with the form of the litany preserved in the Corpus missal. This text has not been preserved in a missal or breviary, but in a musical manuscript known to scholars as the Winchester Troper, which is to be found in the Bodleian Library as MS Bodley 775.[1] Owing to the fortunate fact that the litany copied into this manuscript names Aetheldred as king of the English, its date can be fixed with certainty to the years 978-1016; and the author of the notice of this manuscript in the *Summary Catalogue* thinks it probable that the section ff. 8-121^v was written at Winchester before December 980. The litany occurs on ff. 18^v-19^r, and is worth citing in full:

Peccatores te rogamus audi nos.

Ut pacem nobis dones.

Ut domnum apostolicum in sancta religione conservare digneris.

Ut aecclesiam tuam immaculatam custodire d.

Ut Aetheldredum regem et exercitum Anglorum conservare d.

Ut sanitatem nobis dones.

Ut pluviam nobis dones.

Ut caeli serenitatem nobis dones.

Ut aeris temperiem bonam nobis dones.

Ut fructum terre nobis dones.

Fili dei, te rogamus.

The litany of Holy Saturday preserved in the Corpus missal comes very close to this short litany of the Winchester Troper, and may also be cited in full for the sake of verbal comparison.

Peccatores te rogamus audi nos.

Ut pacem nobis dones.

Ut domnum apostolicum nostrum in sancta religione conservare
    digneris.

Ut aeclesiam tuam immaculatam custodire d.

Ut regem Hibernensium et exercitum eius conservare d.

Ut eis vitam et sanitatem atque victoriam dones.

Ut sanitatem nobis dones.

---

[1] For a full description, see F. Madan and H. H. E. Craster, *Summary Catalogue o, Western Manuscripts in the Bodleian Library in Oxford*, Oxford 1922, II (1). 425-7, n.2558.

Ut pluviam nobis dones.

Ut fructus terre nobis dones.

Ut aeris temperiem nobis dones.

Ut nos exaudire digneris.

Fili dei te rogamus.

It will be seen that there are slight divergencies between the two forms which make it certain that neither text can be the immediate source of the other; but the verbal correspondences are very close indeed. The Irish litany adds a petition which is met in other Frankish litanies, *ut eis vitam et sanitatem atque victoriam dones;* and omits (perhaps by an error of the scribe) the petition for fine weather. The order of the two petitions for mild weather and for the fruits of the earth is inverted in the Irish, as compared with the Winchester version; but the wording of the petitions is almost identical in both texts. So close a correspondence suggests very strongly some historical connection; and it so happens that a connection between Winchester and Irish churches (especially Munster churches) is very probable at the close of the tenth and the first years of the eleventh century.

Brian Boruma is remembered to-day chiefly for his victory over the Norsemen at Clontarf in the year 1014, when he himself was killed in the hour of victory. But his career as king, first of Munster, then of all Ireland, goes back to the year 976 when he succeeded his elder brother Mathgamain as king of Munster.[1] Mathgamain and Brian were the two sons of Cennétig, who was king of the small kingdom of In Déis Tuaisceirt in the neighbourhood of Limerick and the river Shannon. In 972 Mathgamain conquered the town of Limerick, which was then a Norse settlement, and he was recognised as king of Munster in the following year. He was captured and put to death in 976, and Brian had then to assert his right to his brother's kingdom by force of arms. This he did with ever-increasing success in Munster, and in the year 1002 he received formal recognition from the other Irish kings as high-king of Ireland (*árdrí Érenn*). Three years later, in 1005, the Annals of Ulster tell us that Brian made a hosting to Armagh with the kings of Ireland; that he left twenty-two ounces of gold on Patrick's altar; and that he went back from Armagh to Munster bringing with him the hostages

[1] For a brief account of this aspect of Brian's career, see my comments in *History of the Diocese of Killaloe*, 90-5.

of Ireland. His position as high-king was not challenged until his death in 1014.

Brian's relations with the church of Armagh were very close in the last years of his life, and it seems almost certain that the office of steward of Patrick in Munster (*maor Pádraig i Mumain*) owes its origin to the formal guarantee of the rights of Patrick's church in Munster which Brian made, with unusual solemnity, at Armagh during his visit to that city in 1005.[1] We have, unfortunately, no trustworthy account of Brian's religious policy apart from one or two entries in the Annals of Ulster, and a famous entry in the Book of Armagh, which records Brian's formal guarantee 'on behalf of all the kings of Cashel' (*pro omnibus regibus Maceriae*).[2] An account of his victories written in lavishly extravagant terms of panegyric has come down to us in an Old Irish, almost certainly Dalcassian, narrative known as *Cogadh Gaedhel re Gallaibh*.[3] In this narrative we read that 'by him (Brian) were erected noble churches in Erinn, and their sanctuaries'; and that 'he sent professors and masters to teach wisdom and knowledge, and to buy books beyond the sea and the great ocean, because their writings and their books were burned in every church and sanctuary where they had been, and were thrown into the water by the plunderers, from the beginning to the end.'

Brian Boruma was a Munster king, and Munstermen at all times had easy access to southern England. Winchester was at that time the chief seat of the kings of England, and it does not seem in any way improbable that some of the 'professors and masters' whom Brian sent across the sea should have found their way to Winchester, and have brought back with them mass-books and other service-books of that English church. If that conjecture be thought probable, it should be noted that the Corpus missal, with its two Irish companion service-books, the Drummond missal and the Rosslyn missal, may well throw much-needed light on the early history of

[1] This is the correct date of Brian's visit to Armagh. Owing to an error by the editor, W. M. Hennessy, of vol. I of the *Annals of Ulster*, Rolls Series 1887, the date of each annalistic entry is given a year too early; this error has been corrected, as from the year 1057, by B. McCarthy, editor of vols. II and III, and is also everywhere corrected in the index in vol. IV.

[2] The full text is found in *The Book of Armagh*, ed. John Gwynn, Royal Irish Academy 1913, 32; see also ibid., ciii.

[3] *Cogadh Gaedhel re Gallaibh*, ed. J. H. Todd, Rolls Series 1867. For the words cited in the text, see ibid., 139.

what became later the fully developed Sarum rite. In support of this conjecture, which is no more than a conjecture for lack of more positive evidence, it should be noted that Brian's close connections with the church of Armagh in the last years of his life may explain the fact that this missal seems to have been compiled for the use of a church which had some special devotion to the two Roman apostles, SS Peter and Paul; and also that the name Tomas O Sínachan, which has been written in formal style on f. 2^v of the manuscript, is a name which appears only once in the Irish annals, but then as that of a family which had, for a time at least, the position of *maor Pádraig i Mumain*. If we accept the date suggested by the two French scholars for the script and decoration of this missal, we may fairly assume that the liturgical contents of the book are older than the copy which has come down to us; and that the form of mass here preserved is a form that was used in Ireland in the eleventh, perhaps even the early eleventh century.

In view of what has been said, it may perhaps be helpful to review briefly the various dates that have been assigned to this manuscript by earlier scholars. Warren, as we have seen, dated the manuscript tentatively between the years 1152 and 1157. A date *c.* 1150 was proposed by J. T. Gilbert in his introduction to the second volume of the *National Manuscripts of Ireland*.[1] In 1852 Coxe suggested a date as early as the late tenth century in his catalogue of manuscripts preserved in the Oxford colleges. In 1868 J. O. Westwood described the handwriting of the Corpus missal as of the twelfth or thirteenth century.[2] Warren's edition of the Corpus missal was reviewed at length by a very competent Irish scholar, Dr B. McCarthy, in 1880.[3] He was, as far as I know, the first scholar to point out the probability that the missal might be connected with the ecclesiastical policy of Brian Boruma, and he summarises his argument as follows: 'Upon these various grounds, palaeographic, liturgical and historic, we have come to the conclusion

[1] J. T. Gilbert, *Facsimiles of the National Manuscripts of Ireland*, Dublin, II (1878), intro. lvii, item L.

[2] J. O. Westwood, *Facsimiles of miniatures and ornaments in Anglo-Saxon and Irish manuscripts*, London 1868, 96.

[3] *Irish Ecclesiastical Record*, Third Series, I (1880), 505-14. In 1886 McCarthy published an important paper on the Stowe Missal in *Transactions of the Royal Irish Academy*, XXVII (1886), 135-268, which has not received the recognition it deserves.

that the Missal was compiled between the year 1002 [*recte* 1005], the date of the foregoing entry (in the Book of Armagh), and 1014, the date of the Battle of Clontarf.' In 1881 Father Sylvester Malone dealt with some of the problems connected with this missal, and gave it as his opinion that 'there are solid grounds for assigning the date of this Missal to between the middle and the end of the ninth century.'[1] Wickham Legg, writing in 1897, gave it as his opinion that 'the Rosslyn and Corpus missals may with some hesitation be assigned to the 14th century.'[2] In 1921 another Irish priest, Father E. J. Quigley, discussed the evidence for the date of the Stowe and Corpus missals in three somewhat discursive essays in the *Irish Ecclesiastical Record*.[3] Since he chose as the title for these essays 'The Clones Missal,' it is plain that he follows in the main the conclusions of Warren, whose edition he cites throughout. But Father Quigley had the great merit of visiting the Bodleian Library, and of consulting palaeographical experts at Oxford. Here is his report of what was said to him in 1920 or 1921: 'Mr. Falconer Madan, late librarian of the Bodleian in Oxford, holds that it (the Corpus missal) was written between the years 800 and 900 A.D. Dr Lowe, the present Reader in Palaeography in Oxford, holds with Dr Coxe that the manuscript was written in the end of the eleventh century or the early twelfth century.'[4] Kenney, writing in 1929, is wholly dependent on Warren's edition of 1879. Apart from the recent paper by Dr F. Henry and Madame G. L. Marsh-Micheli, the only other discussion of the date of this missal known to me is in the typescript report on the liturgical manuscripts of the Bodleian Library which was compiled some years ago by the Dutch Franciscan scholar, Dr S. J. P. van Dijk. He describes the missal briefly as an Irish monastic manuscript of the late twelfth century.[5]

With this wide variety of expert opinion as to the date of the

---

[1] These words are cited by E. J. Quigley, in *Irish Ecclesiastical Record*, Fifth Series, XVII (1921), 607.

[2] Wickham Legg, ed. cit., III, intro., 1410.

[3] Cf. *Irish Ecclesiastical Record*, Fifth Series, XVII (1921), 381-9, 496-503, 603-9.

[4] Ibid., 607.

[5] Dr Van Dijk's typescript report, I. 131. *Cf. Latin Liturgical Manuscripts and Printed Books: Guide to an Exhibition held during 1952*, Bodleian Library Oxford 1952, 27 and Plates X and XI. I am very much indebted to my friend Dr R. W. Hunt of the Bodleian Library for his help in my work on various Irish liturgical manuscripts in the Library.

manuscript, it might seem tempting to differ from the conclusions of the two French scholars who have based their conclusions almost entirely on the decoration of the missal, and argue that the missal now preserved in the Bodleian Library is in fact a manuscript of the early eleventh, not the mid-twelfth century. Certainty in such matters is not easily obtained, unless some lucky chance—such as the mention of the name of Aetheldred in the litany of the Winchester Troper—gives ground for a more positive dating. But it should be remembered that, whilst arguments from the script of liturgical books are bound to be weak and uncertain, an argument based on the place of artistic decoration in a known sequence of illustrated manuscripts is entitled to serious consideration. For this reason I accept in general the date given by these two French scholars as most probably correct, and I prefer to treat the Corpus missal as a twelfth-century copy of an earlier service-book, whose contents and general character are most easily explained as being due to the activities of Irish ecclesiastical reformers in the first years of the eleventh century.

Jews and Christians
in the Constantinian Empire

JAMES PARKES

Director of the Parkes Library, Barley, Royston, Herts.

THE fourth century introduced no new features into the Christian opinion of Jews and Judaism. Yet it is extremely important because it standardised an existing attitude at the earliest moment when the Church had the power to express its view in law and practice, and not merely in the pulpit or in theological argument. It thus set the tone which determined future relations for more than a millenium; and, as Christendom became more and more the total environment of life in the western world, so the attitude towards the Jews adopted by the Church in the early centuries came to determine the whole condition of Jewish life over the whole realm of Christendom. The Church became the arbiter of life and death, of the permission to carry on even the most meagre and restricted existence under a Christian prince.

It is important to emphasise this Christian aspect of the matter, because there is a tendency among some writers to regard the calamities which Jews undoubtedly suffered under Christian rule merely as the continuation of prejudices which were already manifest in the pagan world. They are, thus, considered either as a consequence of the general imperfection of human nature, or, more precisely, as a result of Jewish life and practice, since that is the common factor between the pagan and Christian worlds. In both cases a distinctive Christian element is overlooked, an element in which the pagan world had no part and in which Jewish conduct was without significance.

To say this is not to claim that Jews are in themselves perfect, or that they can cause no offence to their neighbours by their imperfections. The claim is that the reactions of their neighbours in

69

the pagan world do not explain their subsequent history in the Christian world. In the pagan world reactions were both favourable and unfavourable: and, in both cases, were related to the actual contemporary and local facts of different situations. In Egypt, and particularly in Alexandria, hostility originally began out of the Jewish celebration of Passover, which was a celebration by no means complimentary to Egyptian pride. A rival story appeared within a century of the founding of Alexandria in which the story of the Exodus was told as the expulsion of a group of disease-ridden foreigners in the interests of public hygiene. In Greek cities of the Roman Empire hostility was natural if wealthy Jews, by the privilege of Julius Caesar, escaped taking their share of the burdens and expenses of the decurionate. In the other balance must be set the attraction of the Diaspora synagogue to that healthy and decent element in the population among whom the Pauline mission was conducted and the Gentile Church founded. The god-fearers were not the dregs of the hellenistic world, and the New Testament tells us of two cases where a non-Jewish officer was powerfully attracted to the local Jewish community; and this would not have happened had Jews simply conformed to the descriptions of them in Roman satirical literature.

If we cannot consider the history of Jews under Christian domination to be simply a continuation of their history as minorities under pagan rule, it is equally impossible to explain it by saying that it was the inevitable consequence of the intolerance of monotheism. For Jews have a long and varied history under Islam, which was perhaps an even more intolerant monotheism than Christianity; and that history was completely different. It ended with centuries of the direst oppression and misery. But it never experienced the same active and continuing hostility of the ecclesiastical authorities, and popular religion never invented stories akin to the accusations of medieval Christendom—the charges of ritual murder, the poisoning of wells, or the vast conspiracies to destroy the Christian world. The oppression and misery were primarily due to a stagnant society and were shared to a great extent by the Muslim poor themselves.

The history of Jewish-Christian relations is *sui generis*, and for the understanding of it the fourth century is of capital importance. A complex relationship has, of course, many causes interwoven into its fabric. But one factor, at least, is fundamental and this is brought out by the contrasting histories in the pagan and Islamic worlds. This factor is the Christian need, for its own theological and apologetic purposes, of the Old Testament, which it (in common with the Jews) regarded as of direct divine origin. Christian history of the Jews differs from pagan history in that the pagan attitude was based on contemporary Jewish conduct and not on an interpretation of what was held to be a divinely authoritative description of Jewish character and history. But it also differs from Islamic history, because Islam did not wish to take over the Old Testament and incorporate it into the sacred literature of Islam.

The consequences of this Christian necessity one can see from almost any patristic writer; but, rather than collect quotations from many sources, I would give a summary of the argument of one of the most important figures of the period of Constantine, Eusebius, son or adopted son of Pamphilus, and bishop of Caesarea in Palestine. Born about 265, he died about 340. In theology he was a moderate conservative; but his importance lies not so much in the originality of his theology as in his encyclopaedic knowledge and his lucid exposition of Church history and tradition. Among other writings, he composed, just at the time of the peace between Constantine and the Christian Church, two substantial apologetic works, *The Preparation of the Gospel* and *The Demonstration of the Gospel*. The first is mainly concerned with a defence of Christianity *vis à vis* Greek philosophy, and the second (of which only half survives) is an exposition of its relation to Judaism, and of the fulfilment of Old Testament prophecy in the Incarnation.

In the seventh book of *The Preparation* and in the first two books of *The Demonstration* he expounds his conception of Judaism and its relation to Christianity. According to Eusebius, Christians are neither Greeks nor Jews but heirs of an older and purer belief, indeed, of the original faith of mankind—'the most ancient organisation of holiness, and the most venerable philosophy of mankind' (*Dem.* I, 2). This religion is described by Moses in the book of Genesis, and those who adhered to it are called Hebrews. It is not right to call them Jews, or their religion Judaism, since they lived by faith, and knew nothing of Jewish practices. They did not know the Sabbath, those who preceded Abraham were not even circumcised, and they did not need elaborate rules and regulations to keep them in the paths of righteousness. They were pre-incarnation Christians.

Indeed they knew the Son already before his Incarnation, and it is the eternal Christ who appeared to them either in the guise of an angel, or in the voice of God. At one point (Psalm 105: 15) they are themselves called 'Messiahs' or 'Christs' (i.e., anointed ones), just as today those who accept the Incarnation are called Christians (*Dem.* I, 5).

These Hebrews are, indeed, the physical ancestors of the Jews, although they must be clearly distinguished from them. What happened was this. After the noble and glorious Hebrew, Joseph, died in Egypt, the members of his family settled in that country and gradually forgot the wonderful religion which they had inherited. They adopted the appalling and beastly habits of the Egyptians (*Dem.* I, 6). Moses, the Hebrew, rescued them from the wild, savage, and completely lawless life which they had learned from their Egyptian neighbours, and was inspired both to write the story of their Hebrew ancestors and to give them an extremely strict and rigorous law in the hope of bringing them back to better ways.

Moses insisted that every one of his regulations must be integrally observed, and laid under a curse those who should transgress even the slightest. But, as it was impossible for anybody to observe all the regulations without exception, all Jews were, and still are, constantly under a curse. Moses, however, did not intend this life under laws to be more than a temporary expedient and, even so, only intended it for those Jews who lived in Palestine itself. For Jews who lived outside the country could not begin to observe its regulations about visits to Jerusalem, for example, and could not therefore have ever been intended to practise Judaism.

At the same time as the mass of the Palestinian Jews were confined within the performance of the law, there continued an élite of Hebrews who were constantly chiding and denouncing them, and prophesying to them their final and complete ruin. This would come about because they would reject their Messiah. He would come to bring their law to an end and to make a new covenant, which only a very few of them would accept but which would bring light to the Gentile world. In this way the original pure religion of the Hebrews would become the religion of mankind. With this insistence on the inevitability of the Jewish rejection of the Messiah, it is not surprising that Eusebius rarely emphasises the crime of deicide which other writers delight to hurl against the Jews. He states, of course, that it was the fact that they did not accept the Messiah which brought about their complete and final ruin, but it was their rejection of his teaching rather than the crucifying of his person which he appears to emphasise. This may be due in part to the loss of those books of *The Demonstration* which deal with the crucifixion, resurrection and ascension; but *The Preparation*, which is complete, and of which Book VII is devoted to detailing the distinction between Hebrew and Jewish history, and the deplorable nature of the latter, also pays more attention to the rejection than to the crucifixion.

According to Eusebius, there was not a single decent or righteous *Jewish* character in the whole of the story. All the virtuous characters, whether before or after Moses, were Hebrews, and so pre-incarnation Christians. Moreover, since the Bible was divinely inspired, it was clear that God himself never expected them to be anything but disgusting and reprobate, since He continuously foretold their rejection of the truth and consequent ruin. Even the fragmentary remnant referred to by various prophets as being saved or restored did not refer to a pious minority among the Jews. It referred rather to the persistence of Hebrews among them, and so in the end came to cover only the twelve apostles and a few other Christians. Eusebius on a number of occasions insists that they were so few that they could easily be identified and counted.

In contrast to the Jewish story, the Old Testament contained the splendid record of the pre-incarnation Christians, and the splendid promises which God made to them. It is in this dichotomy that the ultimate evil root of the abnormality of Christian antisemitism resides. Had the Church accepted that its own pre-incarnation history consisted of good men and bad, promise and denunciation, a reasonable balance would have been preserved. Had it recognised that the same was true of the divinely inspired record of the Jews there would equally have been a balanced tradition. But the Church continued to assume the division of the record into the story of two separate 'races,' one wholly good and the other wholly evil, and this was transmitted in century after century of Christian teaching until it bore its evil fruit in the massacres of the First Crusade.

The elaborate scheme of Eusebius is not so fully worked out by other writers; and, in quoting him, I am not implying that the

Church of his contemporaries or successors consciously drew directly on his writings. I have quoted him because he represents the most complete systematization of an attitude which we can see growing from the battle of the Testimonies onwards, and can trace in subsequent centuries until we reach the medieval picture of the Jew as the physical offspring and willing servant of the Devil.

The strange system which he described coldy and logically is, for example, produced with heat and emotion by other fourth century Christian leaders. We can see it from two of the greatest, Hilary of Poitiers in the West and John Chrysostom in the East; and, geographically between them, we can see it put into practice, with a horrifying contempt for legality, by a third, Ambrose of Milan. Hilary, in a commentary on Psalm 52, says that the strong man who boasts of mischief 'is that people which has always persisted in iniquity and out of its abundance of evil has gloried in wickedness.' Chrysostom, in a series of six sermons preached at Antioch in 387, and in two similar discourses, reaches a height of obscene abuse and denunciation which has no parallel until one comes to the ravings of a Hitler or a Goebbels. The sermons stand in the most incomprehensible and paradoxical relation both to his reputation for sanctity and to the veneration in which he was held. But the most striking thing about them is that not one word of the torrent of abuse he pours on the Jewish people and their religion is concerned with the conduct of the Jews of Antioch of the fourth Christian century. It is all taken, and magnified, from the denunciations of the Old Testament, a fact which would not necessarily be clear to the congregation to which they were addressed. When Chrysostom tells these Christians that their Jewish neighbours 'sacrifice their sons and their daughters to devils; outrage nature; overthrow from their foundations the laws of relationships; are become worse than wild-beasts, and, for no reason at all murder their own offspring to worship the avenging devils who are attempting to destroy Christianity,' (I, 6) he by no means makes it apparent that he is quoting from a Psalm (106: 35-7) which was written the best part of a thousand years before and, even then, referred with poetic licence to the period of the Judges nearly a thousand years before it was written.

With Ambrose, the statesman bishop of Milan, this attitude to Jews passes into the sheer abuse of his episcopal power of excommunication to force the emperor himself to condone an illegal act. The bishop of Callinicum in the eastern provinces had led a mob which had burned down a synagogue. Theodosius the Great ordered the bishop to be punished for this violation of law and public order. Ambrose publicly refused him the sacraments in the cathedral of Milan until he had rescinded the order. He described the synagogue as a miserable hovel, a home of insanity, a place of unbelief which God himself had condemned; and he asked contemptuously who wanted the act of the bishop to be avenged—'God whom they have insulted or Christ whom they crucified?'

This attitude of three leading theologians of the fourth century is something which is the direct product of the conflict over the possession of the Old Testament. This is brought out admirably by *The Preparation of the Gospel* of Eusebius, a work which, apart from Book VII, is concerned with Greek philosophers not with Jews and Judaism. But the whole argument of the greater antiquity and purity of the religion of the 'Hebrews' would be entirely meaningless if, in fact, it was an argument in favour of Judaism and not of Christianity. The Church had put herself in the position where she was obliged to deny the right of the Jews to the possession of their scriptures. There had for some time been nothing new to add to the bitter argument about the prophecies of the birth and nature of the Messiah. But, once the Church began to make a claim on the loyalty of *all* the subjects of the Empire, it was no longer as necessary to wrest the Messiah from the Jews as it was to affirm the spiritual primacy of Christianity over all other systems of human thought, in particular over the philosophy of the Greeks. And to do this she had to appropriate to her exclusive possession all that she needed to quote from the historic Jewish Scriptures. It was of the greatest importance that she could show that even Moses (who was a pre-incarnation Christian) antedated anything that Greece had produced, whereas *she* had existed centuries before Moses was born.

This necessity was emphasised by the fact that the Jewish contemporaries of the fourth century Church were by no means disposed to accept the Christian claim in silence. Up to 313 it was they and not the Christians who had professed a *religio licita*. After the Empire had made peace with the Church they still remained a *religio licita* and they still retained, during the whole period under consideration, the basic citizenship which they had received under Caracalla in 212. They were well able to express their opinion of

Christian arguments, and there is ample evidence that they did so, and that the Church found them vigorous opponents, exercising especially their influence on potential converts to Christianity.

If there can be said to be facts behind the abuse of Chrysostom, it would be that Jews and Christians were too friendly in Antioch; and that Jews were the most effective spearhead of the argument against the truth of Christian theology. The Jew of whom the medieval Church was afraid was a bogey she herself had created. But in the earlier centuries this was not so. Jews could and did speak out their minds on what they considered the contradictions and absurdities of Christian theology. They were genuine opponents; but they needed to be understood and answered, not defamed and denigrated.

From the moment that the followers of Jesus as Messiah separated themselves from the rest of the Synagogue, and that the Synagogue in turn repudiated them, dispute and conflict were inevitable. The times being what they were, it was, humanly speaking, equally inevitable that it should be exceedingly bitter. From the reply of Origen to Celsus, we know that already the scurrilous life of Jesus which became the *Sepher Toledoth Jeshu* was being shaped in Jewish circles. There was plenty to add fuel to the fire of anger between the two opponents. But that which had a permanent effect was not the anger or the bitterness, but the complete deformation of the historical relationship by the Christian Church, expressed in the division of the Old Testament into the history of two contemporaneous but separate races of *Hebrews* and *Jews* which Eusebius systematised and other Christian leaders accepted.

Toleration of Christianity by Constantine dates from 313, and in 315 the Church was already showing her determination to bring her power to influence legislation into the battle against Judaism. There is a law of 18 October 315 which shows both the reality of the Jewish pressure referred to in the previous paragraph and the contemptuous attitude of the Church to her opponent. The law (Cod. Theod. 16.8.1) runs as follows:

Constantine to Evagrius:
We desire the Jews and their elders and patriarchs to be informed that if after the passage of this law anyone who flees from their gloomy sect to the worship of God is pursued by them with stones or any other molesta-

tion, as we know is at present happening, the offender shall be immediately consigned to the flames with all those who have taken part in the offence. But if any person shall join himself to their evil sect, and give himself up to their assemblies he shall suffer the same punishment.

The addition of a punishment for conversion to Judaism might well be considered an unjustifiable interference. Moreover, the language itself is deliberately offensive. Judaism is described as a *feralis* or *nefaria* sect, and the synagogue is given a term which is never applied to a religious building, but is army slang for a brothel.

The two other matters which engaged the attention of the Constantinian lawmakers in the interests of Christianity are the access of Jews to the decurionate and the protection from conversion to Judaism of non-Jewish slaves with Jewish masters. As to the first, Jews had originally been excused the burdens of local and civic government by the fact that it conflicted with their monotheism. This had, in its time, been reasonable, but with the passage under Constantine of polytheism from an imperial religion to a despised superstition, the reason for excusing Jews vanished. On the other hand, the curial office was the most detested in the Empire. Persons of curial rank were forbidden to travel or leave their districts to settle elsewhere. The office was made hereditary and, thus, might complete the ruin of an impoverished family, for its expense continued to be considerable. There is evidence that Christian officials had to be held back from denying the Jewish community the exemptions recognised to others. For three laws, of 321, 330 and 331 (Cod. Theod. 16.8.3, 2 and 4), repeat the immunities of Jewish clergy and communal officials, and this repetition suggests that it was not readily obeyed. Fifty years later a law of Gratian, Valentinian and Theodosius (Cod. Theod. 12.1.99) abolished all exceptions and immunities so far as Jews were concerned.

The last law of Constantine dealing with Jews refers to the circumcision of a Christian or non-Jewish slave (16.9.1 of 335). The slave gets his freedom and the Jew loses his possession. The constant repetition of laws dealing with non-Jewish slaves (see the index in my *Conflict of the Church and the Synagogue*, p. 391) indicates that the slave trade, as well as the possession of slaves, involved a number of wealthy Jews at the time. The fact that the Gentile Christian Church began largely among the poorer classes of the Mediterranean world probably explains the acute awareness of the problem once the clergy had access to legislative power.

The Councils of the Church during the fifty years following 313 illustrate the extent of the actual problem dealt with in these pages, for they deal entirely with the close association between Jews and Christians of all ranks in the affairs of daily life. A list of them is its own commentary:

c.300   Canon 16
Elvira   Catholic maidens are not to be given in marriage to heretics unless the latter are willing to join the Catholic church. It is unfitting for Jews or heretics to receive such brides, for there can be no fellowship between a believer and an unbeliever. Parents who offend against this canon shall be excluded from communion for five years.
Canon 49
We warn the owners of property that they must not allow the fruits which they have received by the action of grace from God to be blessed by Jews, lest they render our own Christian blessing without effect. Any offender will be excluded from the Church.
Canon 50
Any ecclesiastic or layman who partakes of food with the Jews is to be excluded from communion that he may amend.
Canon 78
Any married Christian who commits adultery with a Jewess or heathen is excluded from communion. Any other may be restored after five years' punishment.

341   Canon 1
Antioch   Any bishop, priest or deacon, who causes confusion to the congregation and disturbance to the churches by eating the Passover together with the Jews (or 'on the same day as the Jews') shall be considered expelled from the church.

360   Canon 16
Laodicea   The gospels as well as other portions of scripture are to be read upon Saturday.
Canon 29
Christians must not Judaise, and rest on the Sabbath, but work on that day. But, if possible, they must rest as good Christians on Sunday. If they are found Judaising, let them be anathema.
Canon 37
It is not lawful to receive gifts from Jews or heretics for the feasts, or to share the feasts with them.

Canon 38

It is not lawful to accept unleavened bread from the Jews or to take part in their impious ceremonies.

It is fitting to end with this picture. Nothing, I believe, can excuse the attitude taken by the Church in her hour of triumph. Nothing can justify the appalling travesty of history fixed by the calm and unemotional arguments of Eusebius, or graven in the memory by the tempestuous emotion of Chrysostom. But it is at least partly explained by the strength of the Jewish community at that time, and by the close, indeed intimate, relations which existed between ordinary Jews and Christians. The canons indicate it sufficiently without my taking time by offering in evidence the anecdotes, grave and gay, which have survived from the period.

Reflections upon the study of the General Councils in the Fifteenth Century

E. F. JACOB

Emeritus Chichele Professor of Modern History, University of Oxford

---

THE twentieth General Council of the Roman Church may provide a sufficient excuse for reflecting on some earlier assemblies of this kind, particularly those of the fifteenth century.[1] One may well enquire what the twin-headed Church of 1409 has to do with the unified body of today. Historical parallels and analyses may be stretched too far, and the Church has indeed turned its back upon the events of the period 1378-1449; but there is always a connection between unity and reform, and we have been reminded recently that they go hand in hand. If the present Council has no longer the task of reconciling a divided body, it has in front of it, just as in those fifteenth-century councils, the problem of internal reorganization and of presenting the result to the outside world.

In the period of the councils with which we deal there was for many years no unity of the head and the utmost discrepancy of view upon the methods of achieving reform. Christendom had received in the Schism a shock from which no-one seemed able to recover. But it was a shock that aroused an extraordinary effort, a determination to tolerate weary years of absence in lands far from home on the part of those participating in the council and, moreover, one that brought about a period of self-examination in which not only

---

[1] Since this was written, Mgr. Jedin put into my hands (at Trento) his admirable discussion of Conciliarism (H. Jedin, *Bischöfliches Konzil oder Kirchenparlament?* Vorträge der Aeneas Silvius Stiftung an der Universität Basel, II, 1963) with valuable bibliographical notes to which readers may be referred.

professional theologians but also the moderate wayfaring man took part. It is common now to see conciliar activity against the background of law and administration: it must also be seen in the light of contemporary Christian humanism and Christian spirituality; and the leaders of the movement, whether from Paris, Salisbury, Deventer, Windesheim or the universities of Vienna and Cracow, to name only a few centres, were people who put the individual, and the bearing of his life upon the society of the Church, into a new context. It is this bent which altered the contemporary attitude towards positive law and ceremony, and ranked the humbler academics with the professional administrators. The new attitude is well stated by Gerson in his *De Unitate Ecclesiastica*:

The Fifth Consideration:
The unity of the Church in one vicar of Christ does not for its attainment at the present time require a literal observance of the outward terms of positive law, or of ordinary processes in summonses, accusations, denunciations, or similar matters. This General Council may proceed summarily, and with the good and important [principle] of equity. It shall have sufficient judicial authority to use ἐπιείκεια, i.e. the power to interpret all positive law, to adapt it for the sake of accomplishing the union more speedily and more advantageously, and, if need be, to abandon it [positive law, including the canon laws] because it was instituted for the peace and well-being of the Church. If it had been instituted properly and not by any tyrannical malignity, it should not militate against the Church, lest the power that has been conferred on human institutions bring about the destruction rather than the edification of the Church. In fact the power of using ἐπιείκεια with regard to a matter of doctrine [*doctrinaliter*] belongs principally to those learned in theology, which in relation to other [sciences] is fundamental [*architectoria*] and thereafter with those skilled in the science of canon and civil law, as they have to take their basic ideas from the principles of divine and natural law.[1]

This attitude is, needless to say, derived from Aquinas[2] and was taken up by other conciliar thinkers when they were considering how to break through the canonical rule that it is the pope alone who summons the general council. The initiative, they argue, under existing circumstances, comes from the Church at large.

[1] In the translation of J. K. Cameron, *Advocates of Reform*, ed. M. Spinka, S.C.M. Library of Christian Classics, XIV (1953), 143.

[2] See W. Ullmann, *The Origins of the Great Schism*, London 1948, 198 f; and his *Principles of Government and Politics in the Middle Ages*, London 1961, 293-4.

The assemblies for which the historian's sources are most abundant are Constance and Basle along with Ferrara-Florence (1438-9). For Pisa in 1409, the publication of the *Acta* by Dr Vincke in *Römische Quartalschrift*[1] brought that Council into line with the other three and demonstrated its character as a great legal process against Gregory XII and Benedict XIII. As the process was, with minor exceptions, practically the only serious work undertaken by the Council, Pisa stands apart from the other ecumenical councils of the fifteenth century.[2] Its interest lies more in the wealth of preliminary treatise rather than in the results (which were unhappy) or in its day-to-day progress. A possible further exception is Siena where the protocol is largely missing and only the Sienese archives can supply the gaps. For Constance, Basle and Ferrara-Florence, both official *Acta* and personal narratives have survived, for the latter in a Greek version as well as in the Latin, while there is a Greek historian's commentary of high importance. Each council presents its own documentary problems, but perhaps only for Ferrara-Florence can they be said to be scientifically exposed from a documentary point of view.[3] For Constance the way onward was brilliantly pointed by Finke, working on the basis of von der Hardt, but even his magisterial works—the *Quellen und Forschungen zur Geschichte des Konstanzer Konzils* (Paderborn 1889) and the introductions prefixed to the various sections of the *Acta Concilii Constanciensis*—mark only the beginnings of modern manuscript study[4] and no Jedin can arise to write fully the history of this Council before further discovery and examination of manuscript sources has taken place. In the case of Basle it was fortunate that a scholar like Johannes Haller was available to begin the edition of the notaries' manuals, and even more to give in the masterly first volume of the edition (1896) an introduction to the historians of the Council and to the available correspondence in the papal archives and

---

[1] XLVI (1938), 81-331.

[2] It is omitted from *Conciliorum Oecumenicorum Decreta*, compiled by the Centro di Documentazione, Istituto per le Scienze Religiose, Bologna 1962.

[3] Cf. the series edited by G. Hofman, *Concilium Florentinum: Documenta et Scriptores* (Orientalia Christiana) which contains the *Acta Graeca* of the Council, ed. Fr. Joseph Gill, S.J. There is an excellent bibliography of sources in J. Gill, *The Council of Florence*, Cambridge 1959, 416-20.

[4] Some of these problems are discussed by C. M. D. Crowder, 'Le Concile de Constance et l'édition de Von der Hardt', *RHE*, LVII (1962), 409-45.

elsewhere. It is the relation between the official *Acta* and the narrative historians which presents some of the best opportunities for study. Thus, in the case of Constance, for example, a close study of Cardinal Guillaume Fillastre's diary, which, as Finke pointed out, is in many respects more accurate than the protocol itself[1] and is now available for English readers in the excellent version of Dr Loomis,[2] is much to be desired.

Fillastre, who gave practical shape and form to the ideas of his colleague at Constance, Pierre d'Ailly, cardinal of Cambrai, was an observer who was also one of the main actors during the whole of the Council's existence and nothing is more illuminating than his account of the confusions and complications of February and March 1415 and of the period June to October 1417. The dean of Rheims, cardinal of St Mark, is a particularly interesting figure because he was both a French ecclesiastic and a curialist, foreseeing in some of the reforming measures presented to the Council's commissions of reform the decline in authority of the Sacred College, and because he himself became practically the author of its resurrection. In him, the patriotic anti-Lancastrian and far-seeing administrator are found combined, and it is natural that he should view any attempt to control the policy of a Roman Church apart from the Sacred College with the gravest suspicion. He believed in the corporate direction of events by the College. He was not opposed to reform and he had a high sense of the duty of *reformatio capitis*, but he was determined that the process should be directed from the top, and, whatever he may have thought about the members, it was there that the change must start. In the election of Martin V he played a leading role, for in the end it was only his accession and that of Foix to Cardinal Odo Colonna that made Martin V's election secure. The passage in which he narrates this is one to be remembered:

Note that when the accession occurred, a procession of the General Council and City Clergy, among whom were some two hundred innocent children of the city wearing their surplices, was passing in front of the conclave chanting the hymn 'Veni Creator'. It was heard clearly from the conclave. The electors were praying on their knees and many were stirred to tears. Afterwards the transfer of votes was completed and the

---

[1] *Acta Concilii Constanciensis*, Münster 1923, II, 8.

[2] In *The Council of Constance: the Unification of the Church*, ed. J. H. Mundy and K. M. Woody, Records of Civilization, LXII, Columbia 1961, 200-447.

election held according to rule. All who had left the chapel were recalled and the election resumed, the candidate elect standing on the altar and the electors in their seats. All and everyone, cardinals as well as the rest, voted in turn for him. He was asked to consent and did so humbly. Then all in order of their rank came forward to kiss his foot, his hand and his mouth and thus accepted him as Roman and Supreme Pontiff and in honour of St. Martin (for it was St. Martin's Day) he was advised to take the name of Martin and he agreed.[1]

Fillastre realises that this was the most notable moment in the long process of *unio capitis* which had been sought since the cardinals came to Pisa. Viewing the election of John XXIII after Alexander V had died at Bologna, he merely observed, 'it is said that the election was corrupt, and certainly was so as regards the merits of the man elected.'[2] Here he followed the opinion of his time. Recent research on the relations of John to Ladislas of Naples and the condottiere regime in northern Italy has shown how difficult it is to pass clear and categorical judgements upon John XXIII.[3]

To Fillastre we owe the story of the deepening distrust of the French, Italians and Aragonese for the tactics of the Anglo-German bloc that had come to formal existence after the Treaty of Canterbury in 1416: a difference cleverly exploited by himself and the majority of the Sacred College to prevent the emperor from carrying out his projects of reform. It is impossible that with all this significant observation Fillastre's constitutional day-book can ever be neglected. But Ulrich of Richental, from whose chronicle Finke drew so much colour in his famous but too little known *Pictures from the Council of Constance*, deserves just as much comment, and to write him down, as has commonly been done, as a superficial observer of the ceremonial side of the Council and of local detail in the markets and streets of Constance is short-sighted and unhistorical. The extraordinary honour accorded to the emperor which is reflected upon throughout the whole narrative is a practical illustration of the position of the emperor as given in Dietrich of

---

[1] *Council of Constance*, 428, from *Acta Concilii Constanciensis*, II, 159.

[2] Finke, *Acta*, II, 14.

[3] Fillastre is reporting current views about John XXIII's character, but as P. D. Partner, *The Papal State under Martin V*, London 1958, 20 f. points out, John, while legate in the Romagna, had proved himself an administrator of character and ability in contrast to Gregory XII who had become the creature of Ladislas of Naples.

Niem's *Viridarium* and requires pondering, if his imperial journey for peacemaking in Europe is to be understood.[1]

It is to the Council of Basle that one must rather look for modern studies of the relationship of chronicle to record. For this Council there are a number of narrative accounts by contemporaries. The historian who commands greatest acclaim is John of Segovia, the Salamanca graduate, whom we know in two capacities: as an advocate of peaceful understanding with Islam, and as the composer of a chronicle less partisan and more generously conceived than Fillastre's account. The first of these aspects has been dealt with by Dr Cabanelas Rodríguez in his *Juan di Segovia y el problemo Islamico*, published at Madrid in 1952, and recently by Professor R. W. Southern;[2] the second, though with frequent references to Cabanelas Rodríguez, by Uta Fromherz (Basle 1960). The latter is an important treatise upon a man who steadily grew in stature as the Council of Basle proceeded. In 1440 he was made cardinal St Calixtus by Felix V whose election he supported, and he remained an ardent conciliar to the end of the Council. That he had a clear and accurate recording mind can be seen from the fact that in 1440 he was given, along with certain others, the task of editing the acts of the Council of Constance; and after Felix's departure from the Council he was made overseer for the papal finances at Basle, a post of which, because of its difficulties, he was to complain bitterly.

The chronicle of John of Segovia is drawn from his own experience as well as from the official *Acta*. He was incorporated on 8 April 1433 under his own hand, since the embassy of the king of Castile did not arrive till August 1434, delayed because the king wanted to see which side, the pope or the Council, was going to win in the debate over the papal dissolution. In the first year of his stay he belonged to the household of the Spanish Cardinal Cervantes, and was assigned to the Deputation of the Faith. That is why in his chronicle such stress is laid upon the *reduccio Bohemorum* and later upon the dogma of the Immaculate Conception. In the famous debate in general congregation of 5 December 1436 over the place for the prospective council of Greeks and Latins, he recorded a vote for the cautious formula: Vienna; if the Greeks wish, Avignon;

[1] Recent work on this important curialist is noticed in E. F. Jacob, *Essays in the Conciliar Epoch*, 3rd ed. Manchester 1963, appendix to ch. 2, 'Dietrich of Niem'.

[2] R. W. Southern, *Western Views of Islam in the Middle Ages*, Cambridge Mass. 1962.

Pavia, Florence, Udine, Savoy and Siena or a place on which the two sides agree—as Dr Fromherz remarks, *ein sehr vorsichtige Formulierung*.[1] Aeneas Sylvius in one of his letters remarked that Segovia belonged to the party of the legate (Cesarini) who was already voting in the papal interest, but this, as Haller showed, was most unlikely: he certainly voted with the majority led by Cardinal Aleman, who proposed Avignon as the meeting place and it was after this that he began to appreciate Cesarini's progressive alienation from the conciliar majority. He took no active part in the second process of the Council against the pope in 1437: he still had too great an admiration for the remarkable president, Cesarini, to join in the conciliar hue and cry,[2] and one of the most touching things in the chronicle is the delicacy and skill with which he delineates the legate's attempts to mediate, even at an advanced stage in the dispute, between the Council and Eugenius IV. The subtlety of spirit which Voigt attributed to Cesarini,[3] here was illustrated at its best. But it was of no avail. Cesarini left a deeply regretful—not a resentful—Council in January 1438, and a new phase in the proceedings of Basle had begun.

Segovia had to throw in his lot with the radicals and to state the case, moderately, for the deposition of Eugenius IV. Aeneas Sylvius in his historical commentary on the Council of Basle has depicted a scene from the discussion, after Cesarini had gone, over the eight conclusions why the pope should be deposed as a heretic:

Inter tot tamen strepitus turbulentasque vociferationes non defuit spectato et optimo viro Johanni Segovia ex gymnasio Salamantino Theologo, audientia, quoniam et illum conciliares avidi audiebant, quasi ex suis unum, et alii virtutem hominis, summamque bonitatem etiam inviti venerabantur. Tanta est enim virtuti innata authoritas, ut etiam in hoste colatur; verumque illud Vergilianum in eo fuit:

Tum pietate gravem, ac meritis si forte virum quem
Conspexere, silent arrectisque auribus adstant.

Omnes namque (ut assurrexit Johannes) silentium tenuerunt.[4]

In voting for a new election after the deposition of Eugenius IV, Segovia insisted on a sixty-day delay, which he said was prescribed

[1] Uta Fromherz, *Johannes von Segovia als Geschichtsschreiber des Konzils von Basel*, Basle 1960, 29.

[2] Fromherz, op. cit. 101 ff.

[3] *Aenea Silvio de' Piccolomini*, Berlin 1856, I, 216.

[4] Fromherz, op. cit. 31.

by *honestas*, rather than on the quick election suggested by *utilitas* (sectional interests). It is natural therefore that after the election of Count Amadeus of Savoy as Felix V, a man of his authority and standing should play a part in the attempt to win the German electors from their neutrality. To be an advocate of the Council to the end required more than a sense of opportunism. Aeneas Sylvius had the opportunist's *flair* for judging the exact moment. Segovia had stood firm from 1445 on, trying to bring about a new council so as to effect the reform repeatedly put off. The faith which sustained him was a belief that the Church itself was the competent authority with power derived immediately from God and Christ. It is itself the *suprema potestas;* it is *illimitata, nullis circumclusa terminis;* what is unlimited can of its very nature only be one. *Plurificacio omnino sibi repugnat.*

. . . quod ecclesia universalis sit primum et unicum eius supreme potestatis adequatum subiectum, ad ipsum demonstrante irrefragabiliter necessarie evidencia racionis, non minoris entitatis fore subiectum pre accidente, quod in illo fundatur. Cum igitur suprema potestas ecclesie accidens sit, subiectum profecto, a quo dependet, maioris erit entitatis. Est autem potestas ecclesie, sicut et regimen ipsius, continua permanens, invariabilis seu immobilis, eterne sibi competens et usque ad seculi consummacionem, propter quod assignari illi opportet subiectum eiusmodi condiciones habens; non vero tale est papa aut generale concilium, neutro eorum continuo permanente. Erit igitur ecclesia primum per se ac principale subiectum et adequatum supreme ecclesiastice potestatis.[1]

Segovia ascribes to the Church and its power a fundamental unity; he sees in it more than the *congregatio fidelium;* unity belongs to the concept and the very being of the Church; it is involved in its existence and does not arise as a secondary effect from the multitude of individual believers. Here one might compare Nicholas of Cues who thinks of the *unitas concordantiae* as an end to be striven for by all believers, and one without which the Church has no authority.[2] To Segovia unity is a reality inherent in the concept of the Church and he makes no distinction between *mater ecclesia* and *populus fidelis.* To the *fideles* belong the bishops and the hierarchy as well as the lower ranks.

Does not this doctrine of the Church as supreme ecclesiastical

---

[1] The quotation is in Fromherz, 131-2.
[2] Fromherz, op. cit. 50.

power fail to take into account the very patent facts of division from 1437 onwards[1]? Segovia would only imply that it is *the Church as a whole*, not the hierarchy or any section of it, which must display its unity in action, and, if the present Council is failing, contrive a fresh assembly under an undoubted pontiff. Confronted with the fact of the success of the transferred Council at Ferrara-Florence he could claim that these were the tactics of a minority: the true council suffers a *passio*, it is assailed by the papal dissolution, yet among the Fathers there is *persistencia*, princes in number adhere to it, and marks of confidence give it genuine *consolacio* or *comfortatio*.[2] To him Basle is a suffering body, patient as the physical body of Christ was and now, as his *corpus mysticum*, has to be.

One other aspect of Segovia which has been the subject of recent research is his attitude towards Islam. Here Darío Cabanelas Rodríguez has emphasised Segovia's deep interest in bringing about harmony between the Church and Mohammedanism: converting if possible the Moorish princes of Spain, and if that was impossible, showing the fundamental resemblances between the two religions. In 1431, after a successful campaign of John II of Castile against the Moors, he held a disputation at Medina del Campo, John's headquarters, on the Moorish charge against the Christians that they had two gods, father and son, and that God had abandoned his son to die rather than rescuing him. Segovia's reply to the charge constitutes the first of his treatises dealing with the persons of the Trinity. In 1453, when he had become bishop of St Jean de Maurienne, he wrote for the priory of Aiton a number of works on Islam, especially a translation of the Koran and the treatise *De gladio spiritus*. It is in this that he gave the story of his disputation at Medina del Campo, followed by twelve *intelligentiae* on the doctrine of the Trinity and seven *questiones* or *animadvertentiae* on the doctrine of the Incarnation. The treatise belongs to the latter part of 1453.[3] In September that year, to Segovia's deep disillusionment, Nicholas V proclaimed a new crusade; Segovia had been hoping to send the new treatise to the pope but clearly this was now useless; he tried in 1458 to influence Aeneas Sylvius (Pius II), but without avail, by sending some of his treatises.

[1] Fromherz, op. cit. 149.
[2] Fromherz, op. cit. 21.
[3] Fromherz, op. cit. 42 ff.

In the *De gladio spiritus* Segovia recognises that the Crusades were a mistake: it is true that the capture of Jerusalem was important but its maintenance imposed a severe strain, and after its capture the attempts to recover the Holy Places did nothing but harm. This seems to echo the complaints made at Constance of Christian incursions into Slavonic territories.

How were the Mohammedans to be brought to a knowledge of the Trinity and the Incarnation? At bottom lay a problem of the sources, and while many passages in the Koran could be interpreted in the Christian sense, the Bible and the Koran are so fundamentally different that only an appeal to reason could convince the Mohammedans. Segovia has to show that the word of God became Man and to produce a rational proof for the existence of the Trinity. These arguments bring to mind the vision of Cusanus, *De pace fidei*, where, in a disputation conducted by the Word, St Peter and St Paul, representatives of the various religions were brought to a knowledge of the truth and professed that they were not aware of it previously: they discover *religio una in rituum varietate*.[1] Unlike Segovia, Cusanus in his later days held that in the end such a unification can only come through the immediate intervention of God. He does not think that he can make out a strong rational case, but his Christian disputants, St Peter and St Paul, ask for the Divine help to influence the conflicting sects. The dialogue is deeply interesting because the aim is to bring the parties to a single religion,[2] whereas Segovia is in the end content with a *convivencia humana*, perhaps somewhat on the Delhi model, that is, an understanding to live and work and perhaps pray together, rather than a formal unity. Here I must quote the observation of Uta Fromherz: 'Ideas like his could only arise at that time in the mind of a Spaniard who from his experience knew the possibility of friendly intercourse with the Mohammedans and in whose world Islam was far from dangerous and to be regarded as a philosophical problem.' [3] It is to be noted that both Segovia and Cusanus regard Mohammedans as tinged with Nestorian heresy and Cusanus declares in the Introduction to his *Cibratio Alchoran* that 'the sect of the Mohammedans arose in the same spirit as the

[1] *De pace fidei*, ed. R. Klibansky and H. Bascour, *Medieval and Renaissance Studies*, Supplement III, London 1956, 7.

[2] 'Veritas veri cultus,' ibid. 62.

[3] Fromherz, op. cit. 50-1.

Nestorians, with like mind and with equally potent eloquence.' [1]
Cusanus knew Segovia and corresponded with him and, like
Cusanus, Segovia was aware than an accurate establishment and full
understanding of the text of the Koran must precede any attempts
to argue against the sectaries.

One turns back to Constance to discover an important fact,
based on principle. At Basle dialectic had become the supreme test.
In Constance the work of the reforming commissions was discussed
and argued, but little attempt was made to talk with those who held
views different from the Church. The process against Hus and
Jerome was conducted by dogmatic statements and although we
know that Bishop Robert Hallum did his best to convince the
Bohemian, it was statement rather than argument which was
employed. The great difference at Basle and at Ferrara-Florence
was that the Church had consented to discuss and defend, on a
carefully delimited basis, tenets which for centuries had been
regarded by her as essential and fundamental. These were not only
matters of belief but also of administrative and judicial order, and
attention was coming to be focussed on the significance of this
change and of the place taken in the disputes by the ordinary
academics, by the doctors and masters incorporated in the deputations.[2] The fact of their being able to influence the discussions

---

[1] Ibid., 51.

[2] P. Ourliac, 'Sociologie du Concile de Bâle,' *RHE*, LVI (1961), 19 ff. The influence of
a university 'middle' element can be seen, for instance, in the career at Basle and else-
where of Dr Thomas Ebendorfer, a theological professor, one of the representatives of
the university of Vienna at the Council. Ebendorfer's diary was printed in 'Monumenta
Conciliorum Generalium,' ed. E. Birk, I (1857), 701 ff. His life is studied by Alphons
Lhotsky, *Thomas Ebendorfer, Ein österreichischer Geschichtsschreiber, Theologe und
Diplomat des 15 Jahrhunderts*, Schriften der Monumenta Germanica Historica, XV,
Stuttgart 1957. The strong support of the Council (and of the earlier fifteenth-century
councils) given by the academics derived largely from their conviction of the need for
reform. It was specially evident among the Germans at the time of Basle, and can be
heard in the famous document known as the 'Reformatio Sigismundi' and the con-
comitant literature: cf. Lothar Graf zu Dohna, *Reformatio Sigismundi, Beiträge zum
Verstandnis einer Reformschrift des funfzehnten Jahrhunderts* (Veröffentlichen des
Max-Planck Instituts für Geschichte), Göttingen 1960. Vienna, as the letters of Peter of
Pulka show, was urging this strongly at Constance. The function of academics as
ambassadors in conciliar diplomacy (though varying in their support according to
national instructions) is well illustrated in R. H. Trame, S.J., *Rodrigo Sanchez de
Arévalo, 1404-1470*, Catholic Univ. of America, Washington 1958, 16-62, a study of the
Salamanca theologian, and, of course, by the career of Ebendorfer himself, especially
at the diets of Nuremberg and Frankfurt, 1444-5.

was an important advance for the middle and lower ranks of the clergy.

This change was reflected in, and made possible by, the passage from the 'nation' to the 'deputation' system. A 'nation' system was one of administrative convenience and political necessity, forced upon the Council by the need for counteracting the numerous votes of Italian prelates supporting John XXIII. Fillastre's diary shows that it was not easily accepted. The impatience of Sigismund for a favourable French vote in favour of John XXIII, giving adequate guarantees of resignation, led to an atmosphere of doubt and distrust and alienated the cardinals, who, like D'Ailly, were convinced of the need to uphold the central control and direction of the Council by themselves. But it is interesting to note that in his memorandum *De Ecclesiae et cardinalium auctoritate*, read in one of the churches in Constance on 1 October 1416, D'Ailly maintained that the government of the Church should not be regarded as an unmixed monarchy: that it had elements of aristocracy and of democracy, and that, in Aristotelian style, a mixture of the two, or 'polity,' is best. Now at the Council of Constance polity, on the whole, went under; the predominant authority of leaders of Church and State in the 'nation' delegations and their liability to be directed by their own monarchs ruled out in many cases the more democratic discussions which we know to have taken place at Basle; and with the Bohemians who appeared at Constance there could be no other method than the genuine give and take of opinion. There was wrangling in the general sessions at Constance over procedural points, but there was no one there like Cesarini to steer the argument.

A principal advance made by modern conciliar history is to be found in the study of debates and treatises, read or published, and positions advocated in the Basle Assembly. The Council had deserted the way of dogma and admitted the way of argument. It is this change which, combined with the contemporary political situation in France, made inevitable the failure of the English representatives at Basle to influence the course of the proceedings or to lend themselves to the pacification of Europe at which the Council was aiming. A significant attestation is found in Dr Schofield's discussion of the reception of the Basle envoy Gerardo Landriani, bishop of Lodi, who came in June 1432 to secure Henry VI's adherence to the Council and the subsequent failure of the English delegation to make any impression.[1] Landriani, on the whole, found both the English Council and the bishops friendly, and arrangements were made for the departure of a powerful delegation, but on 28 January 1433, Henry VI wrote a letter to his ambassadors, while they were still on the way, showing how meagre and inaccurate was the information about the Council that was available in England and how slow were the movements of the English delegation compared with those of the Bohemians, who had been in the Council since 4 January. 'Still more astonishing', remarks Dr Schofield, 'is the evidence contained in this letter (it is from Emmanuel College MS 142) that the King had heard for the first time of the Council's adoption of "deputations" instead of "nations" only after his ambassadors had left England.' He therefore sent them fresh instructions:

> We remember having instructed you at your departure from our realm of England that, on coming to the place of the Council, you should there participate and co-operate with others, especially in the cause of the faith and for bringing back the Bohemians. However, since we have heard that the same Council has decided to proceed not by nations but deputations, we perceive in such case it is to be feared the decrees of the said Council must proceed from and be enacted by a majority not of nations but of persons. And as the Bohemians, for whose reunion you have principally been sent, have not yet come to the place of the Council—so it is said— we wish you in the absence of the same Bohemians from the aforesaid place, also to absent yourselves and to remain in some convenient place until our orators come to join you and can arrive simultaneously at the same place [i.e., of the Council].[2]

They were sent to the Council and very nearly in the same breath told to absent themselves! In the summer of 1433 Henry VI protested against the oath of incorporation by which the entrants undertook to work for the Council's honour, to give good advice, not to disclose individual votes, and, this is most important, to maintain and defend the Council's decrees. Henry VI on 17 July wrote to the Council complaining of this oath and described it as unprecedented, contrary to the teaching of Christ and degrading to the temporal rulers whose ambassadors were expected to submit to it. Now this

---

[1] 'The First English Delegation to the Council of Basel,' *JEH*, XII (1961), 167-05

[2] Schofield, art. cit. 180-1.

oath had been adopted by the Council at the beginning of February 1432, which was the month in which the system of the four deputations had been accepted. These deputations and incorporation became the two main obstacles to English participation in the Council. Only in the debates on the four articles of Prague were the English allowed to participate in the Council's work. Despite the ineffectiveness of their stand against the Hussites the English were deeply interested in the Council's offer of mediation in France and had made it the basis of provisional plans for diplomatic work at Basle by a later section of the delegation. These plans were ultimately frustrated. Generally speaking, if the first part of the delegation had been allowed to accept the deputation system and be incorporated,[1] the influence of this country in the peace negotiations of the Council would have been substantially greater than it, in fact, turned out to be.

The attitude of this delegation may in the end have been determined by the fact that representatives of Charles VII of France had already been incorporated before the English arrived. The Council was anxious for the adhesion of any power that could help it. It had to compete against papal efforts in the same direction and the struggle with Eugenius was the whole time in the background. The English Council was interested in Basle as a method of refuting the Hussites and perhaps of procuring the extradition of one of their leaders, the renegade Peter Payne, and it was envisaging the Council as possible mediator for a satisfactory settlement in France. On reform it does not appear to have uttered any instruction at all. Recent work on the diplomatic history of the three years has pointed to the failure at Basle as an important factor in the depression suffered by the English cause in France.

The study of conciliar thought has been invigorated and to some extent revolutionised by modern work on the impact which the canon lawyers made upon contemporary political theory, in particular the theory of the *plenitudo potestatis*. The canon lawyer is not by definition a political theorist: he is essentially a commentator on texts and cases; and these, for their elucidation, depend in part upon the opinions of his canonist predecessors and in part upon

---

[1] 'No member of the English delegation was incorporated—a point that has not been sufficiently stressed': Schofield, art. cit. 183.

concrete instances within his own range of view. It is not his business to embark upon general questions which are matters for the theologian; but in the later Middle Ages the canonist was continually concerned with the practical problem of authority, most of all of what the pope could or could not do by reason of the plentitude of his power. Here I may be allowed to quote a passage written elsewhere:

> The canonists could deal with this by two different methods. On the one hand, and here they act strictly within their own field, they could insist with Huguccio that any reasonable theory of Church government must be founded on a clear distinction between the authority inherent in the whole *congregatio fidelium* and the powers that could be exercised by the institutional *ecclesia Romana* which he identified with the Pope and cardinals. Secondly, the canonist could subscribe to a theory put forward by Hostiensis of the distribution of authority within an ecclesiastical corporation in the same way as the bishop is part of the corporation of his cathedral church, sharing with the canons the responsibility for guiding its affairs and possessing practical powers to act on its behalf; so that the Pope is part of the college of cardinals, and in turn pope and cardinals stand in a like relationship to the *universitas fidelium* in which ultimate sovereignty resides. To establish this it was necessary to show that the *universitas fidelium* was a *universitas* in the most legally precise sense of the term, and this was demonstrated by Huguccio when he asserted that the Church as a whole was subject to the same rules of corporation structure as any lesser chapter or college.[1]

But there was another, an extra-legal way of combatting the *plenitudo potestatis*: to set against it the need for moral action and moral restraint and to maintain that the pope is bound by the faith that he owes to the Catholic religion and to the Church as its organ, to uphold the example of Christ. His ideal in fact must be the *imitatio Christi*. How characteristic of the Christian humanism of the fifteenth century! If the pope falls away from this, action can be taken against him by the whole body of the Church. It is in pursuit of these moral ends, recently summed up by Ludwig Buisson as *caritas*, that process can be undertaken.[2] Thus certain great fifteenth-century canonists departed from the cautious distinctions

[1] Jacob, *Essays in the Conciliar Epoch*, 3rd ed. 1963, 240-1. This is based upon B. Tierney, *Foundations of the Conciliar Theory*, Cambridge 1953, chs. 2 and 3.

[2] Ludwig Buisson, *Potestas und Caritas*, Cologne 1958, chs. 4 and 5 (especially 269).

made by their predecessors and subscribed to what is practically a subjective doctrine justifying resistance to the papal plenitude.

These extra-legal, almost 'nature-rightly,' doctrines are found embodied in the work of men like Petrus de Anchorano, prominent at Pisa, who died in 1416, Antonius de Butrio (d.1408) and, need we say, in the great Zabarella (d.1417) whose gloss on the Schism in his commentary on the Clementines is known to all conciliar scholars. Zabarella, of course, knew all the strictly legal arguments for the control of papal plenitude. These jurists set the standard for their noteworthy successors, John of Imola and Nicholas de Tudeschis, better known as Panormitanus. Zabarella taught both of these men and it may be remembered that Nicholas was auditor-general of accounts in the Apostolic Camera at the beginning of the Council of Basle. He stood for Eugenius IV in the Council when he (Nicholas) had joined it, and then followed the conciliar majority and passed over to the side of Felix V, who made him cardinal. He is a most important canonist, not only for his mastery of the sources, but also because he thinks out familiar problems in a fresh way and carries them a stage further.

In the early stages of this development it is action against the pope on the ground of his heresy which is demanded and argued. This goes back to a gloss of Huguccio on the words *nisi deprehendatur a fide devius* (*Dist.* 40, 1, 6) as Dr Tierney has shown.[1] The concept of heresy widens in Conrad of Gelnhausen, Petrus de Anchorano and Zabarella. The pope is heretical if he remains long in schism; if, in fact, there is *error et pertinacia*, and, as Anchorano stresses, action against him is justified because of the *crimen periurii fraccionis voti*. Panormitanus delivered a very clear opinion. If the pope sins he can be warned according to the evangelical rule, 'If thy brother sin against thee' etc. Supposing his sin is public and the Church sustains scandal therefrom, if despite warning he will not abstain, it must be told to the Church, i.e. to the council representing it, and by it he can be punished, particularly if he refuses to reform. This charge of scandal can be applied to the pope not merely for persisting in the schism and so incurring the charge of heresy, but for persistant refusal to reform his administration: thus the papal system of reservations came in question at Constance.

[1] Tierney, op. cit. 57-8, and Appendix i.

In 1415, the French nation in a special *Deliberatio* made *annates* the subject of their complaint. Excesses in administration, evil administration of the spiritualities and temporalities of the Church were joined together in the document deposing John XXIII for dishonourable life and morals, scandalising the Church of God and the people of Christ. John had persisted in this conduct 'after due and caritative admonition and so had rendered himself notoriously incorrigible'. Here is the moral rather than the legal revolt against the plentitude of power.[1] But it was all the more difficult to bring the charge of scandal against a pope of upright life like Eugenius IV when he declined to reform the curial system. This was a matter of finance and technique, and John of Torquemada could very well stand out against the conciliar majority when such extra-legal sanctions were applied. Once Eugenius IV had been led, his hand forced by the Council, to sanction Cesarini's method of securing the *reduccio Bohemorum*, what strictly legal justification had the Council for their action against, and eventual deposition of, Eugenius? The papal lawyer could argue that even if *maior pars concilii* resisted a papal transfer of the Council of Basle to Ferrara-Florence, and voted for the continuance of the Council in a meeting place chosen by them, it was not necessarily the *sanior pars* that did so. The history of the passage of Cesarini and others including Cusanus to the papal side in 1437-8 illustrates the fears of men who saw the dangers in these subjective criteria that were sweeping the Council.

For some of us this has a certain paradoxical interest when we recollect that in England Archbishop Henry Chichele who in 1431-2 had held firm by Eugenius and persuaded his Convocation to follow that pontiff, Chichele, who had refused to apply in England the *annates* decree of the Council (1435), sent down to Oxford among his first present of legal books to the library of his new college, the Commentaries of Anchorano, de Butrio, Zabarella and Panormitanus. Perhaps the fact is that in many leading canonists one can find material wherewith to build a theory of resistance to the papal power. But whether this theory should pass from a series of isolated comments and glosses into political action, and Christendom be torn on such an issue, is not for a historian, least of all for the writer of this paper, to say. One statement of opinion may

[1] Buisson, op. cit. 209.

perhaps be put in the form of a question: Is not the Church at its finest (*optime se habet*, as the *Monarchia* puts it), not when it is presenting an ironclad unity to its critics, but when it is applying its dialectic to the choice between conflicting ideas and cannot yet clarify its mind in its internal differences? In other words, when the possible intellect is being exercised to the utmost in a supremely spiritual cause?

The Gospel of Philip

R. McL. WILSON

*Lecturer in New Testament Language and Literature,
St Mary's College, St Andrews*

THE document with which this paper is concerned was discovered in 1945 or 1946 in the Gnostic library of Nag Hammadi, in the same codex as the more famous Gospel of Thomas. Unlike Thomas, however, it has so far attracted comparatively little attention—largely because it affords no scope for the seekers after sensation. It has been held by reputable scholars that Thomas goes back at least in part to a tradition independent of our canonical Gospels, but Philip has never been regarded as anything but a Gnostic work. Yet it is not thereby devoid of interest or of significance.

The text was first made available in a photographic edition published in Cairo in 1956 by Pahor Labib,[1] and on the basis of this a German translation was published in January 1959 by H. M. Schenke.[2] Apart from references in general surveys of the content of the discovery, such as those of Puech and Doresse, and an article by Puech in the new edition of Hennecke's *NT Apokryphen*,[3] the literature devoted to Philip amounts to my knowledge to three articles only—or rather two and a half, since one of them is devoted in part to Thomas.[4] An English translation was published in April

[1] Pahor Labib, *Coptic Gnostic Papyri in the Coptic Museum at Old Cairo*, Cairo 1956.

[2] *TLZ* 1959; reprinted in Leipoldt-Schenke, *Koptisch-gnostische Schriften aus den Papyrus-Codices von Nag-Hammadi*, Hamburg-Bergstedt 1960.

[3] Puech in *Coptic Studies in Honor of W. E. Crum*, Boston 1950, and in Hennecke-Schneemelcher, *NT Apokryphen* I, Tübingen 1959 (Eng. trans., London 1963); Doresse, *The Secret Books of the Egyptian Gnostics*, London 1960. For the literature relating to the discovery see S. Giversen, 'Nag Hammadi Bibliography, 1948-1963' in *Studia Theologica*, XVII (1963), 139 ff.

[4] R. M. Grant, 'Two Gnostic Gospels,' *JBL*, LXXIX (1960) 1-11; id., 'The Mystery of Marriage in the Gospel of Philip,' *Vigiliae Christianae*, XV (1961) 129 ff.; E. Segelberg, 'The Coptic-Gnostic Gospel according to Philip and its Sacramental System,' *Numen* VII (1960), 189 ff.

1962 by C. J. de Catanzaro,[1] and another translation with an introduction and notes is in the press.[2] An edition of the Coptic text with a new German translation has been prepared by Dr W. C. Till.[3]

A Gospel of Philip is mentioned by Epiphanius, but the extract which he quotes does not appear in the Nag Hammadi text, so that he would seem to be referring to a different work.[4] That there should have been two Gospels of Philip need occasion no surprise—there were at least two Gospels of Thomas, and two Gospels of the Egyptians, and three different apocrypha in the Nag Hammadi library are placed under the aegis of James.

The document is certainly Gnostic, although it does not altogether fit into the standard pattern of Gnostic theory as presented in the histories of doctrine. It has, for example, close links with Valentinianism as described by Irenaeus. According to the Valentinian myth, Sophia-Achamoth at one point conceived a spiritual progeny in the likeness of the angels who accompanied the Saviour. These are ultimately the Gnostics, who are destined in the final consummation to be reunited with their angelic counterparts in a celestial marriage. At one point in Philip we find the prayer 'Thou who hast joined the perfect, the light, with the Holy Spirit, unite the angels with us also, the images.'[5] There are frequent references to the 'bridal chamber,' the Bridegroom and the Bride, although as R. M. Grant has noted it is not always clear whether these references are to marriage here on earth or to the heavenly unions of the aeons of which human marriages are the earthly counterpart; nor, it may be added, is it clear whether the references are to marriage as such or to a 'sacrament' dignified by the name of 'the bridal chamber.' Again, if it is a sacrament, there is no very obvious indication as to the form of the rite, although Schenke finds reason to believe that the core of the 'mystery' consisted in the holy kiss.[6] 'The perfect' it

[1] *JTS*, NS XIII (1962), 35 ff.

[2] R. McL. Wilson, *The Gospel of Philip*, London 1962.

[3] W. C. Till, *Das Evangelium des Philippus. Koptischer Text mit Übersetzung und Wörterverzeichnis*, Berlin 1963.

[4] Epiphanius, *Pan.* xxvi, 12, 2-3. According to Doresse (op. cit. 225), the passage appears in the Nag Hammadi Gospel of the Egyptians.

[5] Pl. 106, 11-14 Labib, the end of 'saying' 26 in Schenke's division, which has been followed in the remaining references.

[6] Leipoldt-Schenke, op. cit. 38. Segelberg thinks this probably correct.

is said, 'conceive through a kiss and give birth. Because of this we also kiss one another. We receive conception from the grace which is among us' ('saying' 31).

The first point of importance, then, about this document is that it provides a measure of confirmation of the reliability of Irenaeus. It is sometimes suggested that as an opponent of Gnosticism he must have been biased, painting the Gnostics always in the blackest colours, even to the point of misrepresentation. It cannot be said that Philip completely vindicates his accuracy, or that he can now be claimed as at all points infallible, but it does show that he knew what he was talking about. At several points, in fact, his account of the Valentinian theory is an indispensable tool for the understanding of the text. On the other hand, Philip does not seem to fit exactly into his description of any of the branches of the Valentinian school, and it would be rash to claim that he might have known this Gospel. There are points of contact with what he tells us of the Marcosians, but it is by no means certain that the document should be linked specifically with this group.

Another pointer to Valentinianism appears in 'saying' 39 of Schenke's division: 'Echamoth is one thing and Echmoth another. Echamoth is simply Sophia, but Echmoth the Sophia of death'— which makes a distinction between the higher Sophia of Valentinianism, the aeon whose primal lapse set the whole cosmic process in being, and Sophia-Achamoth, the Mother who is responsible for this material world. Generally speaking, then, this text is probably to be described as of Valentinian origin, although, as Schenke observes, we must allow for the possibility that it may contain elements from other sources.

But there are also problems. For one thing, the closest parallels so far noted at some points are to be found in the writings of Irenaeus himself, not in his accounts of Gnostic heresies but in his *Demonstration of the Apostolic Preaching*. This is not, I think, to be taken as an indication either that Irenaeus was himself infected with Gnosticism or that Philip was comparatively orthodox. It seems to point rather to a period when the issues as between Gnostic and orthodox were not yet clear-cut. In any case, it serves as a reminder that whatever they drew from other sources, and whatever these other sources may have been, the Valentinians at least were strongly influenced by Christian doctrine. Perhaps we may go even further, and suggest that Gnosticism was more of an inner-Christian development than has sometimes been thought—that Burkitt and Casey and more recently Mlle Pétrement were nearer to the truth than some distinguished German scholars.[1] At any rate this would seem to be the case for the Valentinian form of Gnosticism. It is certainly the impression left by Philip.

As Grant observes, there are indications of a movement from Judaism through Christianity to Gnosticism. At different points in this new gospel we find the statements: 'He who has not received the Lord is still a Hebrew' ('saying' 46). 'When we were Hebrews, we were orphans and had (only) our mother, but when we became Christians we obtained a father and a mother' (6). The author thus clearly considers himself, and the group to which he belongs, to be Christian. Again, 'if anyone goes down to the water and comes up without receiving anything and says "I am a Christian," he has taken the name at interest. But if he receive the Holy Spirit he has the gift of the name' (59). The point of this statement is that he who has the name on loan will have it required of him, whereas he who has the gift has it as an inalienable possession. Elsewhere we find 'this one is no longer a Christian, but a Christ' (67, cf. 44).

Philip is not a coherent and systematic text, although it is perhaps open to question whether Schenke was not unduly influenced by the example of Thomas when he made his division into 127 'sayings.' Occasionally the thought does appear to run on from one 'saying' to another, and there are whole sections which appear to be linked not merely by catchwords but by a common theme. Here, however, much remains to be done. There are no obvious signs of dislocation, nor are there indications to suggest the stitching together of older texts originally distinct, as in the Gospel of Mary.[2] Rather do we seem to find a constant return to certain favourite themes: sacrifice, the bridal chamber, the sacraments—especially Baptism and the Chrism, the mystery of Adam and Eve, the veil of the Temple. It is said, for example, that the sacrificial animals were offered up alive, but when they were offered they

---

[1] F. C. Burkitt, *Church and Gnosis*, Cambridge 1932; R. P. Casey, *JTS*, XXXVI (1935), 45 ff., and in *The Background of the New Testament and its Eschatology*, Cambridge 1956, 52 ff.; S. Pétrement, *Revue de Métaphysique et de Morale*, LXV (1960), 385 ff.

[2] Cf. Till, *Die gnostischen Schriften des koptischen Papyrus Berolinensis 8502*, Berlin 1955; Wilson, *New Testament Studies* III (1957), 233 ff.; Puech in Hennecke-Schneemelcher, op. cit. 251 ff.

died; man, in contrast, was offered to God dead, and he lived (14).
Or again we read that those to whom sacrifice was offered were no
gods (50). The sacraments of this group appear to have been five in
number, and the Chrism ranked above Baptism: 'The chrism is
superior to baptism, for from the chrism are we called Christians,
not because of the baptism; and Christ is (so) called because of the
chrism' (95).[1] The story of Adam and Eve receives a new interpretation: 'When Eve was in Adam, there was no death; but when
she was separated from him, death came into being' (71). 'Those
who have united in the bridal chamber will no longer be separated.
Because of this Eve separated from Adam, because she was not
united with him in the bridal chamber' (79).

New Testament allusions are fairly frequent, but not always
easy to detect; and sometimes, as with the Genesis story, the text
is provided with a highly original exegesis. After alluding to John
6:53 ff. in the form 'He who shall not eat my flesh and drink my
blood has no life in him,' Philip goes on to explain 'His flesh is the
logos, and his blood the Holy Spirit' (23). So far from presenting
the Gospel story, however, this gospel is completely remote from
the earthly ministry of Jesus, although there are allusions to such
episodes as the Baptism, possibly the Transfiguration, and the
Cross. The first of these is a reference to Mt. 3:15 in a context,
unfortunately fragmentary, which also includes something about
going down to the water (89). The second must be considered
doubtful. The Transfiguration naturally comes to mind when we
read 'when he appeared to his disciples in glory on the mount he
was not small' (26), but this is, after all, a Gnostic text and a mountain is frequently the scene of appearances of the Risen Christ to his
disciples in Gnostic works.[2] The reference to the Cross is placed in
the mouth of Philip, who is mentioned only at this one point, no
other disciple being named at all. 'Philip the apostle said: Joseph the
carpenter planted a garden because he needed the wood for his
trade. It was he who made the Cross from the trees which he
planted. And his seed hung on that which he planted. His seed was
Jesus, but the planting was the Cross' (91). The nearest parallel to
this appears to be a Bogomil text which affirms that the tree was

[1] Cf. Theophilus, *Ad Autol.* i. 12. Tertullian also derives the name of Christ from
the chrism (*De Bapt.* 7; cf. Iren. *Dem.* 53).

[2] Cf. Puech's survey of the Gnostic Gospels in Hennecke-Schneemelcher.

planted in Paradise by Satanael, who then existed alone with God.[1]

The text runs to more than thirty pages of some thirty-five lines each, so that time would not suffice even to read it, much less to comment on it. One final passage must suffice. It is commonly said that the Gnostics denied the resurrection of the body, and indeed Puech has used this as part of his argument for an older and non-Gnostic form of the Gospel of Thomas.[2] What then are we to make of a Gnostic text which affirms 'It is necessary to rise in this flesh, in which everything exists' ('saying' 23; pl. 105, 18-19 Labib)? The explanation seems to be that the author of this text was not a Docetist but the exponent of an inverted Docetism. It is our flesh which is phantasmal, and the flesh of Jesus which is the true. The context quotes 1 Cor. 15:50 and alludes to John 6:53, which may help to provide an explanation for the Church's rejection of the Pauline doctrine of the resurrection in the course of the second century, and its emphasis, as in Tertullian, upon the resurrection of the flesh.[3] For Philip here seems to reproduce Paul with a remarkable fidelity.

The significance of this document, then, lies in its confirmation of Irenaeus, in its provision of evidence for Gnostic manipulation of the Scriptures, and also in a few glimpses which it provides of what Gnosticism meant for its adherents. To us it seems merely fantastic; to them it was a saving faith. He who has received the light of *gnosis* cannot be detained by the hostile powers, 'and none shall be able to torment one of this kind even if he dwell in the world. And again when he goes out of the world he has already received the truth ... The world has become the aeon' (127).

[1] D. Obolensky, *The Bogomils*, Cambridge 1948, 273.

[2] Hennecke-Schneemelcher, 221 f.

[3] The doctrine of the resurrection would appear to have been a very live issue in the second century. The earliest stage of development seems to have been a defence of the doctrine in the face of pagan opposition (e.g. Athenagoras), but later we find references to denial of the resurrection within the Church. The necessity of a resurrection *of the flesh* is affirmed by 2 Clem. and Justin, and especially by Tertullian. From some of the Nag Hammadi texts, as yet unpublished, it would appear that the Gnostics adapted the Pauline doctrine for their own ends: it is necessary to rise in the flesh, but only to strip off the garment of the body and put on the heavenly robe. But it was perhaps not so much the doctrine itself as the implications of the denial which were important to the 'orthodox' (cf. E. Evans, *Tertullian's Treatise on the Resurrection*, London 1960, xi).

Augustine's Visit to Caesarea in 418

GERALD BONNER

Department of MSS., British Museum

I N discussing the reason for Augustine's visit to Caesarea in 418, a clear distinction should be made between what we know for a fact and what we can deduce by inference. Furthermore, we should not regard incidents which were a consequence of the visit as constituting its pretext. The episode for which it is best remembered is Augustine's encounter with the Donatist Bishop Emeritus, and the saint's unsuccessful attempt to persuade him to return to Catholic unity.[1] But the meeting between the two protagonists of Catholicism and Donatism seems to have been fortuitous. Again, Augustine was able, while at Caesarea, to prevail on the citizens to discontinue the *Caterva*, the organised local brawl, hallowed by tradition though by nothing else, which came to resemble a miniature civil war.[2] But Augustine had not made a special journey to Caesarea to speak against the *Caterva*. His own explanation of the visit is that he went to Caesarea on the orders of Pope Zosimus to settle some 'ecclesiastical necessity' which had arisen there,[3] and this assertion is echoed by his biographer, Possidius.[4] Thanks to the survival of the minutes of Augustine's debate with Emeritus, which

[1] *Retract.* Bk. II, cap. lxxvii (51): 'Aliquanto post conlationem, quam cum hereticis Donatistis habuimus, orta est nobis necessitas pergendi in Mauretaniam Caesariensem. Ibi apud ipsam Caesaream Emeritum, Donatistarum episcopum, uidimus, . . . qui in eadem causa maxime laborauerat.' CSEL, xxxvi, 187-8.

[2] *De Doctr. Chr.* Bk. IV, cap. xxiv (53): 'Denique cum apud Caesaream Mauretaniae populo dissuaderem pugnam civilem, vel potius plus quam civilem, quam *Catervam* vocabant . . . Et ecce jam ferme octo vel amplius anni sunt, propitio Christo, ex quo illic nihil tale tentatum est.' PL, xxxiv, 115, 116.

[3] *Ep.*190, i, 1: 'Quamuis tuae sanctitatis nullas ad me ipsum datas acceperim litteras, tamen, quia illae, quas ad Mauretaniam Caesariensem misisti, me apud Caesaream presente uenerunt, quo nos iniuncta nobis a uenerabili papa Zosimo, apostolicae sedis episcopo, ecclesiastica necessitas traxerat . . . .' CSEL, LVII, 137-8: *Ep.*193, i, 1: ' . . . cum uero inde digressi sumus, perreximus usque ad Mauretaniam Caesariensem, quo nos ecclesiastica necessitas traxit.' CSEL, LVII, 168.

[4] Possidius, *Vita Augustini*, 14.3: ' . . . quo eum venire cum aliis eius coepiscopis sedis apostolicae litterae compulerunt, ob terminandas videlicet alias ecclesiasticas necessitates' (ed. Pellegrino, p.86).

took place on 20 September, it is possible to fix the date of the visit fairly exactly. From the same source, we have the names of some of the bishops who were with Augustine on that occasion: Deuterius, the metropolitan of Caesarea; Alypius of Thagaste; Possidius of Calama; Rusticus of Cartenna; Palladius of Tigava; and others, who are not named.[1] And this constitutes the whole of our exact knowledge. Beyond this, we proceed by inference.

It would, clearly, be of interest if we could arrive at some convincing theory about the nature of the ecclesiastical necessity which caused Zosimus to request Augustine to go to Caesarea; but Church historians in general have (very wisely) been reluctant to speculate. Thus Eugène Portalié, in an article in the *Dictionnaire de Théologie Catholique* which has become something of a standard reference, merely says: 'Augustin [est] venu à Césarée en 418 chargé, par le pape Zosime, d'une mission restée secrète.'[2] Paul Monceaux was a little more speculative: 'Dans l'été de l'année 418, Augustin fit un assez long séjour à Caesarea. Il y était venu comme légat du pape Zosime, avec deux de ses collègues et amis, Alype de Thagaste et Possidius de Calama, pour régler des affaires ecclésiastiques. Avec cette mission des trois Numides, coincidait probablement la convocation d'un concile Césarienne; à ce moment, en effet, la plupart des évêques de la province se trouvaient réunis à Caesarea.'[3] Dr Frend finds the visit evidence for a spectacular growth of papal authority: 'Evidently there had been some major ecclesiastical conflict among the Catholics at Caesarea, and Augustine, accompanied by Alypius and other friends among the Numidian episcopate, went as Papal Legate to investigate—an astonishing piece of evidence for the growth of Papal authority in the African provinces in the last decades of Roman rule.'[4] Frederick

---

[1] *Gesta cum Emerito*, 1: 'Gloriosissimis imperatoribus Honorio duodecimo et Theodosio octauo consulibus duodecimo Kalendas Octobres Caesareae in ecclesia maiore cum Deuterius episcopus metropolitanus Caesariensis una cum Alypio Tagastensi, Augustino Hipponiensi, Possidio Calamensi, Rustico Cartenitano, Palladio Tigabitano et ceteris episcopis in exedram processissent....' CSEL, LIII, 181.

[2] DTC. art. 'Augustin,' cols. 2295-6. (Eng. trans. 1960, 53).

[3] *Histoire littéraire de l'Afrique chrétienne*, VI, 1922, 174.

[4] W. H. C. Frend, *The Donatist Church*, Oxford 1952, 294. Cf. P. Battifol, *Le Catholicisme de S. Augustin*, 5e éd. Paris 1930, II, 438: 'La mission donnée par le pape Zosime à Augustin de se rendre à Césarée de Maurétanie, pour agir là avec les évêques de la province dans l'affaire que nous avons dite, est un indice d'un politique que le Siège apostolique inaugure en Afrique. Au cours du IVe siècle, en effet, on ne trouve pas trace d'une intervention semblable du Siège apostolique en Afrique.'

van der Meer, in his admirable study of Augustine's pastoral activities, *Augustinus de zielzorger*, says briefly: 'Once, at the bidding of Pope Zosimus, he went as far as Caesarea in Mauretania, though we do not know why,' [1] and a similar restraint is shown by other scholars. [2]

So far, we have dealt with historians who stick to facts about Augustine's visit and do not speculate. Abbot Chapman, in dismissing a theory of van Espen to which reference will be made hereafter, suggested that it was 'presumably with regard to Donatism that Augustine was sent by the Pope,' [3] but gave no evidence to support this view, which seems to be based unconsciously upon the misleading idea that because Augustine debated with Emeritus, he must have gone to Caesarea primarily for that purpose. Chapman

[1] F. G. L. van der Meer, *Augustinus de zielzorger*, Utrecht-Brussels 1947, 24 (Fr. trans. *Saint Augustin: Pasteur d'ames*, 1959, i, 42; Eng. trans. *Augustine the Bishop*, 1961, 13). See also 210 (Fr. trans., I 363; Eng. trans., 236). Elsewhere (362), van der Meer speaks of Augustine going to Caesarea at the bidding of the pope and of a provincial synod: 'Toen hij—nu acht jaar geleden, zegt hij, dus in 418—met een opdracht van den paus en eene van der synode naar Caesarea van Mauretanië was gereisd . . . .' (Fr. trans. II, 202; Eng. trans., 410 does not mention the provincial synod). Van der Meer does not specify the synod, but presumably has in mind a canon of the Council of Carthage of 1 May 418: 'Item placuit, ne diutius universi episcopi qui ad concilium congregati sunt tenerentur, ab universo concilio judices ternos de singulis provinciis eligi, et electi sunt de provincia Carthaginiensi, Vincentius, Fortunatianus, et Clarus; de provincia Numidia Alypius, Augustinus, et Restitutus; de provincia Byzacena, cum sancto Donatiano primate Cresconius, Jocundus, et Æmilianus; de Mauretania Sitifensi Severianus, Asiaticus, et Donatus; de provincia Tripolitana Plautius, qui ex more legatus unus est missus, qui omnes cum sancto sene Aurelio universa cognoscant.' *Codex Canonum Ecclesiasticorum*, canon 127: PL, LXVII, 221D-222A. It is tempting to regard this sub-committee as being appointed in response to Zosimus's request to re-hear the disputed ecclesiastical cases in Mauretania; but it may be observed that the list does not include Possidius of Calama, Rusticus of Cartenna or Palladius of Tigava, who were at Caesarea with Augustine in September (*Gesta c. Emerito*, 1, cited above, 105 *n.*1).

[2] E.g. P. Battifol, *Le Catholicisme de S. Augustin*, 5e éd. 435, 436: 'Cette mission d'Augustin en Maurétanie Césarienne est étrange: la Maurétanie Césarienne, en effet, est une province régulièrement constituée, elle a son concile provincial, elle a son primat, et on sait qu'Augustin est très attentif au droit de chacun en ces matières . . . On ne sait rien de plus de l'affaire pour laquelle Zosime a envoyé Augustin à Césarée. On voit seulement que l'évêque d'Hippone n'a pas refusé à Zosime de marcher, et aussi bien qu'en cette occurrence il a la confiance du Siège apostolique'; G. Bardy, *Saint Augustin: L'homme et l'oeuvre*, 7e éd. Paris 1948, 408: 'Zosime lui témoigna sa reconnaissance en le chargeant d'une mission, dont nous ignorons la véritable nature, à Césarée'; Michele Pellegrino (ed.), *Possidio: Vita di S. Agostino*, Edizione Paoline 1955, 210, cap. xiv *n.*3: 'Agostino parla di questo viaggio, intrapreso per incario di papa Zosimo, senza dire di quali affari dovesse trattare.'

[3] John Chapman, *Studies on the Early Papacy*, London, 1928, 189 n.1.

may be right or wrong, but, since he does not produce any evidence, there is little to be gained by arguing with him.

There is, however, one closely-argued and interesting theory which deserves consideration—that put forward by the Belgian canonist Zegar Bernhard van Espen (1646-1728) in the essay 'In Synodos Africanas,' printed posthumously in the third volume of his collected works, published at Louvain in 1753. Van Espen sought to find the cause of Augustine's visit to Caesarea in a famous episode of African Church history, which has been the subject of a good deal of controversial writing, but which is not usually related specifically to the career of Augustine: the case of Apiarius. This person, a presbyter of the diocese of Sicca Veneria in proconsular Africa, was condemned by his bishop, Urbanus, for an unspecified offence or offences, sometime in late 417 or early 418. He departed to Italy and appealed to Pope Zosimus, in whom he found a sympathetic auditor. Zosimus took up the case, threatened Urbanus with excommunication if he did not retrace his steps and sent Apiarius back to Africa, accompanied by three legates, Faustinus, bishop of Potentia in Picenum, and Phillip and Asellus, presbyters, who brought with them a set of written instructions called the *Commonitorium*.

Van Espen argued as follows. From the *Acta* of the Council of Carthage of 25 May 419, it appears that Zosimus's legates arrived in Africa about the middle of 418, were received at a preliminary council fairly soon after their arrival, and there produced their *Commonitorium*. But the records of the preliminary council of 418 have perished, while those of the Carthaginian Council of 25 May 419, in which it is mentioned, say nothing about its place or the members who composed it, apart from Augustine and Alypius. We know, however, from Augustine's writings that, about the time when the Roman legates arrived in Africa, he and certain other bishops were required by letters of Zosimus to go to Caesarea *ad terminandas Ecclesiae necessitates*. Now these papal letters can hardly have referred to the Pelagian heresy, which had been condemned by the emperor by an imperial rescript of 30 April 418, by the Carthaginian Council of 1 May 418, and by Zosimus himself in the *Tractoria* which he issued shortly afterwards; and, since we know of no affair, other than that of Apiarius, which affected Roman and African relations at this time, it follows that the ecclesiastical necessity which took Augustine to Caesarea was the case of the presbyter Apiarius.[1]

There is a tidiness about van Espen's suggestion which is appealing and it has enjoyed a certain degree of popularity. It was accepted by Dr Bright (if we can judge from a footnote in *The Roman See in the Early Church*),[2] by B. J. Kidd,[3] and, more recently, by Dr Cross, in an article 'History and Fiction in the African Canons' in *The Journal of Theological Studies*.[4] It has, however, been opposed by Abbot Chapman in a single, obvious, and common sense question: 'why in Mauretania of all places?'[5] and it is difficult to see what answer van Espen could have given to this question. Apiarius was not a priest of Mauretania and Caesarea is not an obvious first port of call for a Roman delegation. Van Espen's elaborate theory has the remarkable effect of darkening counsel by words with knowledge. He resembles the witness at the Oxford assizes of whom a former Lord Chief Justice is said to have asked caustically: 'Has this witness been introduced merely to make the case more complicated?'

Secondly, van Espen's assumption that, once the Pelagian controversy was settled, the only remaining bone of contention between Rome and Africa was the Apiarian affair, shows evidence of wishful thinking coupled with the belief that the documents we possess give us a complete history of the events of the early-fifth century. If, however, we recall how fragmentary are our sources for the Apiarian affair[6] and how great a part chance has played in their

[1] Z. B. van Espen, 'In Synodos Africanas' in *Opera Omnia*, III, Louvain 1753, 273-4.

[2] William Bright, *The Roman See in the Early Church*, London 1896, 142 *n*.1: 'It is in his *Dissertatio in Synodos Africanas* that van Espen treats of these councils. The council of which he says "Sat obscurum est cuius loci" is the first held on the affair of Apiarius; but he thinks it was at Caesarea in Mauretania, where we know that Augustine took part in a meeting of bishops.'

[3] B. J. Kidd, *A History of the Church to A.D. 461*, Oxford 1922, II, 164; idem, *The Roman Primacy to 461*, London 1936, 98.

[4] F. L. Cross, JTS, XII (1961), 241.

[5] Chapman, loc. cit.

[6] Cf. T. G. Jalland, *The Church and the Papacy*, London 1944, 288: 'In attempting to evaluate the evidence [for the Apiarian affair], let us constantly bear in mind the fact that our documents are scarcely adequate as a basis for a complete reconstruction of the affair. On the Roman side there is actually nothing beyond the fragments of a *commonitorium* delivered by Zosimus to his legates and a short letter of Boniface I to the same; while on the side of the Africans, besides some local canons of uncertain date, we have to make what we can of the corrupt and incomplete acts of the plenary African council

survival, we should be chary of talking about any episode as if it were the only one of its kind taking place. It would be possible for a furious controversy to have occurred and to have left no record for our present age.

Paradoxically, I want to use this second argument against Van Espen's theory, to suggest that there may be a clue to the reason for Augustine's visit to Caesarea in the documents at our disposal, though not such a definite one as van Espen hoped to supply. I may add that my suggestion is not original, but was (so far as I know) first put forward by F. W. Puller in 1900 in the third edition of *The Primitive Saints and the See of Rome;* but I have not, hitherto, seen Puller's arguments related to Augustinian studies.

The *Commonitorium* which Pope Zosimus gave to his legates has not survived as a whole, but apparently it contained four main points for discussion: (i) the right of bishops to appeal to the bishop of Rome; (ii) that bishops should not make inopportune visits to the imperial court; (iii) that presbyters and deacons should have the right of appeal from the judgement of their ordinary to neighbouring bishops; and (iv) that Urbanus of Sicca should be excommunicated, or even sent to Rome, 'unless he should correct those things which seemed to need correcting,' viz. his proceedings against Apiarius.[1]

Of these four items only the fourth specifically concerns Apiarius, while the third (that of appeals by clerics to neighbouring bishops which could, perhaps, cover an appeal to Rome)[2] enun-

of May 25, 419, its synodical letter to Pope Boniface, letters to Carthage from Cyril of Alexandria and Atticus of Constantinople, and finally a synodical letter to Celestine I of uncertain date.'

[1] *Eccl. Occid. Mon. Iur. Ant.*, ed. C. H. Turner, I, 600: ' ... Commonitorium ... in quo eis quatuor quaedam nobiscum gerenda mandata sunt: unum, de appellationibus episcoporum ad Romanae ecclesiae sacerdotem; alterum, ne ad comitatum importune episcopi nauigent; tertium, de tractandis presbyterorum et diaconorum causis aput finitimos episcopos, si a suis excommunicati perperam fuerint; quartum, de Vrbano episcopo excommunicando, uel etiam Romae uocando, nisi ea quae uidebantur corrigenda corrigeret.'

[2] So Kidd, *The Roman Primacy*, 99:' ... and who was nearer neighbour to a bishop of Africa than the bishop of Rome?' but see *contra* Hamilton Hess, *The Canons of the Council of Sardica*, Oxford 1958, 65: 'It must be observed that the canons which were quoted by Pope Zosimus actually gave more support to the claims of Carthage than to those of Rome. As Apiarius was not a bishop, but a presbyter, canon 7 would clearly have no application to his case. Canon 17 directs that clerical appeals should be made to neighbouring bishops (*finitimos*), into which category the Roman bishop would hardly fall.'

ciates a general principle. The Africans made much of the case of Apiarius, because he was a scandalous character; but there was nothing in the *Commonitorium* to justify van Espen's argument that the only matter in dispute between Rome and Africa, once the Pelagian business had been settled, was the case of Apiarius. Quite the contrary. The first item (that of episcopal appeals to Rome) and the second (that bishops should not proceed to the imperial court inopportunely) do not concern the disreputable presbyter of Sicca Veneria at all. They do, however, suggest that relations between Rome and Africa at the midsummer of 418 were still very strained. If we look at the situation from Zosimus's point of view, he had every reason to feel displeased with the African bishops. They had shown themselves very difficult over the Pelagian affair; it is more than likely that they had intrigued behind the pope's back to secure the imperial rescript against Pelagianism of 30 April 418,[1] and the second item of the *Commonitorium* may have been framed with these manoeuvres in mind. Then there was Apiarius with a story of unjust treatment by his bishop—no doubt the sort of story calculated to touch Zosimus's impulsive and not unkindly heart. And, finally, there was the affair of the Mauretanian church.

This is the episode where, it seems to me, the hypothesis of Puller is very persuasive. He suggested that, in the early part of 418, or possibly at the end of 417, some dispute occurred in Mauretania, which caused one or more bishops to appeal to Rome. Zosimus, delighted as always to intervene, requested St Augustine and a number of other bishops to go to Caesarea and take part in re-hearing the case or cases about which the appeal had been made. Once the news reached Africa that Zosimus had followed the example of the emperor and the Carthaginian Council of 1 May 418 in condemning Pelagius, the African bishops would have been delighted to do all in their power to satisfy his requests.[2] At the same time they may well have felt it necessary to safeguard their own position (probably with an eye on Apiarius) by making it clear to the pope

---

[1] See G. de Plinval, *Pélage: ses écrits, sa vie et sa réforme*, Lausanne 1943, 320; J. Ferguson, *Pelagius: a Historical and Theological Study*, Cambridge 1956, 110.

[2] F. W. Puller, *Primitive Saints and the See of Rome*, 3rd ed. London 1900, 491-2: 'By that condemnation [of Pelagius and Coelestius] the state of tension between Rome and Africa had been brought to an end, and the African bishops would be full of joy and gratitude, and would be anxious to oblige their Roman colleague.'

that they would not tolerate overseas appeals by the inferior clergy,[1] as they had already decreed at the Council of Carthage of 418: 'The inferior clergy who wish to appeal from their own bishop are to have recourse only to African councils or to the primates of their own provinces. But anyone who shall take it upon him to appeal beyond the seas shall not be granted communion by anyone in Africa.' [2]

The news about this resolution, when it reached Zosimus, may well have decided him to come to a clear understanding with the Africans. Hence the Roman delegation, with its *Commonitorium* with the four points which were to be raised: the first concerning the Mauretanian affair and the principles involved; the second, a reply to the denial of appeals *ad transmarina* by reminding the Africans of their own practices with regard to the imperial court; the third, concerning the right of inferior clergy to appeal to neighbouring bishops against excommunication by their ordinary; and, finally, the Apiarian affair was to be discussed, and Urbanus of Sicca Veneria himself threatened with excommunication if he did not amend his ways.

Zosimus supported his case by citing two canons which he believed, in all good faith, to be of Nicene origin but which were, in fact, canons of the Council of Sardica of 342-3. The subsequent discussion of the authenticity of these canons at the Council of Carthage of 25 May 419 does not concern us here. The immediate

---

[1] Puller remarks, op. cit. 492: [The African bishops] 'seem also to have felt it to be necessary to guard against such appeals in the future by pointing out to Zosimus that appeals of bishops from African decisions to Rome were forbidden by the African canons.'

It is possible that there is a reference to this intimation to Zosimus in the synodical letter of the Council of Carthage to Boniface, dated 26 May 419: 'Quorum omnium [capitulorum *Commonitorii*] de primo et tertio (id est, ut Romam liceat episcopo prouocare, et ut clericorum causae aput suorum prouinciarum episcopis finiantur) iam priori anno etiam nos litteris nostris ad eundem uenerabilis memoriae episcopum Zosimum datis insinuare curauimus ut ea seruari sine ulla eius iniuria pauTisper sineremus, usque ad inquisitione statutorum Nicaeni concilii': *Eccl. Occid. Mon. Iur. Ant.* I, 601); but the general tone of the language seems to suggest that the communication was of later date, after the first interview with the Roman legates.

[2] *Codex Canonum Ecclesiasticorum*, canon 125: 'Item placuit, ut prebyteri, diaconi, vel caeteri inferiores clerici, in causis, quas habuerint, si de judiciis episcoporum suorum questi fuerint, vicini episcopi eos audiant, et inter eos quidquid est finiant, adhibiti ab eis ex consensu episcoporum suorum. Quod si et ab eis provocandum putaverint, non provocent nisi ad Africana concilia, vel ad primates provinciarum suarum; ad transmarina autem qui putaverit appellandum, a nullo intra Africam in communionem suscipiatur.' PL, LXVII, 221C.

point is that the papal legates arrived in Africa in the late summer of 418, bringing with them the *Commonitorium* and suitably briefed for their task.[1] Soon after their arrival they had their first meeting with a representative group of African bishops, possibly at Caesarea in September, if the Mauretanian dispute were serious enough to justify the presence of the papal legates when the appeal was heard, or more probably at Carthage in November or December, after the return of Augustine and his colleagues from Mauretania.

If Puller's hypothesis is accepted—and it is only an hypothesis, though a persuasive one—then we can say that van Espen argued on the right lines, although the particular incident he fixed upon was mistaken. Augustine went, as he himself says, because of some ecclesiastical necessity in the church of Mauretania. That Augustine does not enlarge upon this theme is hardly surprising. No doubt the disputes of the Catholic bishops of Africa among themselves and with the apostolic see were familiar enough to Donatists and crypto-Donatists,[2] and nothing would be gained by washing dirty linen in public. Indeed, Augustine may well have been inclined to dwell upon the diligence with which he was prepared to execute a papal commission, although, as van der Meer has observed, his ultra-montanism was of a mystical, rather than a political, kind.[3] The point is that the ecclesiastical necessity which took Augustine to Caesarea was linked, in the *Commonitorium* of Pope Zosimus, with the Apiarian affair. Both these incidents form part of the dispute between Zosimus and the African Catholic bishops—a dispute which seems to have been well-nigh endemic throughout the whole of Zosimus's brief pontificate.

Finally, in the light of this hypothesis, we shall venture to disagree with Dr Frend that the episode of Augustine's visit to Caesarea is 'an astonishing piece of evidence for the growth of Papal

[1] See the statement of Faustinus of Potentia at the Council of Carthage of 419: 'Iniuncta nobis sunt a sede apostolica aliqua per scriptura, aliqua etiam in mandatis cum uestra Beatitudine tractanda.' *Eccl. Occid. Mon. Iur. Ant.*, I, 569.

[2] Cf. Augustine's remark in *Gesta c. Emerito*, 2: '. . . quidam uidentur de ipsa, ut paulo ante dixi, catholica ueritate dubitare, quidam uero non saltem dubitant, sed adhuc corde positi in parte Donati praesentiam nobis exhibent corporalem, siue uiri siue feminae carne intus, spiritu foris . . . .' CSEL, LIII, 182.

[3] Van der Meer, op. cit. 23-4: 'wellicht was hij minder juridisch ingesteld; in elk geval was hij wel een mystisch doch geen politiek ultramontaan—of, in dit geval, ultramarijn.' (Fr. trans., I, 40; Eng. trans., 12).

authority in the African provinces in the last decades of Roman rule,' and see it rather as another example of Zosimus's unfortunate tendency to intervene in a manner calculated to irritate people who were, by inclination and first principles, very well-disposed to the Apostolic See and to its occupant. The African bishops, for their part, were anxious to carry out the pope's wishes, as far as they could; but they were determined to maintain what they considered to be the traditional practices of African ecclesiastical procedure.

What is Mediana Week?

GEOFFREY G. WILLIS

Vicar of Wing, Buckinghamshire

MEDIANA is a term peculiar to Roman liturgy and is applied to the fifth Sunday in Lent, to the Wednesday and Saturday which precede this Sunday, and to the week embracing these three days. The term first occurs in a letter of Pope Gelasius, written in 494,[1] in which he says that ordinations of priests and deacons should only be performed at certain seasons on Saturday evening, namely the fasts of the fourth, seventh and tenth months, which are the original Embertides, on the first Saturday in Lent, which is in the fourth and later Embertide, and on the Saturday *medianae quadragesimae*. The term occurs again in the next century when Pope Pelagius I (556-561) appointed this *mediana septimana paschae* as a season for ordinations.[2] The text of Gelasius is quoted in the *Liber Diurnus*,[3] of which the earliest manuscript dates from the seventh to the eighth century; in a letter of Gregory II of 715[4]; and in the eleventh Canon of the Roman Council of 743.[5]

The term *mediana* Sunday is found in *Ordines Romani* XXVI; XXVII; XXVIII; XXIX; XXXI; L, xxi, which all state clearly or that it was a Roman peculiarity: 'dominica quam sedis apostolica mediana uoluit nuncupari.' The title is found also in the Epistolary of Würzburg, a Roman book of the seventh century, and in the *Comes* of Murbach and the *Comes* of Alcuin in the eighth century. After this the term disappears from Roman liturgy and it is not found in the Gelasian or Gregorian Sacramentaries.

Mgr Callewaert explains these curious facts by saying that *mediana* is an extraordinary week, like the Ember Weeks, in that it

---

[1] *Ep.* 14 (*ad uniuersos episcopos per Lucaniam*), 11, in Thiel, *Ep. Rom. pontif.*, I, 368-9.
[2] PL, LXIX, 416 D.
[3] PL, CV, 75 A-76 B.
[4] PL, LXXXIX, 502 C-D.
[5] Mansi, *Concilia*, XII, 384.

is united with the following and not with the preceding Sunday. It shares its name with the Sunday which concludes it, instead of taking it from the Sunday which precedes it. *Mediana* week has certain other similarities with Ember Weeks. For instance, in *Missale Romanum* it still preserves three lessons on Wednesday (two Prophetic and one Gospel), though it has lost one of the three on Saturday. *Flectamus genua* and *Leuate* have been preserved on the Wednesday, as on the Ember Days. Moreover, at Rome, from the fourth to the seventh centuries, there were three weeks in Lent which had special solemnity; the first, which was Ember Week, the fourth, which was *mediana* week, and the sixth, which was Great Week. Only for these three weeks in Lent does the *Comes* of Würzburg, which goes back to the early seventh century, provide more than two lessons. These weeks were weeks of more rigorous fasting than the others in Lent, and in the middle of the fifth century St Peter Chrysologus of Ravenna and St Maximus of Turin were aware of this, and disapproved of it. They wanted to establish a rigorous six-week fast, Sundays alone excepted.

Professor Chavasse rejects this explanation.[1] He thinks that the expression *mediana* is inexplicable in a Lent of forty days and can only be explained in terms of a three-week Lent. The only evidence for the existence of a three-week Lent is provided by Socrates, the Greek ecclesiastical historian, writing about 439, who says that Rome has a continuous three-week fast before Easter, except for Saturdays and Sundays, by contrast with other churches, which fast for as much as seven weeks: οἱ μὲν γὰρ ἐν ῥώμῃ τρεις ρπὸτοῦ Πάσχα ἑβδομάδας πλὴν Σαββάτου καὶ Κυριακῆς συνημμένας νηστένουσιν.

Rome certainly had a six-week fast before 385, and by that time it also fasted on Saturdays, which it had not done in earlier times. So Socrates is guilty of two errors in the one sentence. Chavasse accepts his evidence, and argues that in this three-week Lent, from our fourth Sunday until Easter Even, there are three Sundays, our fourth, fifth and sixth; and that the middle Sunday of these three is the fifth, which is the one called *mediana* in these early Roman authorities; and that *mediana* week is then reckoned backwards from that Sunday, and begins on the Monday before, that is on the

---

[1] A. Chavasse, 'La préparation de la Pâque, à Rome, avant le Ve. siècle: Jeûne et organisation liturgique,' in *Memorial J. Chaine*, Lyon 1950, 61-80.

[2] *Hist. Eccl.* V, 22: PG, LXVII, 632.

Monday after the fourth Sunday. It is reckoned backwards because one is counting back from Easter. This would seem to be more subtle than convincing. We may agree that the fifth Sunday in Lent is the middle Sunday of the last three before Easter, but on Chavasse's reckoning *mediana* week is the first of the last three if one counts forwards, and the last of the three if one counts backwards. The middle week of this period would be the one running from the fifth to the sixth Sunday in Lent. And is it really true that the Roman Church reckoned backwards in this way, even if it is the case that the Romans tended to count time backwards for calendrical purposes from the Kalends, Nones and Ides? Moreover, if one counts backwards, Sunday ought to be the seventh day of the week and not the first; so *mediana* week ought to run from the Saturday before the sixth Sunday in Lent to the fifth Sunday in Lent, and this is not the case.

This explanation depends entirely on the evidence of Socrates, which does not appear in this respect to be trustworthy. Long before his time Rome fasted on Saturdays in Lent, and Lent was six weeks in length. Chavasse explains that Socrates is speaking of a period before his own time: the answer to this is that in that case he should not have used the present tense. As soon as Lent appears at all at Rome it has six weeks, forty days from Lent I to Maundy Thursday; and Good Friday and Easter Even are reckoned as part of the Paschal Solemnity concluding on Easter Day, and are not really part of Lent.

I suggest therefore that Socrates may have misunderstood the distinctively Roman practice of Lent as a six-week disciplinary period, connected also with preparation for baptism, in which there were three weeks of special solemnity and more rigid fasting. In these weeks Saturday was a fast in the fourth century, which it was not at Rome in the other weeks of Lent until the fifth century. The three specially solemn weeks are not in fact συνημμέναι, as Socrates says, but discontinuous. One of these weeks is the first week of Lent, and is Ember Week, with ordinations on Saturday night; one is the last, which is Holy Week, with a Saturday Vigil at which baptism was administered; and the middle or *mediana* week of these three is the one which follows *media quadragesima*, i.e. the fourth Sunday, which is the twenty-second day of a forty-day Lent, near enough to the middle. It is quite possible that the fourth Sunday was, as *Laetare* Sunday was to be later in the Roman rite, a more joyful Sunday, which is a break half-way through Lent, and then immediately after it, on Monday, *mediana* week begins. Like the first week of Lent it is a specially solemn week, and like that week concludes with a Saturday Vigil, at which Gelasius and Pelagius at least conferred holy orders. For this reason the fifth Sunday in Lent was, like the second Sunday, a *vacat* Sunday until the seventh century, with no proper liturgy, and it would have, like the Sundays after all Embertides, which long remained vacant, a connection with the week before rather than with the week following.

Donatism : the Last Phase

R. A. MARKUS

Lecturer in Mediaeval History, University of Liverpool

THE purpose of this paper is to question some generally held
assumptions concerning the character of Donatism, and its
relations with the Catholic Church, during the later period of
Byzantine rule in North Africa. The features of the Donatist Church
during its classical period, in the fourth and fifth centuries, are now
well known. They are conveniently surveyed by Dr Frend in his
magisterial study of the movement.[1] He has established, definitively
in my view, that the schism in the African Church had roots far
deeper than historians had previously discerned. The theological
divergence between Catholicism and Dissent, as he put it, 'was
interwoven with other differences, such as geography, culture and
economic circumstance.'[2] 'The two churches were in fact two
societies, differing fundamentally in outlook on both religious and
social questions.'[3]

The struggles between the two churches reached their climax
during Augustine's episcopate, on the eve of the Vandal occupation
of Africa. During their course African Catholicism 'became pro-
gressively more dependent on the Roman see in ecclesiastical
questions and on the Roman authorities for material support . . . At
the death of Augustine the alliance between Church and Empire
had become complete.'[4] It need hardly be stated that this align-
ment between Church and State was one of the issues over which
the two churches stood most sharply opposed. The view I wish to
question is that this description of the situation fits the case as it
stood around A.D. 600; or, in other words, to ask whether the

---

[1] W. H. C. Frend, *The Donatist Church*, Oxford 1952.
[2] Ibid. 333.
[3] Ibid. 332.
[4] Ibid. 324.

situation at this time bears any significant resemblance to the situation as it had been in the first quarter of the fifth century. The life of the African Church during much of the intervening period has to be reconstructed in large part from archaeological evidence. Much of this still remains to be explored; the existing material is fragmentary, and my knowledge of it even more so. I shall, therefore, confine myself to the plentiful literary material contained in the correspondence of Pope Gregory the Great.

Gregory's letters provide ample evidence of the survival of Donatism in Africa at the end of the sixth century; and, especially in Numidia, if we may believe him, even of a revival on a considerable scale and 'spreading daily' (*Ep.* ii, 46; cf. *Epp.* i, 72, iv, 32). Gregory's attempts to counter this resurgence have been often described, admirably by Homes Dudden[1] and by Dr Frend[2]; but the particular complexion of the problems which faced him has not, so far as I know, been studied yet. Gregory's correspondence contains a great deal to suggest that the Donatist revival had led to a situation very different from that obtaining in the heyday of the two churches' stark, embattled stance of mutual hostility in the fourth and early-fifth centuries. Now the two churches appear to have found a *modus vivendi*. Catholics, we learn, widely allow their families and dependents to become Donatists (*Ep.* vi, 34). Donatist clergy are placed in charge of churches by Catholic bishops, and are even alleged to be promoted over the heads of their Catholic colleagues (*Ep.* i, 82). Ex-Donatists could become Catholic bishops, though Gregory drew the line at their becoming primates of their province (*Ep.* i, 75): it may be inferred that the African episcopate would have had no objection. Catholic bishops are willing to issue licences for the consecration of bishops for the local Donatist community. The text of Gregory's letter concerned with a particularly interesting case of this (*Ep.* ii, 46)[3] shows that the Donatist

[1] F. Homes Dudden, *Gregory the Great*, London 1905, I, 414-28.
[2] Op. cit. 309-12.
[3] MGH, *Epp.* I, 147, lines 5-9: 'Propterea igitur petitione insinuaverunt nobis praesentium latores Constantius et Mustelus et asserunt ecclesiae Pudentianae diacones Numidia provincia constitutae Maximianum ecclesiae eiusdem antistitem in loco quo deget, corruptum premio, Donatistarum episcopum nova licentia fieri permisisse . . . .' The explanation *in loco quo deget* would be unnatural if the place were Pudentiana; we should in this case expect some phrase like *in eodem loco*. This situation must have been common in Numidia. In Africa episcopal sees were often located in villages and quite insignificant places. It appears that bishops often preferred to reside in villages outside

bishop in question was at the head of a community in the village where Maximianus, the Catholic bishop, resided, not in his episcopal see. It looks as if the Catholic bishop had simply agreed to the foundation of a new church in a neighbouring village, or to the consecration of a bishop for a church without its pastor, and that the community or the bishop had subsequently fallen under a suspicion of heresy, a suspicion which local people would not have entertained. It is tempting to think that the denomination of a new church founded in such circumstances scarcely mattered; it would have been widely acceptable in the locality under either Catholic or Donatist label—or, more likely, without either. Archaeological evidence might help to decide how far one should take this situation at Pudentiana as typical. It would be interesting to know very much more about churches built during this period: how many can confidently be identified as Donatist? Of those which can be so identified, how many were in places where there was not already a Catholic church in existence? Conversely, how many newly built Catholic churches were in places where there was no Donatist church? From answers to such questions one might form a more reliable impression as to how widely the need was felt—if at all—of separate provision for the two denominations in the same locality.

Gregory was quick to smell bribery behind such instances of compromise with the schismatics. He may not have been far wrong in this; but this will scarcely explain so general a state of affairs. How general the situation was, and how deeply rooted in the life of the African Church, is revealed by an examination of the obstacles that Gregory encountered in his attempts to get things changed. In one of his letters to Numidia, Gregory remarked that Donatism was making inroads on the Lord's flock 'as if it were unrestrained by any shepherd's protection' (*Ep.* iv, 35). From his outsider's point of view, he may have been very close to the truth. From the beginning of his pontificate he had been striving to get the Church and the imperial administration in Africa to combat Donatism; he had tried to get councils to concert action and to punish irregularities

their episcopal sees; cf. *Ep.* i, 72, where Gregory recommends that the primates of African provinces be chosen not automatically by seniority, but that their manner of life be also taken into account; he adds 'Ipse vero primas non passim sicut moris est per villas, sed in una iuxta eorum [i.e. the other bishops of the province] electionem civitate resideat.' Gregory wished the practice of bishops residing away from their sees to be ended, at least in the case of primates.

(*Epp.* i, 72, 75, 82; ii, 46; iii, 47, 48; iv, 7, 32), especially in the ordination of clergy. The civil authorities were not too ready to comply with Gregory's zeal, and were loath to enforce the rigour of the imperial edicts against the heretics (*Epp.* iv, 32; vi, 61). This is scarcely surprising. It fits well into the general pattern of the policies pursued by the authorities during Maurice's reign, exemplified, for instance, in the toleration extended to the Istrian schismatics in the interests of securing their loyalty to the empire during troubled times. In this case, however, the emperor had issued a *iussio* against the heretics (which has not survived: *Ep.* v, 3); but it was not enforced by the administration in Africa, as Gregory later complained (*Ep.* vi, 61). Gregory suspected some highly placed civil servants of heresy, and urged them to appear in Rome in person to clear themselves (*Ep.* iv, 41). What their heresy was is not clear from the letter; but that they thought of themselves as orthodox is beyond doubt, and that they were suspected of sympathy with Donatism is more than likely.

More interesting, however, is the attitude of the generality of African churchmen. What this was we can infer quite dramatically from the fate of one of them, Paul, the bishop of an unknown see in Numidia. This Paul had been 'subjected to annoyance' on account of his anti-Donatist zeal, and had found nobody in Africa to support and assist him. Eventually he managed to make his way to Rome, having had to struggle for at least two years with every obstacle put in the way of his journey by the authorities (*Epp.* iv, 32, 35). When he arrived in Rome he made it clear that his complaint was not that he had become hated by the Donatist minority for his crusade of repression, but that he had incurred general displeasure 'on account of his defending the Catholic faith'; and he added some dark charges against the authorities which Gregory refused to specify (*Ep.* vi, 59). But Paul had not only incurred the displeasure of the civil administration: he had also been excommunicated by a council of his province (*Ep.* vi, 59). In Africa Paul had clearly been regarded as a busybody creating unnecessary trouble by his fussy intransigeance; his fellow-bishops and the imperial authorities were at one on this. The records are silent concerning his ultimate fate, after his case had been referred to the imperial court and from there back again to an African synod (*Epp.* vi, 61; vii, 2). On his return from Constantinople to Africa, to be tried there, Gregory wrote to some Numidian bishops recommending Paul to their love and urging them not to fear influential persons but to deal with him with justice and compassion (*Epp*. viii, 13, 15). Gregory can scarcely have expected much support for Paul's views from the Numidian episcopate. He knew very well the opposition that zeal like Paul's must run into in Numidia. When a synod of Carthage (594), in obedience to an imperial *iussio*, decreed a heavy penalty on clergy who were convicted of laxity in seeking out heretics, Gregory was alarmed: it was all very well to make such decisions in the remote calm of Carthage, but what would be the reaction among the primates of other provinces more directly concerned (*Ep*. v, 3)? The letter he wrote to the bishop of Carthage on this occasion seems to me to betray a fear of an African schism which the policy decreed at Carthage might provoke, if persisted in.

Bishop Paul's case throws much light on the situation in the African Church; it is equally illuminating on the extent of papal influence in Africa. The civil administration was active in restricting its exercise (Gregory had been appealing to African officials to allow Numidian bishops to travel to Rome since 591 (cf. *Ep*. i, 72); it was not until 596 that Paul got away, with two companions); his repeated appeals for its support in repressing heresy fell on deaf ears, and the exarch was the foremost of Bishop Paul's opponents.[1] The secular authorities, however, were not the only obstacle to the effective assertion of papal authority in Africa. Though the papacy encouraged appeals from Africa, it is significant that all these appeals were referred back to local African tribunals by Gregory. Bishop Paul's case was the only one he had tried to get settled in Rome, and through the intervention of the civil authorities this attempt had failed. When a similar case occurred later in his pontificate, involving the primate of Byzacena, Gregory, 'seeing the perversity of men,' declined to judge the case, even though it had been referred to him by the emperor (*Epp*. ix, 24, 27); this, too, ended by being returned for judgement in Africa (*Ep*. xii, 12).

Gregory found it necessary to send frequent reminders to Africa of the authority of the Apostolic See (*Epp*. ii, 46; iv, 41; viii, 31; ix, 27); but no African bishop appears among the addressees of his letter promulgating an imperial decree among the metro-

---

[1] Cf. *Ep*. ix, 27 (discussed below) for another instance, in which a *Theodorus magister* had prevented a case from being heard in Rome.

politans of the Western patriarchate (*Ep.* viii, 10). When a council had eventually assembled in Numidia in response to his reiterated demands, it had made a number of decisions against which Gregory protested as being 'contrary to the tradition of the fathers and the canons,' and which he tried to get rescinded with the aid of the exarch (*Ep.* iv, 7). There can be no doubt that African churchmen in general were as little inclined to view with favour his interventions as was the imperial administration. Gregory could not think of appointing a papal vicar for Africa, as he had done in other provinces.[1] Here he had to be content to rely on a Numidian bishop, Columbus, as his special unofficial agent and informant; and Columbus, though bound to 'St Peter, prince of the Apostles' by a special oath of loyalty (*Ep.* iii, 47), was to find the burden heavy: in 596 he complained to the pope of having become unpopular in his province because of Gregory's frequent letters to him (*Ep.* vii, 2). The African Church preferred to keep Rome at arm's length: Bishop Paul's excommunication, for instance, had been notified to Gregory, who complained about this in pained surprise, not by the primate of Paul's province, but by the exarch of Africa (*Ep.* vi, 59). Crementius, the primate of Byzacena, preferred to appeal from his own provincial council to the imperial court rather than to the pope, while his accusers, far from challenging the appeal and invoking the pope, flocked to the imperial court (*Epp.* ix, 24, 27). Gregory had one further channel through which he had hoped, early in his pontificate, to exert influence in Africa: the rector Hilarus, sent to take charge of the African possessions of the Roman church. But these hopes, too, were destined to be disappointed: in 591 Hilarus is peremptorily commanded to call a council in Numidia and to punish and rectify abuses (*Ep.* i, 82); in the following year Bishop Columbus is told to deal with irregularities at a council to be held under Hilarus's supervision (*Ep.* ii, 46); ten years later, however, the Numidian bishops have to be politely requested to invite Hilarus to their deliberations, 'if matters should so require' (*Epp.* xii, 8, 9). The change of Gregory's tone over the years needs no comment. He had come to accept the limits on the range of his influence which he could do nothing to remove.

[1] This is noted by E. Caspar, *Geschichte des Papsttums*, Tübingen 1933, II, 446. Caspar's summary of the real extent of papal influence in Africa can scarcely be improved on.

Donatism is not mentioned in Gregory's correspondence after 596. It would be quite unwarranted to infer from this that it had expired or was on the decline after this date. The evidence from the first five years of Gregory's pontificate, and from his relations with Africa during the remaining years, does not entitle us to suppose that his efforts could have had such spectacular success. It is very much more likely that the mingling of the two churches advanced unchecked towards something not far short of a complete fusion. An interesting indication of this process of fusion is contained in a formula preserved in the *Liber diurnus*. The instructions issued to newly consecrated bishops contain a prohibition of accepting Africans 'who dare to apply for admission to ecclesiastical orders, in any circumstances, for they frequently turn out to be Manichaeans or *rebaptizati* (i.e. Donatists).' [1] In Rome the distinction between Africans and Donatists was clearly a tenuous one; and it is more than likely that to Italian suspicions corresponded a state of affairs in the African Church such that the distinction between Catholic and Donatist was becoming increasingly unreal. Men who in Rome might be called 'Donatists' appear to have been quite acceptable in Africa in the ranks of the clergy and the episcopate, and, until such a man left Africa, no-one would think of enquiring whether he was a Catholic or a Donatist.

This *Liber Diurnus* formula can be traced back as far as Gelasius I (*Ep.* 15; PL, lix, 137). This suggests that the blending of the two communities in Africa had begun already during the period of Vandal rule. Little is known about the fate of Donatism during this period, but it seems very likely that Donatists and Catholics were

---

[1] *Synodale quem accipit episcopus*, no. 6 in the Vatican codex, pp. 80-81 in the edition by H. Foerster, Bern 1958. Cf. Gregory II's letter to Boniface, MGH, *Epp.* III, 267. I have not been able to consult L. Godard,'Quels sont les Africains que le pape Grégoire II défendit en 723 d'élever au sacerdoce?' *Revue Africaine*, 1861, 48-53. Dr Frend (op. cit., 313) is certainly right in interpreting the reference to the 'rebaptised' as meaning the Donatists. But we cannot conclude, as he does, that 'if this interpretation is true, then there is formal evidence for the survival of Donatism up to the very end of African Christianity.' The Lateran *scrinium* was not an institution noted for a zeal for innovation and change, least of all in Gregory II's time. If it could people the wilds of Thuringia with Roman municipal institutions (as it did in its mode of address), it would not be beyond its powers to fill Africa with Manichees and Donatists. The formula survived as late as the eleventh century (cf. Nicholas II, *Ep.* 25: PL, CXLIII, 1347). More evidence than the use of a fossilised convention is required to establish the survival of Donatism. The formula is already stereotyped by the time of Gregory I (cf. *Epp.* iii, 11; ix, 210) and was obviously a standard product of the papal *scrinium*.

generally not distinguished by the Vandal rulers, and that the two churches were treated alike.[1] Under such conditions it is easy to conceive of their old divisions losing their sharpness. The rise of the Berber kingdoms in the later fifth and early sixth centuries may have promoted this process of merging. Some of their rulers were Christians[2]; and Christian exiles from the Vandal kingdom were active as missionaries among the Berbers of Numidia and Byzacena, particularly among those of the Hodna.[3] Numidia is the region in which the 'Donatist' revival of Gregory's time is concentrated. Of the trouble-spots mentioned in his correspondence only Lamiggiga can be definitely identified; but Bishop Columbus's see was almost certainly Nicivibus,[4] and both these places are in the heart of the area of the Berber kingdoms of the Hodna and the Aurès. It is difficult to resist the inference that the revival of 'Donatism' was related to the resurgence of these kingdoms. Since, however, our only hints of their Christianisation imply conversion by Catholic missionaries, the likelihood is strengthened that what Gregory knew as 'Donatism' was in fact a non-Roman, Berber Christianity.

How far we may generalise from the evidence I have surveyed here is not easy to decide. The narrow range of the literary records can in any case be extended only by archaeological evidence. But the literary evidence seems to me to be sufficient at least to prompt second thoughts about Dr Frend's judgement on the extent to which 'pope Gregory's arm reached into the farthest corners of Byzantine Numidia.'[5] There were clearly severe limits to its strength and to the effectiveness of its reach. The *Autonomiegefühl* of the African episcopate, of which Caspar speaks,[6] seems to me to be closely connected with the new relations between Catholics and Donatists which I have sketched. By the end of the sixth century the African Church had moved very far from the joyful acceptance of the set-up of the imperial *Reichskirche* which the council of Carthage had expressed in 535, welcoming the Byzantine reconquest. Within less

---

[1] Cf. P. Monceaux, *Histoire littéraire de l'Afrique chrétienne*, IV, Paris 1912, 97 f.

[2] Cf. J. Carcopino, 'Un "empereur" maure inconnu, d'après une inscription latine récemment découverte dans l'Aurès', *Revue des études anciennes*, (1944), 94-120.

[4] Cf. C. Courtois, *Les Vandales et l'Afrique*, Paris 1955, 338-9.

[3] Cf. H. Jaubert in *Rec. de Constantine*, (1912) 66-7, 141-4, quoted by Frend, op. cit., 309-10.

[5] Op. cit. 314.

[6] E. Caspar, *Geschichte des Papsttums*, II, 446.

than a generation the African Church had taken the lead in resisting what it regarded as Justinian's attempt to meddle with Chalcedonian orthodoxy, and in denouncing the papacy in so far as it had lent itself to Justinian's purposes[1]. Its resistance could be crushed only by mobilising all the resources of repression that the empire could muster. The stand taken by the African Church on the underlying ecclesiological issues[2] led it to adopt its older stance of 'dissent' (to use Dr Frend's phrase). In this new climate of thought and feeling the gulf between Catholics and Donatists must have appeared less deep than it had been, say, in the first decade of the fifth century, and certainly very much less deep in the eyes of African churchmen than in those of the papacy. If my argument in this paper is right, it must incline us to revise the current views on the nature of Donatism and Catholicism in their later Byzantine phase in Africa. The alliance between African Catholicism and the empire will appear, in this new perspective, as little more than an episode in the tradition of the African Church.

[1] The resistance to the condemnation of the Three Chapters was geographically widespread, involving the provinces Proconsularis, Byzacena and Numidia. I owe this point to my pupil, Miss Susan Proudfoot.

[2] This is apparent from the remarkable study by W. Pewesin, 'Imperium, ecclesia universalis, Rom: der Kampf der afrikanischen Kirche um die Mitte des 6. Jahrhunderts', in *Geistige Grundlagen römischer Kirchenpolitik (Forsch. z. Kirchen- u. Geistesgeschichte,* 11), Stuttgart 1937. Although Augustine had helped to cement the alliance between African Catholicism and the empire, the lineaments of a very different and, indeed, contrary view can also be discerned in his writings, above all in the *De civitate Dei.* How these divergent views were related in his mind and in his intellectual development is a question which still remains to be studied. Significantly, Augustine could be invoked in support of both sides in the course of the controversies during the schism of the Three Chapters.

Birinus and the Church at Wing

ERIC FLETCHER, M.P.

THE recent archaeological revelation that the pre-Conquest church of Wing in Buckinghamshire, on the confines of Wessex and Mercia, dates from the seventh century, has prompted an inquiry into the missionary activities of St Birinus. The archaeological evidence has established that the church of All Saints, Wing, was of basilican pattern, with a shallow apse above a crypt containing a 'confessio,' or chamber for relics, immediately under the altar. As in the arrangement of the church plans associated with the Canterbury mission of St Augustine, a small square altar at Wing was built on the chord of the apse, and not at the eastern end of the church. The construction of the crypt indicates that, following Roman tradition, there were passages descending from the nave to the crypt, and an aperture low down at the eastern side of the 'confessio,' enabling worshippers in a kneeling position to revere the shrine.

There is no literary evidence as to the date when Wing was built. In all essentials it is comparable with the church at Brixworth, in Northamptonshire, which by common consent is also ascribed to the seventh century. The interesting question that therefore presents itself is: under whose inspiration could this remarkable seventh century church at Wing have been constructed? Could it have been St Birinus?

Our only authentic information about Birinus is derived from Bede and the Anglo-Saxon Chronicle. There are various manuscript lives of Birinus dating from the eleventh century and later, but they are unreliable in so far as they expand upon Bede and the Chronicle.[1]

[1] Cf. T. D. Hardy, *Descriptive Catalogue of Materials relating to the History of Great Britain and Ireland* (RS), 1862, I, 236, referring to the *Vita Sancti Birini Episcopi et Confessoris*, probably by Goscelin, and to other works. Cf. also Sir Henry Howorth, *Golden Days of English Church History*, London 1917, I, 35-46. Père Grosjean reviewing

The known facts about Birinus are that in 635, some thirty-eight years after Pope Gregory sent Augustine to Kent, Birinus arrived in the neighbourhood of Southampton Water to convert the heathen in Britain. He came on the advice and with the authority of Gregory's successor, Pope Honorius I. He was first consecrated a bishop by Asterius. Asterius was not, as stated by Bede, bishop of Genoa, although he resided there. He was in fact archbishop of Milan.[1] The first intention of Birinus was to preach the gospel 'to the inner parts beyond the dominions of the English, where no other teacher had been before him.' We do not know whether he had the Midlands in mind, or the Britons of Wales, or whether he was acquainted with conditions in the island, but Bede relates that Birinus found the West Saxons so sunk in idolatry (*paganissimos*) that he decided to preach the word of God to them. He appears to have been well received by Cynegils, king of the West Saxons. Oswald, the Christian king of Northumbria, had earlier in the very same year, 635, invited Aidan from Iona, and installed him and his monks at Lindisfarne near the royal fortress of Bamburgh.

By a coincidence, Oswald was visiting Cynegils, and courting his daughter in marriage, at the moment of Birinus's arrival. Oswald stood godfather to Cynegils at his baptism in the Thame. Then, according to Bede, the two kings gave Birinus the city of Dorchester (which had previously been an important Roman centre) for his episcopal see, and during the next fifteen years, until his death in 650, Birinus as bishop of Dorchester established Christianity among the West Saxons. We have no authentic details of the mission of Birinus—the Apostle of Wessex. There is nothing comparable to the graphic accounts of St Augustine's mission to Kent, to that of St Aidan in Northumbria, or even to that of Cedd in Mercia. Two facts stand out. The first is the statement by Bede that Birinus built and consecrated churches. The second is the undoubted success of his mission. Judging by the subsequent spread of Christianity in Wessex, the foundations laid by Birinus were at least as important, if less dramatic and less well known than those of Augustine. References in the Anglo-Saxon Chronicle show that the influence of

a more recent book by T. Varley, *S. Birinus and Wessex: From Odin to Christ*, Winchester 1934, observes that 'certain parts of Mr Varley's book depend more on imagination than on truth': *Analecta Bollandiana*, LIII (1935), 147.

[1] C. Plummer, ed. *Venerabilis Bedae Opera Historica*, Oxford 1896, II, 142.

Birinus extended from Wessex to the neighbouring kingdom of Mercia.

No traces are known to remain of any of the churches built by Birinus, whether at Dorchester or elsewhere. Wing is thirty miles from Dorchester, and may have been within the territory in which the missionary activities of Birinus took place, and over which he exercised episcopal jurisdiction for twenty-five years. If Birinus built any stone churches at all, they would have been built in the Roman fashion. Birinus came from Rome. His inspiration was Roman. He is referred to in the Anglo-Saxon Chronicle as 'the Roman bishop.' The Church in Wessex, as established by him, was not under the control of Canterbury, but was directly responsible to the pope. Can it be that this had been well considered, and that it had been thought more likely that the mission would be successful if it were kept entirely distinct, so as not to arouse any jealousies between the West Saxons and their rivals in Kent? Pope Honorius, the patron of Birinus, had himself undertaken extensive work in beautifying and restoring many churches in Rome.[1]

It may well be that the result of the Birinus mission has been exaggerated by patriotic dwellers in Wessex, and we must recognise that during the latter half of his epsicopate both Wessex and Mercia were under pagan rule. Cenwalch was still a pagan when he succeeded Cynegils as king of Wessex in 643, and so was Penda, king of Mercia and overlord of Wessex till his death in 656. The conditions for the establishment, or maintenance, of a large missionary community at Wing could not have been encouraging.

If one has to dismiss, on grounds of general historical probability the speculation that the seventh-century church at Wing may have been built by Birinus, it still remains to consider under whose inspiration it was built. Birinus was succeeded in the see of Dorchester in 650 by Agilbert, brother of Telchide the first abbess of Jouarre. Agilbert was a Frank. He was consecrated a bishop (without see), in France; he studied in Ireland, and was called to be bishop of Dorchester by King Cenwalch, who had then been converted. Agilbert was a strong supporter of Rome, but, owing to his ignorance of the English language, he left the defence of the

---

[1] F. Gregorovius, *History of the City of Rome* (English translation), London 1902, II, 118 ff. Extant letters of Pope Honorius testify to his enthusiasm for promoting missionary work.

Roman position at the Synod of Whitby, 664, to Wilfrid. He consecrated Wilfrid at Compiègne, and, having quarrelled with King Cenwalch, he eventually became bishop of Paris. Nothing is known of his career in the see of Dorchester, but he built for his sister Telchide the celebrated crypt at Jouarre, considerable remains of which are still to be seen. The most recent contribution to our limited knowledge of Agilbert is that by Père Grosjean.[1]

On the whole, it seems far less likely that a church such as Wing was built by Agilbert than by Birinus.

A third, and more plausible, possibility is that Wing should be included among the monastic foundations for which the enterprising and peripatetic Wilfrid, during his ambitious and adventurous career in so many parts of England, is so justly famous. In the words of his biographer, Eddius, dealing with Wilfrid's activities, in the heyday of his powers and influence, during the years 666-9: 'Wilfrid however, returned to his post of abbot of the monastery and humbly dwelt once more in Ripon for three years, except for the frequent occasions when Wulfhere, king of the Mercians, out of sincere affection for him, invited him into his realm to fulfil various episcopal duties. The Lord raised up for Himself this most kindly monarch, who, amongst his other good deeds, for the benefit of his soul, granted our bishop many pieces of land in various places, on which he forthwith founded monasteries for the servants of God. He lived in honour, dear to all men, and, after fulfilling episcopal duties in various places, returned to his own land with masons and artisans of almost every kind, and there, by introducing the rule of St Benedict, he greatly improved the ordinances of the churches of God.'[2]

We know from other sources that during most of his reign Wulfhere at this period exercised Mercian control, not only over the Chiltern area, but over the entire country as far south as the Thames, including Kent. There is therefore no inherent difficulty about supposing that Wing was one of the places where Wilfrid was given a piece of land for a monastery. We also know that after

---

[1] See appendix to 'La date du Colloque de Whitby', *Analecta Bollandiana*, LXXVIII (1960), 269.

[2] Eddius, ch. xiv, in J. Raine (ed.), *Historians of the Church of York and its Archbishops* (RS), I (1879); translation by B. Colgrave, *The Life of Bishop Wilfrid by Eddius Stephanus*, Cambridge 1927.

Wilfrid's quarrel with King Aldfrid in 692, he repaired to Ethelred, king of Mercia, and for a time was given charge of the see of Leicester, and exercised episcopal functions over the Middle Anglians. During the whole of this period he maintained a retinue of followers, including masons and artisans.

Bearing in mind that, with the exception of Wilfrid's crypts at Hexham and Ripon, the only known Anglo-Saxon crypts are those at Repton and Wing, until the time of Wulfric's Octagon at St Augustine's, Canterbury, the historian may well consider that the basilican church, with its apse and crypt, at Wing is more likely to have been built in the time of Wilfrid than that of Birinus.

Primitive Decretal Collections in the British Museum

CHARLES DUGGAN

Reader in History, University of London King's College

ECCLESIASTICAL historians are already aware of the richness of the British Museum in canonical manuscripts of all kinds. The Royal Library alone preserves at least one copy of the greater number of major canonical collections, as well as an imposing range of the works of leading commentators, decretists and decretalists alike, glosses and *summae*, together with the fascinating, if minor, canonistic exercises known as *distinctiones*, *abbreviationes*, *casus*, *quaestiones*, *transformationes* and *notabilia*.[1] A history of the canon law of the medieval Church could in most essentials be written on the basis of these considerable and varied sources. What is perhaps rather less familiar is the particular value of these manuscripts to the historian of the medieval English Church, both in a positive and a negative way: negative in the sense of the ample evidence provided of a rapid and wide-spread reception of ecclesiastical common law in England; and positive in the sense of the record preserved of the initiative and originality revealed by English canonists, and of the contribution which they made in turn to the law of the Universal Church. The copies or abridgements of the ninth-century *Pseudo-Isidore* and Lanfranc's related collection, now in the Museum but belonging originally to English Cathedral chapters in the early-twelfth century, reveal as significantly as any other evidence the dissemination of canon law in the post-Conquest

---

[1] Cf. G. F. Warner and J. P. Gilson, *Catalogue of Western Manuscripts in the Old Royal and King's Collections*, III (1921): *King's Manuscripts and Indexes*, under 'Canon Law,' 112-4; S. Kuttner, 'Repertorium der Kanonistik, 1140-1234,' *Studi e Testi*, LXXI (1937,) 126, 128, 143, 148, 219, 220, 229, 231, 235, 251, 259, 269-70, 322-44, 477-8, etc. Kuttner lists forty-two volumes in the British Museum each including at least one canonical work from the period 1140-1234.

English Church.[1] The *Quaestiones disputatae*, one of several items in the Royal MS 9 E.VII, record the literary work of English canonists of the later-twelfth century in the circle of John of Tynemouth, Simon of Southwell and others of their school[2]; the copious and systematic lecture notes of Walter Cachepol and an associated group of English decretalists, filling the voluminous Royal MS 9 E.VIII, throw much revealing light on the academic skill of English canon lawyers in the later-fourteenth century[3]; and many other examples of a similar kind could be cited. But second to none of these in interest or importance are the primitive decretal collections of the later-twelfth century, unrivalled numerically in any other single library, English or continental, and preceding in date of composition or technical style the publication of Bernard of Pavia's *Breviarium extravagantium*, or *Compilatio Prima*, completed in or about 1191.[4]

Gratian's *Decretum* had marked a turning point in the history of canonical codification. The literary exposition and interpretation of this quasi-authoritative text began almost immediately after its completion and wide propagation in the mid-twelfth century.[5] Working on this textual basis as an adequate summary of previously defined law, or *ius antiquum*, and influenced also by the rapid development of papal appellate jurisdiction, reflected in the ever-swelling stream of decretals issuing from the papal Curia and the

[1] See especially Z. N. Brooke, *The English Church and the Papacy from the Conquest to the Reign of John*, Cambridge 1931, 57-83, 231-45, 247, *et passim*.

[2] Royal MS 9 E.VII, ff. 191-9. Cf. S. Kuttner and E. Rathbone, 'Anglo-Norman Canonists of the Twelfth Century: an Introductory Study,' *Traditio*, VII (1951), 317-21. The volume includes the *Summa* of Johannes Faventinus and a commentary on part of Gratian's *Decretum*; it belonged originally to St Augustine's Canterbury.

[3] Royal MS 9 E.VIII, 198 fols. transcribed on paper. The main element is a set of lectures delivered by Walter Cachepol († 1369) on the Gregorian *Decretales*, the *Liber Sextus* and the *Clementinae*; the notes are preceded on ff. 1-26 by an alphabetical table of topics, and provide a tabulation on f. 172. In addition to Cachepol, the catalogue lists numerous English canonists whose views are referred to in the volume. Cf. A. B. Emden, *Biographical Register of the University of Oxford to A.D. 1500*, Oxford 1957, I, 337.

[4] For *Compilatio Prima*, see E. Friedberg, ed. *Quinque Compilationes Antiquae necnon Compilatio Lipsiensis*, Leipzig 1882; R. Naz, 'Compilationes (Quinque Antiquae)' in *DDC*, 1942, III, 1239-41; etc.

[5] Among many recent studies on Gratian's work, see Kuttner, 'Graziano: L'Uomo e l'Opera,' in J. Forchielli and A. M. Stickler, edd. *Studia Gratiana*, I (1953), 17-29; A. Vetulani, 'Le Décret de Gratien et les premiers décrétistes à la lumière d'une source nouvelle,' *Studia Gratiana*, VII (1959), 273-353.

elaboration of the system of papal judges delegate, the canonists now conceived a new kind of compilation, composed predominantly of the most recent papal rescripts. These works in fact record the gradual accumulation of a corpus of ecclesiastical case law, based on the most up-to-date authoritative judgments, and are known conventionally as *libri extravagantium*, or *libri decretalium*, or more simply as decretal collections. Their formative period extended from the mid-1170s to *c*.1191, culminating at that later date in the publication of Bernard of Pavia's *Compilatio Prima*, mentioned above.[1] With Bernard's work the technical and juristic development of decretal codification reached its full maturity, and the subsequent history of decretal collections is common knowledge. It is for the preceding seminal period that the British Museum collections provide such valuable evidence.

About fifty collections survive in manuscript from this creative phase for the whole of the Western Church, and these are classified in two main styles as primitive or systematic in technical composition. The best of the primitive collections are divided into books, and further sub-divided into titles, on a subject-matter basis; but the systematic collections reveal, in addition to such advantages, a dismemberment and re-classification of the component parts of the longer decretals, which often included many constituent chapters of varied interest in a single letter, a ruthless elimination of passages of non-juridical value, and a thoroughly mature and professional treatment of the whole work. Roughly half the total number of extant collections of all kinds fall within the primitive range; and these in turn can be separated into family or regional groups on a basis of their established provenance or textual inter-connections. More than half of all surviving primitive collections known at present are of English origin, composing three distinct but also inter-related groups, described as the 'English,'

---

[1] Excellent summaries of these developments are provided in W. Holtzmann, 'Über eine Ausgabe der päpstlichen Dekretalen des 12. Jahrhunderts,' *Nachrichten von der Akademie der Wissenschaften in Göttingen, Phil.-Hist. Kl.* 1945, 15-36; idem and E. W. Kemp, *Papal Decretals relating to the Diocese of Lincoln in the Twelfth Century*: Lincoln Record Society, 1954, XLVII, ix-xvii; Kuttner, 'Notes on a Projected Corpus of Twelfth-Century Decretal Letters,' *Traditio*, VI (1948), 345-51; A. van Hove, *Prolegomena ad Codicem Iuris Canonici*, Malines-Rome 1945, 345-57. See also my *Twelfth-Century Decretal Collections and their Importance in English History*, University of London Historical Studies, 1963, XII, for a more detailed examination of many points dealt with very briefly in this essay.

'Bridlington' and 'Worcester' families respectively. And, in a similar way, the continental primitive collections fall into three regional categories, identified by present usage as the Roman or 'Tortosa,' the French and the Italian groups. From an overall total of fifteen extant English primitive collections, no less than eight are now in the British Museum library, including four of seven members in the 'English' family, one of two 'Bridlington' survivors, and three of six collections composing the 'Worcester' group. In addition to these English collections, one member of the Roman or 'Tortosa' family, the Eberbach Collection, is also found in the BritishMuseum now, though it was in all probability a work of continental provenance originally. To sum up this statistical survey: roughly one sixth of all decretal collections surviving from the creative period of their development, or one third of all extant primitive collections from the same period, are now in the British Museum. The palaeographical details of these manuscripts and their bibliographical references are supplied in an appendix below; and their authorship and provenance have been already explored in separate studies.[1] It is enough here to state briefly the salient features of the English primitive collections, and indicate their interest for historians of the English Church.[2]

Four members of the primitive 'English' family reveal with perfect clarity the earliest technical phases in the development of decretal collections in England and the sources on which their authors drew. The Worcester II Collection is among the most basic and original collections now surviving, being perhaps as early as 1175 in date of composition. It is a very short work, comprising no more than ten decretals in all, of certain Worcester provenance and dependent partly on the judicial records of Roger, bishop of Worcester, 1164-79. The Canterbury Collection is in reality three quite separate sections, containing sixty-two, five and twenty-two items respectively, independent alike in composition and transcription, but bound up together with other canonical works in a single volume. Its first group of decretals drew significantly on Canterbury archives; and its third section is supplemented with the canons of

[1] Holtzmann, *Nachrichten*, 15-36, especially 21ff.; idem and Kemp, *Lincoln Decretals*, xi-xvi; Kuttner, *Repertorium*, 272ff.; idem, *Projected Corpus*, 345-51; etc.

[2] Duggan, *Decretal Collections*, especially ch. 4: 'The English Decretal Collections,' 66-117.

the Third Lateran Council of 1179. The latest likely date of composition of any of its component parts is 1179-81. The Rochester Collection is a close relation of the Canterbury Collection, but is a more finished or polished work, and transcribed as an entity. Following the canons of the 1179 Lateran Council, roughly the first half of the 'Rochester' decretals are affiliated to the opening sequence in the Canterbury Collection, but these are supplemented with further letters down to 1193, making a total of about one hundred and twenty-five items in addition to the conciliar decrees. It is evident that the Rochester Collection drew on both English and continental sources to expand an English work already existing. The Royal Collection, of uncertain provenance, comprises one hundred and twenty-six decretals or canons in all. Despite its unattractive format and occasional careless details, it is technically more advanced than the other collections in its group, revealing many of the typical features of systematic codification. It has no decretals later than 1181 in date of issue. All four collections are correctly described as primitive: none has achieved a consistent or clearly defined classification of subject-matter, though there is some concentration of decretals of cognate interest in the Canterbury, Rochester and Royal Collections, while the last-named work was assembled with considerable professional skill. The principal interest of these collections lies in their provenance: the Worcester II Collection is clearly of Worcester origin; the Canterbury and Rochester Collections reveal a partial dependence on Canterbury archives, and are completed from the comparable records of Worcester and Exeter more significantly than those of other English sees; the Rochester Collection drew also on non-English sources; the Royal Collection suggests less obviously such immediate regional influences, but it also includes a large proportion of letters received at Canterbury, Worcester and Exeter, with those addressed to Exeter being most significantly grouped in this instance.

The 'Bridlington' family is represented among the Museum manuscripts by the Claudian Collection, which, with the Bridlington Collection in the Bodleian Library, was derived from an English archetype now lost. It is a large and well-integrated work, set out in two hundred and sixteen numerated items, many with several component chapters, and incorporating three groups of conciliar decrees. The collection portrays the typical 'Bridlington' style with an elaborate system of rubrics for the individual items and some of their constituent parts, a brief gloss commentary and a marginal apparatus of cross-references of a very elementary kind. The first half of the collection was derived from the family archetype, composed about 1181 or shortly after, and dependent on English sources for roughly nine-tenths of its total contents. This 'Bridlington' stock records a Canterbury-Worcester-Exeter predominance of decretals, similar to that noted already in the 'English' works listed above. But the Claudian Collection is completed with further letters down to 1185-7 in date of issue; this supplementary section depended on both English and continental sources, and in one note-worthy sequence of thirty marriage decretals seems clearly derived from a non-English work. Stylistically, the collection advances little beyond the 'English' group already discussed. It has no overall pattern of composition to suit a subject-matter classification, but there is some grouping of letters of related interest, and a measure of technical skill is revealed by occasional decretal dissection and textual abbreviation in the later stages of composition.

The 'Worcester' family is in some respects the most interesting group of English primitive collections. Apart from the very large number of decretals which it preserves, many being re-discovered for the first time in 'Worcester' manuscripts, it also records the evolution of a distinct line of technical development in style and composition. The earliest 'Worcester' phase is exemplified by the Worcester Collection, completed in or shortly after 1181 and devised in seven books on a broad basis of subject-matter classification. The volume incorporating the Worcester Collection includes further letters independent of the main 'Worcester' transmission, continuing the accumulation of material down to 1187 or later. It has clearly some authentic Worcester connections, and almost certainly belonged to a member of the *familia* of Baldwin, successively abbot of Ford in the Exeter diocese, bishop of Worcester and archbishop of Canterbury (†1190).[1] A different line of development from the family archetype is seen in the 'Cheltenham' Collection, in which several separate sources and strata of composition can be distinguished, continuing its elaboration down to 1193 or soon after. The archetypal 'Worcester' matter is set out in this instance

---

[1] Duggan, 'The Trinity Collection of Decretals and the Early Worcester Family,' *Traditio*, XVII (1961), 506-26.

10

under many rubricated titles, and supplemented from other sources including a member of the influential Bamberg-Leipzig group of continental systematic collections.[1] In contrast with this, the final phase of the main 'Worcester' tradition is found in the Cottonian Collection, a large work whose several component books disclose a readjustment of the archetypal decretals to secure a more precise arrangement of topics; the books are thus sub-divided into titles and they are also supplemented with further decretals down to 1193 in date of issue. The manuscript is unfortunately damaged by fire and partly illegible, but a large proportion of the lost material can be reconstructed by comparison with a closely related collection in the Peterhouse library in Cambridge. The Cottonian and Peterhouse Collections were completed in that order in or after 1193. The 'Worcester' collections are of more complex ancestry than the 'English' and 'Bridlington' works, and their regional sources are more concealed by the redistribution of letters to suit an analytical concept of subject-matter arrangement; but it is clear that both English and continental collections were intermingled in their composition. The 'Worcester' family in its different phases was linked with important lines of transmission in the systematic tradition—perhaps with the seminal *Appendix Concilii Lateranensis* (*c*.1181-5),[2] and certainly with the Anglo-Norman *Tanner*, *Abrincensis* and *Sangermanensis*, composed about the close of the century,[3] and so left its traces in the principal sources of decretals of the late twelfth century.

One further collection completes the total of nine primitive works preserved in this single library. The Eberbach Collection is a member of the Roman or 'Tortosa' group, and is non-English in authorship and possibly also in transcription. It is certain that the manuscript belonged at an earlier period to the Cistercian abbey of the Blessed Virgin Mary in Eberbach, and was transferred to England in more recent times. The work is set out in twenty-five parts, comprising one hundred and eleven chapters in all, of which

---

[1] For the Bamberg, Leipzig and other related collections, see Friedberg, *Die Canonessammlungen zwischen Gratian und Bernhard von Pavia*, Leipzig 1897; and, more recently, W. Deeters, *Die Bambergensisgruppe der Dekretalensammlungen des 12. Jahrhunderts*, Doctoral dissertation, Bonn 1956.

[2] Duggan, 'English Canonists and the *Appendix Concilii Lateranensis*; with an analysis of the St John's College, Cambridge, MS 148,' *Traditio*, XVIII (1962), 459-68.

[3] Cf. Holtzmann and Kemp, *Lincoln Decretals*, xii-xv.

the final twenty-seven are canons of the 1179 Lateran Council; its date of completion is c.1179-81. Though by general agreement a work of continental, if debated, origin, the collection can be broken down statistically to provide conclusions of much interest to English historians: at least thirty-two of its first forty-seven decretals were received by English ecclesiastics, and of these no less than twenty were received at Canterbury, while only about one tenth of the decretals in the second half of the work have English inscriptions.[1] This evidence suggests that the Eberbach Collection preserves an expansion of an English archetype in the hands of a continental canonist, a conclusion supported by similar evidence in various other collections in the 'Tortosa' and French groups.[2]

Judged in a context of the total evidence of a similar kind surviving in English and continental libraries, the collections discussed above support conclusions of the highest significance. The origins of primitive decretal collections have been much discussed by continental scholars. Studies by Heckel, Holtzmann, Vetulani and many others have traced the formative influence of the Curia and the papal registers, and evaluated the evidence for the view that there existed a central source of supply from which semi-official archetypes were dispatched widely through the schools.[3] There is no doubt that influences of this kind have left their traces in some collections, and many in fact incorporate express citations from the central registers. But the earliest stages in the emergence of decretal codification can be explained by no single factor simply. The total corpus of decretals surviving from the late-twelfth century records a fusion of many diverse strands of development; and in this fusion the English collections played a distinct and important part. The English collections of the most primitive kind reveal no central or Curial stimulus or source of supply. They disclose on the contrary a creative initiative displayed by English canonists in accumulating

[1] Holtzmann, 'Die Collectio Eberbacensis,' *Zeitschrift der Savigny Stiftung für Rechtsgeschichte, Kanonistiche Abteilung*, XVII (1928), 548-55; idem, *Nachrichten*, 21; Kuttner, *Projected Corpus*, 346; Duggan, *Decretal Collections*, 126-28.

[2] Ibid. 124-35.

[3] Cf. Holtzmann, 'Die Register Papst Alexanders III. in den Händen der Kanonisten,' *Quellen und Forschungen aus italienischen Archiven und Bibliotheken*, XXX (1940), 13-87; Vetulani, 'L'Origine des collections primitives de décrétales à la fin du XIIe siècle,' *Congrès de Droit Canonique Médiéval*, Louvain 1959, 64-72; etc.

the most recent rescripts which they themselves received, and reflect at that stage little assimilation of comparable works produced by other schools, though they were later expanded from non-English sources. They are, without question, the works of English authors, reflecting the activities of English judges delegate and assembled in their primary phases on a basis of English archives. The seminal period in their development was the decade following the death of Becket (1170); and the most striking feature of their growth is a dependence on the judicial records of Exeter, Worcester and Canterbury. The political and juristic implications of this evidence, and its relationship with the course of papal jurisdiction in England after the Avranches settlement in 1172, have been fully discussed in a separate volume.[1] Briefly, it may be suggested that the prelates of these sees were principally, but not exclusively, instrumental in making papal jurisdiction effective in England in that period of settlement; and that the greater juristic concern of the canonists in their circles is reflected in their interest in recording the decretals received by English bishops. The British Museum collections of the English primitive families provide a major part of the evidence by which these conclusions can be sustained; and the Eberbach manuscript preserves a single, though not unique, example of the formative influence of such English works on collections of the same style and period produced in other schools. The creative impulse displayed by English collectors and its resulting impact on significant lines of transmission in continental groups of collections left a lasting mark on the corpus of decretal law surviving from the late-twelfth century. This corpus in turn played its part in shaping the contents of the famous collections of the following century. And in this way the English canonists had made a decisive and permanent contribution to the law of the Universal Church.

[1] Duggan, *Decretal Collections*, 118-51: in the supplement on MSS, appended below, all references to this volume are identified as *Decretal Collections*; in most instances, details are also found *sub nominibus* in Kuttner, *Repertorium*; Holtzmann, *Nachrichten*; idem and Kemp, *Lincoln Decretals*; and *DDC*.

MANUSCRIPTS

1 *The 'English' Family*

(a) The Worcester II Collection: *Wigorniensis Altera :* Royal MS 11 B.II, ff. 97^r-102^r. Vellum: 10$\frac{1}{8}$ x 6$\frac{7}{8}$ ins; double cols. of 34 lines. Initials of inscriptions, decretals and chapters alternately blue and red to f. 98va; many inscriptions and initials omitted; well-written in several stages in similar hands. Cf. *Decretal Collections*, 46, 69-70, 152-4 and Plate I. MS also includes tracts on legal and theological subjects: *Summa* of Paucapalea; commentary on part of Gratian's *Decretum ;* etc. Belonged to Worcester Cathedral Priory: f. 1, 'Liber monasterii Wygornie.' Cent., xii-early xiii.

(b) The Canterbury Collection: *Cantuariensis :* Royal MS 10 B. IV, ff. 42va-58vb and 59vb-65ra. Vellum: 10$\frac{7}{8}$ x 7$\frac{7}{8}$ ins. In four parts: (i) Running on from tract *Quoniam in hac :* Decretals, ff. 42va-58vb; double cols. of 33 (aver.) lines; rubricated inscriptions and initials; some inscriptions omitted; marginal rubrics in black in three hands, mostly in flourishing style; (ii) Decretals, ff. 58$^{ra\_vb}$, independent of previous section; double cols. of 33 and 41 lines; rubricated initials on f. 58^v; transcribed in two or three stages; (iii) Running on from tract *Iudicum est :* Decretals, ff. 59vb-61vb; double cols. of 41 lines; decretal initials omitted to f. 60rb, thereafter rubricated; some inscriptions erased or omitted; (iv) Canons of 1179 Lateran Council, ff. 62ra-65ra; double cols. of 41 lines; rubricated initials and titles; texts and rubrics suggest transcription in stages. Cf. *Decretal Collections*, 48, 73-6, 162-73 and Plate III. MS includes treatises on civil and canon law: *Ulpianus de edendo ;* tract by Peter of Blois; etc. Belonged perhaps to Christ Church Canterbury. Cent., xii-xiii.

(c) The Rochester Collection: *Roffensis :* Royal MS 10 C.IV, ff. 137ra-155ra. Vellum: 13$\frac{3}{4}$ x 8$\frac{1}{2}$ ins; double cols. of 48 lines. Very fine transcription including: (i) Canons of 1179 Lateran Council, ff. 137ra-139vb; (ii) Decretals, ff. 139vb-154rb; (iii) One appended decretal, f. 155$^{ra\_rb}$. Finely written throughout, with some changes of hand; initials of canons and decretals in red and blue, with flourished initials on ff. 142ra, 152va and 155va. Cf. *Decretal Collections*, 76-8 and 173-87. MS includes abridgement of Gratian's *Decretum*. Belonged to Rochester Priory: f. 1, 'Decreta abreviata de claustro Roffensi per A. precentorem.' Cent., early xiii.

(d) The Royal Collection: *Regalis :* Royal MS 15 B.IV, ff. 107va-118vb. Vellum: 8 x 5$\frac{5}{8}$ ins; double cols. of varying number of lines: 55, 46, 50, 51, 36, etc. Transcribed with much variation of hand and spacing; no rubrication except 'ABCD' on f. 117^r; no marginalia, but some titles incorporated in main transcription; extraneous matter on ff. 107^v, 109^r and 109^v. Cf. *Decretal Collections*, 81-4 and Plate II. MS includes works on logic and grammar, letters of Peter of Blois, formulary-book for judges delegate, etc. Original provenance uncertain. Cent., xii and xiii.

Other members of the 'English' family are: (i) The Belvoir Collection: *Belverensis:* Oxford Bodleian Library, MS e Mus. 249, ff. 121-35; (ii) The Fountains Collection: *Fontanensis:* Oxford Bodleian Library, MS Laud Misc. 527, ff. 24-45; (iii) The Durham Collection: *Dunelmensis:* Durham Cathedral MS C. III. 1, ff. 5-18. Cf. *Decretal Collections*, 68-84.

2 The 'Bridlington' Family

The Claudian Collection: *Claudiana:* Cotton MS Claudius A.IV, fols. 189ra-216ra. Vellum: 9¼ x 6⅝ ins; double cols. of 40 lines. Well-written throughout; items numbered in red in sequence to no. 216; numerous rubricated headings for decretals, canons and some component chapters; marginal rubrics in black and apparatus of cross-references, some details lost through trimming of fols.; initials of inscriptions omitted; Roman caps. I, II and III at bottom verso of three completed quires of eight fols. Cf. *Decretal Collections*, 84-91 and Plate IV. MS now includes: *Tractatus de Calendario*, statutes of Queen's College Oxford, Gratian's *Decretum* and a brief account of holy places in Jerusalem. Provenance uncertain; cf. f. 187^v: 'precium istius libri, xii sol.' Cent., decretal collection: end xii.

The other member of the 'Bridlington' Family is the Bridlington Collection: *Bridlingtonensis:* Oxford MS Bodley 357, ff. 80-133; *Decretal Collections*, 84-95.

3 The 'Worcester' Family

(a) The Worcester Collection: *Wigorniensis:* Royal MS 10 A.II, ff. 5^r-62va. Vellum: 9 x 5¾ ins; double cols. of 40 lines. List of book headings on f. 4^v; written in good small hand throughout; arranged in seven books, each starting on fresh fol. recto with rubricated heading and illuminated initial phrase in first decretal; initial letter of some books omitted by illuminator; book numbers in blue and red at top of each fol.; blank fols. between component books, with one later insertion on f. 21^v; items numbered in red through each book; initial letters of items alternately blue and red, with some elaboration; rubricated inscriptions and many rubrics in red; negligible contemporary marginalia, but some references in much later hand, and occasional line-drawings. Supplemented by: (i) Decretals, ff. 1^r-3^r: double cols. on 1^r and 2^v-3^r, and single on 2^r, in typical English hand, differing from main collection; (ii) Decretals, ff. 62^v and 63^v, double cols., in at least three hands; ending in mid-decretal on f. 63^v. Headings 'Decretales epistole' and 'Decretales epistole due' appear on ff. 1^r and 4^v respectively. For fuller discussions, see H. Lohmann, 'Die Collectio Wigorniensis,' *ZRG., Kan. Abt.,* XXII (1933), 36-187; P. M. Baumgarten, 'Papal Letters relating to England,' *English Historical Review,* IX (1894), 531-41; Duggan, *Trinity Collection,*

506-26; idem, *Decretal Collections*, 49-51, 95-8, 110-5 and Plates V and VI. Provenance: Worcester and (?) Canterbury, belonging perhaps to Archbishop Baldwin († 1190). Cent., late xii.

(b) The 'Cheltenham' Collection: *Cheltenhamensis:* Egerton MS 2819, ff. 18ra-102vb. Vellum: 10 x $7\frac{1}{8}$ ins; double cols. of 36 lines. Set out under sixteen rubricated groups of titles, from 'De symoniacis *etc*,' f. 17vb, to 'De penitencia,' f. 96ra; beautifully written throughout, in several stages; inscriptions rubricated but some omitted; decretal initials alternately in red and blue; light marginal gloss and rubrics in black in contemporary hands, with cross-references and citations from Gratian; ff. 101^{v}-102^{r} embellished with green, red and gold initials; final decretal a later addition (1193+), f. 102ra-^{vb}. For relevant literature, cf. Kuttner, *Repertorium*, 298; and *Decretal Collections*, 98-103 and Plate VII. MS includes: civil law tracts, collection of legal maxims, canons of 1179 Lateran Council and group of decretals opening with one of Innocent III. Provenance unknown: cf. f. 1^{v}: 'Noverit universitas vestra quod ego Robertus Parvus dedi et concessi Petro Ruffo'; modern owners include William Shaw Mason († 1853) and Sir Thomas Phillipps († 1872). Cent., late xii and early xiii.

(c) The Cottonian Collection: *Cottoniana:* Cotton MS Vitellius E. XIII, ff. 204^{r}-288^{v}. Vellum: $5\frac{1}{2}$ x $8\frac{1}{2}$ ins; double cols. of varying number of lines: 47, 48, 49, 51, etc. Well-written throughout, but much damaged by Cotton fire of 1731 and partly illegible; opens with canons of the councils of Tours (1163) and Lateran (1179), followed by decretals arranged in several books; each book begins with elaborate decretal incipit in red and blue, with line ornamentation on lower fol.; material arranged in titles within the books, but headings omitted by rubricator; negligible marginalia; work transcribed perhaps by several hands. MS includes the history by Florence of Worcester. Provenance uncertain. Cent., late xii- early xiii.

Other members of the 'Worcester' family are: (i) The Trinity Collection: *Trinitatis:* Trinity College Cambridge MS R. 14.9, ff. 82-8; (ii) The Klosterneuburg Collection: *Claustroneoburgensis:* Klosterneuburg Stbl. MS XXXII.19, ff. 36-87; (iii) The Peterhouse Collection, *Peterhusensis:* Peterhouse Cambridge MSS 114, 180, 193 and 203, first and final quires. Cf. Duggan, *Trinity Collection*, 506-26; idem, *Decretal Collections*, 95-117.

4 *The Roman or 'Tortosa' Family*

(a) The Eberbach Collection: *Eberbacensis:* Arundel MS 490, ff. 210ra-221rb. Vellum: 11 x $16\frac{1}{4}$ ins; double cols. of 61 lines. Beautiful later copy; initial letters of inscriptions in red and blue, with some elaboration; rubricated marginal division signs: A I to A XXV; slight marginalia, mostly textual emendations. Analysed by Holtzmann, *Eberbacensis*, 548-

55; cf. Ch. Lefebvre, *DDC*, 1953, V, 134-7; and *Decretal Collections*, 126-8. MS includes Gratian's *Decretum*. Belonged to the Cistercian abbey of the Blessed Virgin Mary in Eberbach. Cent., catalogue suggests xiv.

Other members of the Roman or 'Tortosa' family are: (i) The Tortosa Collection: *Dertusensis;* (ii) The Alcobaça Collection: *Alcobacensis.* For details, see Holtzmann, 'Beiträge zu den Dekretalensammlungen des zwölften Jahrhunderts,' *ZRG., Kan.Abt.*, XVI (1927), 39-77; idem, *Nachrichten*, 21; Kuttner, *Projected Corpus*, 346; and *Decretal Collections*, 126-8.

5 ADDENDUM: *The Frankfurt Collection*

One final twelfth-century collection, a systematic work outside the scope of the present report, completes with *Compilatio Prima* the total number of such works in the British Museum: the Frankfurt Collection: *Francofurtana:* Egerton MS 2901, ff. 1-97. Vellum: $9\frac{1}{2}$ x $6\frac{1}{4}$ ins; one of three related manuscripts, the others being: (i) Frankfurt a.M., Stbl. cod. Barthol. 60, ff. 2-85; (ii) Paris, Bibliothèque Nationale, lat. 3922 A, ff. 173-209. Cf. Kuttner, *Repertorium*, 295-6; Holtzmann and Kemp, *Lincoln Decretals*, xiv; Lefebvre, *DDC*, 1953, V, 878-84; and *Decretal Collections*, Plate VII. Belonged in xvii cent. to the Imperial monastery of St Maximin in Trier; then successively to Frederick North, 5th Earl of Guilford, Thomas Thorpe, Sir Thomas Phillipps and George Dunn. Original provenance: continental with English or Anglo-Norman supplements. Cent., late xii.

The Archbishopric of Lichfield

C. J. GODFREY

Rector of Donhead St Andrew, Shaftesbury, Dorset

IT must have been exceedingly galling to Offa, king of Mercia from 757 to 796, greatest of eighth-century English rulers, one comparable in terms of personal ascendancy with Charlemagne, that his midland kingdom, though politically the master, was ecclesiastically the servant of Kent. The archbishop of Canterbury, he would be well aware, kept princely state and coined his own money, and with the decline of the Kentish kings held an increasing political power. A hostile archbishop could be a serious obstacle to the overlordship of the Mercian king in Kent, and indeed Jaenbert, archbishop during the greater part of Offa's reign, was a supporter of the Kentish king, Egbert II, a ruler distinctly shaky in the matter of loyalty to Offa. It seems to have been about 765 that Offa's overlordship was recognised in the south-eastern kingdom, and from this time onwards he would be increasingly restive under the commanding position of the archbishop of Canterbury. It seems clear that Offa decided to reduce this power, and this could best be done by the establishment of an archbishopric for Mercia, able to rival or even outdo Canterbury. A precedent had already been set in 735, when the bishop of York, Egbert, secured the pallium, and Offa doubtless thought that his dignity deserved what the much inferior kingdom of Northumbria had obtained. So much was possibly in his mind; all he wanted was a favourable opportunity to implement his plan.

An undated letter probably written c.784,[1] by Pope Hadrian I to Charlemagne, refers to a report that Offa had suggested to Charlemagne the removal of Hadrian in favour of a Frankish pope.

---

[1] F. M. Stenton, *Anglo-Saxon England*, Oxford, 2nd ed. 1947, 213-14; A. W. Haddon and W. Stubbs, edd. *Councils and Ecclesiastical Documents relating to Great Britain and Ireland*, 3 vols., Oxford 1871, III, 440-2 (hereafter referred to as *Councils*).

Not that he really believed such a story, comments Hadrian. Charlemagne was easily able, at Offa's request, to deny the report. Still, the contagion of suspicion clung to Offa, and Hadrian was slightly uneasy in his mind. It seems probable that the despatch of papal legates to England in 786[1] was in part at least a consequence of Hadrian's anxiety over the attitude of the powerful Mercian king. This seems to be the specific and practical motive behind the famous visit, while at the same time the pope realised that it offered him an excellent chance to investigate the state of affairs in the far-distant English Church.

Offa, far from resenting the mission, saw in it a golden opportunity to implement his scheme for an additional archbishopric. The legation was led by two prelates prominent in the papal service: George, bishop of Ostia, and Theophylact, bishop of Todi, who duly arrived in Kent, where they were received by Archbishop Jaenbert. They then proceeded to the hall of Offa, who gladly welcomed them. The Northumbrian annalist Simeon of Durham says that the legates restored the ancient friendship existing between England and the Catholic faith introduced by Gregory through Augustine.[2] The statement is puzzling, perhaps, but we cannot believe that it implies any coolness between the eighth-century English Church and the papacy. It suggests rather that the legates had fully satisfied themselves of the personal loyalty of King Offa to Rome. The embassy however was no mere visit of goodwill, and the legates bore with them a body of statutes for consideration and adoption by the English Church.

A preliminary council was held, at which not only Offa but also Cynewulf, king of Wessex, was present. A Northumbrian council followed, at which the proposed statutes, twenty in number, were adopted; and a Mercian council was then convened by Offa, at which the twenty canons were read out both in Latin and the Germanic vernacular ('tam Latine quam theodiscae'), so that not only the ecclesiastics but also the laymen present might understand.

---

[1] Simeon of Durham, *Historia Regum*, s.a., ed. T. Arnold, *Symoneonis Monachi Opera Omnia* (RS), II, 1885; *Councils*, III, 443.

[2] 'Antiquam inter nos amicitiam et fidem catholicam quam sanctus Gregorius papa per beatum Augustinum docuit': *Councils*, III, 443. The joy of Offa, said the legates in their subsequent report, was due to the reverence in which the king held the see of St Peter. The report, sent to Pope Hadrian, is in *Councils*, III, 447-62, and in D. Whitelock ed., *English Historical Documents* I 1955, 770-4 (hereafter referred to as *E.H.D.*).

The canons, covering a variety of topics, including the correct time to administer baptism, the selection of ordination candidates, the communal life of the clergy and the honour due to earthly kings, were again adopted.

It appears that the mission concluded with a general synod of the whole English Church, at which Offa vowed to donate each year 365 mancuses for the support of the poor and for the provision of lights in St Peter's, Rome.[1] This offering, which has usually been regarded as connected in some way with the origin of Peter's pence, was ostensibly made by Offa as an act of thanksgiving for his victories; but, in reality, it looks very much like an act of personal gratitude to the papacy for the rendering of valuable services. The services rendered were surely a general approval of Offa's plans for the Mercian archbishopric. Offa had written to Hadrian, explaining the idea, representing it as necessary because of the vastness of his realms, and had moreover given the pope to understand that the scheme held the unanimous approval of his subjects.[2] To Hadrian the scheme must have seemed reasonable; the English provinces were very large by continental standards.

Meanwhile, though Offa had been given the signal to go ahead, his scheme was still in the exploratory stages, and there is no mention of it in the report concerning their mission which the legates subsequently drew up. Indeed, the incumbent of the Lichfield see, Higebert, signed this report as bishop, not as archbishop, though of course the act of creating a new province would not be regarded as accomplished until the arrival of the pallium from Rome. About Higebert himself we have little information, and, as far as we know, he played an unassuming part in the distressing controversy which was about to centre around the archiepiscopal see of which he was perhaps a somewhat unwilling occupant. He had possibly been bishop since 779, in which year he appears as 'electus praesul' at the Mercian witenagemot of Hartleford in Gloucestershire[3]; two years later he attested a charter of Offa at

---

[1] See a letter written by Leo III to Offa's successor Coenwulf in 798: *Councils*, III, 523-5; *E.H.D.* I, 793-4.

[2] *Councils*, III, 524; *E.H.D.* I, 793.

[3] *Councils*, III, 437, 446; W. de G. Birch, *Cartularium Saxonicum*, 3 vols., London 1885-93, I, 230 (hereafter referred to as *C.S.*).

Brentford in connection with a claim against the church of Worcester.[1]

In 787, after the legates had presumably returned to the Continent, the proposal to divide the southern province was formally brought forward in synod at Chelsea. Approval was by no means as united as Offa had imagined or represented, and there was an angry session.[2] But Offa had his way and Jaenbert agreed to surrender part of his province.[3] Higebert was duly elected archbishop of Lichfield. Other important matters were also transacted at this Chelsea synod. It was apparently as part of its proceedings that Ecgfrith, Offa's son, was consecrated (in his father's lifetime). This is the first known instance of a royal consecration in England.

In a charter extant for 788 the attestation of Higebert as bishop still appears, immediately after Jaenbert's.[4] But his pallium apparently arrived in the course of the year, and before the end of 788 he attests, as archbishop, a charter of Offa in favour of Rochester cathedral church.[5] He attests as archbishop in 789,[6] and again in 792.[7] In attesting a charter of 793, at an important gathering attended by Offa along with many kings and fifteen bishops, Higebert takes precedence of the archbishop of Canterbury.[8] Attesting as archbishop in 794 he again takes precedence.[9] He attests as archbishop after the archbishop of Canterbury in 798,[10] and before Canterbury in 799.[11] Meanwhile Jaenbert had died in August 792, and Higebert consecrated as his successor, in July 793, a Lindsey abbot named Aethelheard, who was well disposed to the Mercian cause.

[1] *C.S.* I, 241; *E.H.D.* I, 466-7.

[2] *Anglo-Saxon Chronicle*, ed. B. Thorpe (RS), I (1861), s.a.

[3] William of Malmesbury says that to Lichfield were assigned the dioceses of Mercia and East Anglia, i.e. Worcester, Hereford, Leicester, Sidnacester (Lindsey), Elmham and Dunwich; and to Canterbury went London, Rochester, Winchester and Selsey: cf. N.E.S.A. Hamilton, ed., *De Gestis Pontificum Anglorum* (RS), 1870, 16; and W. Stubbs, ed., *De Gestis Regum Anglorum* (RS), 1887, I, 85. This was probably true, though Malmesbury does not mention Sherborne, and we might have expected London to go to Lichfield.

[4] *C.S.* I, 254.

[5] *C.S.* I, 253.

[6] *C.S.* I, 255, 256, 257.

[7] *C.S.* I, 264.

[8] *C.S.* I, 267.

[9] *C.S.* I, 269; cf. 274.

[10] *C.S.* I, 289.

[11] *C.S.* I, 293; *E.H.D.* I, 470-1.

Offa died in July 796, and was in due course succeeded by his kinsman Coenwulf, who was at once faced with the task of suppressing a rebellion in Kent led by a certain Eadbert Praen, a member of the Kentish royal house who was also an apostate clerk in holy orders. As a result of this revolt, the pro-Mercian Aethelheard fled from Kent. Shortly afterwards, Alcuin wrote to him, censuring him in strong terms for thus deserting his flock 'through fear of death or torments,' [1] a grave fault for which he must atone with a penance of prayers, masses and almsgiving. But though the recalling of the runaway archbishop of Canterbury was the primary aim of the letter, its real interest to the historian is its implicit information that the abolition of the Lichfield archbishopric was already under active consideration, so soon after the death of Offa. In order that the Church's unity, partly rent asunder because of the love of power, might be peacefully restored, Aethelheard should take counsel with his clergy and the archbishop of York. Alcuin suggests a compromise solution, namely that Higebert might be allowed to retain his pallium during his lifetime, though he should not consecrate any more bishops.

Significant evidence that Higebert's authority had started to collapse very soon after Offa was dead comes from a profession of obedience to Aethelheard by Eadwulf, bishop of Lindsey. Sir Frank Stenton thinks it was written two years later, in the latter part of 798, following the return of Aethelheard to Canterbury[2]; but it seems more likely to have been written a year or two earlier than Stenton's estimate, and to have been prompted by a sense of loyalty to a chief suffering exile. It was in 796 that the previous bishop of Lindsey had died.[3] The document, which is more than formal in its tone, and glows with loyalty to Aethelheard, is the first of a very interesting and significant series of professions of obedience to Canterbury.

Shortly aftwerwards, King Coenwulf put himself in touch with Rome with a view to ending the Lichfield archbishopric. In 798 he

---

[1] *Councils*, III, 518-20; *E.H.D.* I, 789-90. A letter from Alcuin to Aethelheard in the previous year, calling on him not to forsake his church, implies that Eadbert's scheme to shake off the Mercian yoke was already being plotted before Offa's death: *Councils*, III, 495-6.

[2] Stenton, *Anglo-Saxon England*, 226.

[3] Simeon of Durham, ed.cit. s.a.

wrote to Leo III,[1] pointing out that, contrary to the original decree of Gregory I, the authority of Canterbury (or more strictly of London in the Gregorian plan) had been divided into two provinces, a course produced by Offa's hostility to Kent. It is clear from this letter that Coenwulf himself had decided in favour of a single ecclesiastical province for the southern English, or had resigned himself to it. But he was not prepared to surrender so easily the political advantage aimed at by his predecessor, namely, the disarming of a powerful archbishop of Canterbury. He clearly now had in mind the possibility of transferring the southern metropolitan see from Canterbury to London, in accordance with the original recommendation of Gregory I. This would have placed the southern archbishopric well within his power, which was the real point after which Offa had been striving.

Leo replied promptly.[2] He defended the action of Hadrian in confirming the division of the Canterbury province, on the ground that Offa had represented this as being the unanimous wish of the English clergy. The vast size of the province also seemed to have made it a sensible move. Leo read Coenwulf's letter as a request for the transference of the metropolitical dignity from Canterbury to London, but he refused to agree to so great a departure from long and settled tradition. This was an important decision from the point of view of the future history of the English Church. If the pope had agreed to Coenwulf's implied suggestion, there can be little doubt that the transference would actually have taken place, and London would have become the formal centre of the southern province. The external conditions for attempting this were not unfavourable: Aethelheard had deserted his see, while London appears to have recently fallen vacant by the death of its bishop, Eadbald.[3]

In 798 Aethelheard was able to return and resume his seat in Canterbury. In the following year a step was taken towards the rehabilitation of the mother-see at a council held in Tamworth, at which some lands of Charing and other places in Kent, which Offa had seized and distributed to his thegns, were restored to Christ

---

[1] *Councils*, III, 521-3; *E.H.D.* I, 791-3. For Gregory's decree see Bede, *Historia Ecclesiastica*, I, 29.

[2] *Councils*, III, 523-5; *E.H.D.* I, 793-4.

[3] *C.S.* I, 293; *E.H.D.* I, 470-1.

Church, Canterbury.[1] The next known move was a visit of Aethelheard to Rome in 801, accompanied by Cynebert, bishop of Winchester.[2] Alcuin wrote a letter of commendation to Charlemagne on behalf of the archbishop when the latter set out on his journey,[3] at the same time writing to Aethelheard, telling him that he had made arrangements for him to be met when he landed in France, and advising him to travel as simply as possible lest his splendid retinue unfavourably surprise the emperor.[4]

At the beginning of 802 Leo wrote to Aethelheard,[5] conceding to him and his successors the English churches, in agreement with former custom, to be held inviolably by his metropolitan see for ever. The letter is precise, formal and authoritative in its tone; it is in effect a papal authorisation for the abolition of the Lichfield archbishopric. Leo also wrote to Coenwulf, informing him of his action, while Alcuin in the same year sent a letter of congratulation to Aethelheard.[6]

At a provincial synod held at Cloveshoe on 12 October 803, the archbishopric of Lichfield formally came to an end.[7] With 'very great fraud' Offa had rent asunder the see of St Augustine in Canterbury. It was then decreed that this see should never be diminished, and that there should be no archiepiscopal see in Lichfield itself or anywhere else in the south or midlands, save in Canterbury, where 'the Catholic faith first shone forth in this island.' With the permission of Pope Leo, the charter of Hadrian conferring the metropolitan dignity on Lichfield was declared invalid, on the grounds that it had been obtained through misrepresentations. The bishop of Lichfield attesting on this occasion was Ealdwulf. What had happened to Higebert meanwhile is unknown, but there is a strong likelihood that during the last few weeks he had returned to the monastic life, probably wearied with the controversies which had surrounded his see. An abbot Higebert

[1] *Anglo-Saxon Chronicle*, ed.cit., s.a.

[2] *Councils*, III, 533-4; *E.H.D.* I, 794-5.

[3] *Councils*, III, 532-3.

[4] *Councils*, III, 536-7; *E.H.D.* I, 798-9.

[5] *Councils*, III, 538-9, 540-1.

[6] *Councils*, III, 542-3; *E.H.D.* I, 799-800; *C.S.* I, 310.

[7] *Councils*, III, 545-7; *C.S.* I, 312.

is amongst the attestors of another document issued at this synod, forbidding the election of laymen as heads of monasteries. This act was signed by various diocesan bishops, each of whom was accompanied by a deputation of clergy from his diocese. Thus, Ealdwulf, bishop of Lichfield, was accompanied by Abbot Higebert and five priests. This Higebert was surely the previous holder of the metropolitan see; it is the last we hear of him. Aethelheard himself did not live long to enjoy his restored dignity. He died on 12 May 805, and was succeeded by Wulfred, his archdeacon, the first known English holder of the latter office.

Historians have seen one significant outcome of the Lichfield affair in the series of professions of faith and obedience which runs from *c*.796 to *c*.870. They are peculiar in England to the Canterbury province, and survive in two manuscripts, the early twelfth-century B.M. Cotton MS Cleopatra E.i, and a later Canterbury register.[1] They are the result of a custom, which was established after the controversy, of new bishops being required to make profession of their belief in the Catholic faith and to promise loyalty to their metropolitan. The first of the series, as we have seen, is the profession of Ealdwulf, bishop of Lindsey, a former pupil of Aethelheard. It is a warmly expressed document, instinct with reverence for the see of St Augustine. Allowance must be made for the fact that the new bishop in this case was the former pupil of a man who was at the time, or had recently been, in exile. Personal loyalty to a chief in adversity was a common and highly commendable Anglo-Saxon characteristic. But the document certainly sets the tone of the series as a whole; and, if we are right in assuming that the sentiments expressed by Eadwulf were on the whole typical of those of other bishops, we have the answer to the question why the arch-bishopric of Lichfield did not long survive the death of Offa. It was essentially a deep-seated loyalty of churchmen to the traditions of the see of St Augustine which brought about the collapse of the Mercian scheme. It is an echo of the famous Teutonic comitatus-principle, in action in the ecclesiastical field. These professions were carefully preserved, as a precautionary move on Canterbury's part against any future attempt to split the province. The wars occasioned by the ninth-century Danish invasions interrupted the

[1] Register A, Cathedral Library, Canterbury. The professions have been copied into the volume in a fifteenth-century hand.

series, and the only instance surviving from the post-Danish period is a profession of a mid-tenth century bishop of Elmham.[1] A large selection of these professions is included by Stubbs in the third volume of *Councils and Ecclesiastical Documents.*

The supremacy of Canterbury in the south was never again so seriously challenged, except perhaps briefly during the Becket dispute, while Gilbert Foliot was bishop of London; and indeed its commanding position in the English Church had received a powerful impetus. Though some new southern dioceses were established in later Anglo-Saxon times, it was not suggested that the province, one of the largest in the western medieval Church (rivalled in terms of territorial extent only by Mainz, Toledo and perhaps Cologne), should be divided, and the settlement of 803 has been honoured until the present day.

[1] Eadwulf, who made a profession to archbishop Oda: *E.H.D.* I, 578; W. G. Searle *Anglo-Saxon Bishops, Kings and Nobles*, Cambridge 1899, 48.

11

The Letters of
Pope Innocent III to Ireland

P. J. DUNNING, C.M.

Vice-Principal, St Mary's College, Strawberry Hill, Twickenham

THE purpose of this short communication is to call attention to an attempt to establish a definitive calendar of Pope Innocent III's letters to Ireland, and also to indicate very briefly the value of those letters. The two chief ways in which papal letters have been transmitted are through originals or through copies. Copies of letters have survived in a variety of ways: in monastic or episcopal cartularies, in the rolls of royal chancery, in collections of canon law, but for this period mainly in the official papal registers.

The dispersal of monastic archives during the Reformation period, together with the deliberate destruction of papal letters after 1536, partly explains why comparatively few original papal letters of medieval popes to the British Isles have survived. For Ireland, only five original letters of Innocent III are at present known to exist. Two of these are confirmations of property: one to the monastery of St Andrew of Stokes of its possessions in Ireland;[1] and the other to the convent of Graney.[2] The three remaining letters are connected with the peace settlement between Pope Innocent III and King John. They are the exhortation of 28 October 1213 to the prelates and nobles of Ireland to remain faithful to the king[3]; the letter of 4 November 1213 conferring the kingdoms of England and Ireland on the king[4]; and the solemn privilege of 21 April 1214 conferring the same.[5] The original of Innocent III's

---

[1] Eton College, Stogursey Charters, ed., T. D. Tremlett and N. Blakiston, *Somerset Record Society*, LXI (1949 for 1946), No. 151.

[2] B.M. Add. MS 4792, ff. 114-15.

[3] P.R.O. Papal bulls, 19 (18).

[4] B.M. Cotton MS Cleopatra E.I, f. 149.

[5] B.M. Cotton Charter, VIII, 24.

letter of 9 December 1200 to the members of the Arrouaisian congregation in Ireland was extant in the eighteenth century when Jean Baptiste Queinsert, a Benedictine scholar of the congregation of St Maur, made his inventory of the archives of Artois, Flanders, Hainault and Picardy, but it has since disappeared.[1]

The main source for copies of letters is the registers of Innocent III, now contained in Reg. Vat. 4, 5, 7, 7A and 8. The registers for the fourth, seventeenth, eighteenth and nineteenth years are completely missing, and the register for the third year is very defective. However, a table of contents for some of these lost books has survived from the fourteenth century in Reg. Vat. 8A. The extant volumes of the register of Innocent III contain forty-four letters to Ireland; and the fourteenth-century table of contents from the lost books gives a synopsis of twelve further letters.[2] When W. H. Bliss edited the first volume of the *Calendar of the entries in the Vatican Register relating to Great Britain and Ireland* in 1893, he ignored Reg. Vat. 8A, omitted three *in eundem* letters to Ireland, and failed to notice two important letters contained in Reg. Vat. 5. In consequence, he lists only thirty-nine letters to Ireland for this pontificate. August Potthast's comprehensive summary—*Regesta Pontificum Romanorum*—had been issued some years before, in 1874-5, and this great scholar listed the forty-four letters available in the register, together with a summary of the twelve given in Reg. Vat. 8A. He was not, however, aware that the complete text for three of these letters had survived in copies.[3] Potthast included the letter to the members of the Arrouaisian congregation, which had already been published by Gosse and Migne, and he listed three further letters which by his time had also appeared in print:

[1] The copy which Queinsert made is now in the Bibliothèque Nationale, Paris: Moreau collection 101, ff. 3-4. The letter has been printed by A. Gosse, *Histoire de l'abbaye et l'ancienne congrégation des chanoines réguliers d'Arrouaise*, Lille 1786, 430, and PL, CCXVII, 67.

[2] Reg. Vat. 8A also lists two letters from the third year of the pontificate which have survived in the defective register for that year (Reg. Vat. 5).

[3] The text of the letter to Archbishop Henry of Dublin, confirming the union of the see of Glendaloch with Dublin, is contained in Archbishop Alen's Register; the text of the pope's exhortation to the king of Connacht to implement the decrees of the Fourth Lateran Council is contained in a thirteenth-century collection of law formularies and papal letters preserved at the Bibliothèque Nationale, Paris; and the text of the solemn *privilegium* to Archbishop Henry of Dublin, dated 18 May 1216, has been preserved in the Dublin register known as the *Crede Mihi*. Cf. P. J. Dunning, 'The Letters of Pope Innocent III to Ireland,' *Traditio*, XVIII (1962), 246-7, nos. 63, 67 and 71.

the letter of confirmation to the prioress and convent of Graney,[1] the solemn privilege of 21 April 1214 confirming the kingdoms of England and Ireland to King John,[2] and a letter of 30 July 1214 to Archbishop Henry of Dublin.[3] These additions brought the total to sixty.

Potthast, however, was not familiar with the extant English and Irish cartularies, and it has since been found possible to add considerably to his number. From English and Irish sources, but also in a few instances from continental sources, the texts of twelve further letters have been collected, together with a large number of quotations from, or synopses of, still further letters. The present total of available material, which includes some letters about which our only information is that they were issued, and some doubtful examples, amounts to ninety letters. A brief calendar of these letters was published in the issue of *Traditio* for 1962.[4] It is worth noting that we know from other sources of some thirty-four letters sent to Ireland during the period, which were not included in the extant registers of the pope. In view of the almost complete destruction of monastic and episcopal records from medieval Irish history, this number is surprisingly high, and indicates that far more letters were in fact sent to Ireland by Innocent III than the ninety of which at present we have information.

Broadly speaking, the papal letters of this period fall into two main groups: the solemn privilege (*privilegium*) and the simpler form of letter (*littera*). The vast majority of letters to Ireland fall into this second group. It is possible to sub-classify these letters in various ways according to their form and content; but, in the brief

[1] The text of the original letter had been published in W. Dugdale, *Monasticon Anglicanum*, edd. J. Caley, etc, London 1817-30, VI, 2, 1125.

[2] The text of the original had been published by both D. Wilkins, *Concilia Magnae Britanniae et Hiberniae*, London 1737, I, 541, and J. Rymer, *Foedera* (1816 ed.), I, I, 119.

[3] A copy of this letter is preserved in Archbishop Alen's register, and in the register of the priory of All Hallows, Dublin. The Rev. Richard Butler published the text in his edition of *Registrum Prioratus Omnium Sanctorum*, Dublin 1844.

[4] In this Calendar the confirmation to the prior and monks of St Andrew at Ards (No. 30) is wrongly described as an original; the original letter is the confirmation of properties, including those in Ireland, granted to the prior and monks of St Andrew of Stokes (Calendar No. 31), and preserved among the Stogursey Charters at Eton College. The priory of St Andrew in Ards was a dependency of St Andrew of Stokes, founded in the late-twelfth century by John de Courci. An earlier, and now outdated, calendar of additions to Potthast and Bliss was published in 1947: Dunning, 'Letters of Pope Innocent III to Ireland,' *Archivium Hibernicum*, XIII (1947), 27-44.

description of the letters which follows, Professor Cheney's four-fold classification according to subject-matter is used for convenience.[1]

A considerable number of letters falls into the first category: privileges and letters of protection and indults in response to petitions (*littere gratiose* or *tituli*). Such letters are mainly of value to the local historian, but occasionally they have a wider significance. For example, the letter of confirmation, of 20 July 1212, to the Hospitallers of their churches and properties in Ireland indicates how closely the foundation of houses of this Order followed the advance of the Norman invader.[2]

The second category comprises decretals, or replies to enquiries on points of law (*decretales* or *rescripta*). The number of such letters to Ireland is small, and we have nothing comparable to Innocent III's famous reply on some eighteen points of law raised by Bishop Eustace of Ely.[3] Two decretal letters are of considerable importance: the pope's reply to the king of Connacht's query concerning sanctuary would seem to have exercised considerable influence ultimately in the forming of the present canon 1179 of the Code of Canon Law[4]; and Innocent III's reply to the question of the archbishop of Armagh concerning the entrance of women *post partum* into the church is of interest in the history of liturgical observance.[5] Innocent III's decision in the Armagh controversy has also attracted the attention of canonists.[6]

The majority of the letters fall into the third category: mandates in judicial and administrative matters (*mandamenta*). While this type of letter provides a wealth of historical information, the facts disclosed must be tested, confirmed and amplified where possible from contemporary native sources.[7] The matter so disclosed is of

[1] C. R. Cheney and W. H. Semple, edd., *Selected Letters of Pope Innocent III concerning England*, Nelson's Medieval Texts, 1953, xix.

[2] Cf. McNeill, ed., *Registrum de Kilmainham* (Irish Manuscripts Commission, 1932), 139.

[3] Text and translation in Cheney and Semple, ed. cit. 68-78.

[4] C. Sept.-Oct. 1200. Reg. Vat. 5, f. 2*v*; Reg. Vat. 8A, f.6*r* ; PL. CCXIV, 875.

[5] C. March, 1198. Reg. Vat. 4, f. 16*v*; PL. CCXIV, 55.

[6] C. Sept. 1202. Reg. Vat. 5, ff. 47*v*-48*v*; PL. CCXIV, 1066.

[7] On the dangers involved in using such letters as sources, see Cheney, 'The Letters of Pope Innocent III,' *Bulletin of the John Rylands Library*, XXXV (1952), 23-43; Dunning, 'The letters of Pope Innocent III as a source for Irish history,' *Proceedings of the Irish Catholic Historical Committee 1958*, Dublin 1959, 1-10.

importance mainly for Irish ecclesiastical history. The most valuable letters of this kind are those dealing with election controversies and with attempts to suppress and annex ancient sees: outstanding cases in Ross, Waterford-Lismore, Dublin-Glendaloch, Tuam-Mayo have already been subjected to detailed analysis.[1] This material also has its significance in English history, for the historian of the reign of King John should not neglect the king's involvement in Irish ecclesiastical affairs, especially during the periods immediately prior to the interdict and the peace settlement. It may be of interest to point out that the incidence of these letters is uneven. For the first three years of the pontificate, we have a large number and a great variety of letters to Ireland, all of them in reply to requests from Ireland or arising from the visits of Irish ecclesiastics to Rome. It is understandable that the number should be smaller in the next few years: firstly, because the register for the fourth year is missing; and, secondly, because the pope's legate (Cardinal John of Salerno) was in Ireland in 1202-3. There is a small steady trickle of letters from 1203 to 1206, but—significantly perhaps—from October 1207 until late in 1212 the number is negligible. A steady stream of letters begins again in 1213, and a particularly large number comes from the period of the Lateran Council.

The fourth category comprises political correspondence (*littere de curia* or *littere secrete*), and the number of such letters to Ireland is relatively small. Of particular importance are the letters to the king of Connacht and the invitations extended to the kings of Connacht, Cork, Limerick and Meath to attend the Fourth Lateran Council. The pope's attitude to the complex feudal relationship between Anglo-Norman England and Ireland is not clearly indicated, but it is possible to suggest a fairly consistent policy.[2]

Does a close study of the activities of Pope Innocent III in this restricted field of Irish history give us a clue to his personality, and some deeper understanding of his policy and aims? Complete

---

[1] Dunning, 'Pope Innocent III and the Ross election controversy,' *Irish Theological Quarterly*, XXVI (1959), 346-59, and 'Pope Innocent III and the Waterford-Lismore controversy, 1198-1216,' ibid. XXVIII (1961), 215-32; idem., 'Irish representatives and Irish ecclesiastical affairs at the Fourth Lateran Council,' *Medieval Studies presented to Aubrey Gwynn, S.J.*, Dublin 1961, 90-113; idem, 'Sidelights on the Bishop of Raphoe from the register of Innocent III,' *Foster John Colgan, O.F.M., 1592-1658: Essays in commemoration of the third centenary of his death*, Dublin 1959, 50-60.

[2] Idem, 'Pope Innocent III and the Irish kings,' *JEH*, VIII (1957), 17-32.

answers to these questions cannot be given in this short paper. Nevertheless, answers can be given, and the lines these might take have been suggested elsewhere.[1] For that reason, a study of Innocent III's dealings with Ireland as revealed in the letters is of some importance in any comprehensive assessment of the great pope's personality and aims.

[1] In the published articles already referred to, and in particular in an unpublished doctoral dissertation presented to the National University of Ireland in 1960 (from which I hope to publish further material in the near future). In October 1962, the Rev. M. P. Sheehy published a critical edition of the letters of Innocent III to Ireland in his *Pontificia Hibernica: medieval papal chancery documents concerning Ireland, 640-1261,* Dublin, I, 93-181. Fr. Sheehy includes one letter (a confirmation to the prior and canons of Holy Trinity, Dublin, *c.*March 1216) which was unaccountably omitted by me in my revised calendar in *Traditio,* XVIII (1962), 229-53. This publication had not been advertised and it came to my notice after the text of this article had been written.

Mixed Marriages in Byzantium in the Thirteenth Century

D. M. NICOL

Lecturer in Classics, University College, Dublin

THE Church always demanded that the two partners to a marriage should be not only of the Christian faith but also of the same creed and dogma. Marriage with infidels and Jews was declared illegal; but so also was marriage with heretics and, in Byzantine law, with 'gentiles,' or those not within the orbit of the Byzantine Church and Empire.[1] The fourteenth canon of the Council of Chalcedon forbade an Orthodox Christian to contract 'a marriage with a heretic woman'; the seventy-second canon of the Council in Trullo repeated this prohibition, adding that such a marriage, if contracted, should be dissolved; and in the twelfth century the Byzantine canonist Theodore Balsamon ruled that the female partners in such marriages should be excommunicated. These warnings were solemnly reiterated in the imperial legislation of Byzantium from the time of Justinian onwards.[2]

Such was the letter of the law. In practice, however, the law could be disregarded in this as in other respects when it suited Byzantine imperial policy. Only rarely were the marital arrangements of the emperor questioned by the patriarch. Leo VI got

[1] Much literature has been devoted to the various canonical impediments to marriage in Byzantine law, but less to the subject of intermarriage between Byzantines and foreigners. Cf. however Ph. Koukoules, Βυζαντινῶν Βίος καί Πολιτισμός, in *Collection de l'Institut Français d'Athènes*, IV, (1951), 93-6, 124-6; R. Guilland, 'Les noces plurales à Byzance,' *Byzantinoslavica*, IX, (1947), 9-30 (reprinted in *Etudes Byzantines*, Paris 1959, 233-61); J. Zhishman, *Das Eherecht der orientalischen Kirche*, Vienna 1864; J. Dauvillier and C. de Clerq, *Le Mariage en Droit canonique oriental*, Paris 1936, 164-7.

[2] G. A. Rhalles and M. Potles, Σύνταγμα τῶν θείων καί ἱερῶν κανόνων, 6 vols., Athens 1852-59, II, 251-4; III, 173, 186, 198-9, 364, give the relevant canons of the councils, with the scholia of the twelfth-century Byzantine canonists John Zonaras and Theodore Balsamon.

himself into serious trouble with the Church by contracting a fourth marriage; and John Tzimiskes was humiliated by his patriarch in 969, when he proposed to marry the widow of his predecessor whose murder he had helped to contrive.[1] But, at least from the tenth century, the Byzantine emperors and members of the imperial family made marriages not only with Franks but also with Khazars, Bulgars and even Turks. Marriages with Saracens or Turks were clearly uncanonical. Marriages with Franks, however, came into a special category. For the Franks, although technically 'gentiles,' were exceptional. Constantine Porphyrogenitus, in a famous passage in the *De Administrando Imperio*, advises his son Romanus most strongly against arranging marriage alliances between members of the imperial family and members of any other nation. The marriage of true Romans with foreigners is a form of sacrilege. But he makes one exception. 'Never,' he says, 'shall an emperor of the Romans ally himself in marriage with a nation of customs differing from and alien to those of the Roman order, especially with one that is infidel and unbaptized, unless it be with the Franks alone; for they alone were excepted by that great man, the holy Constantine, because he himself drew his origin from those parts; for there is much relationship and converse between Franks and Romans. . . . But with any other nation whatsoever it was not to be in the power (of the emperors) to do this, and he who dared to do it was to be condemned as an alien from the ranks of the Christians and subject to the anathema, as a transgressor of the imperial laws and ordinances.'[2]

In the days of Constantine Porphyrogenitus there was no question of the Greek and Latin Churches being in schism, so that intermarriage between Greeks and Franks involved no infringement of the canons of Orthodoxy. But clearly in later years the theological differences between the Churches, so often expressed in mutual accusations of heresy, might have been thought to constitute a canonical impediment to marriage between Orthodox and Catholic. The schism of 1054 might have been expected to cast its blight on

[1] Cf. Guilland, art. cit. 237-47; G. Ostrogorsky, *History of the Byzantine State*, Oxford 1956, 260-1.

[2] Constantine Porphyrogenitus, *De Administrando Imperio*, edd. Gy. Moravcsik and R. J. H. Jenkins, Budapest 1949, 70-6; c.13, ll.104 ff. and *Commentary*, ed. R. J. H. Jenkins, London 1962, 67-9.

the possibility of intermarriage between 'prozymites' and 'azymites' in the eleventh and twelfth centuries. But four of the five emperors of the Comnenian dynasty in the twelfth century—John II, Manuel I, Alexios II and Andronikos—married Latin wives. Manuel, whose Latinophile policy was extremely unpopular in Byzantium, married two—Berthe of Sulzbach and Mary of Antioch.

In the thirteenth century, after the disaster of the Fourth Crusade, one would expect such marriages to be even less likely. For the sack of Constantinople and the dismemberment of the Byzantine Church and Empire by the crusaders made the Greeks wonder whether the Latins, who were known to be different in dogma, were of the same religion at all. Niketas Choniates describes them as the 'forerunners of Antichrist'; and Greek and Latin clergy took to accusing each other of heresy with depressing frequency. In such circumstances intermarriage between Greeks and Latins clearly should not have occurred, according to the letter of canon law. Yet the surprising thing is that, for all the ill-feeling and religious bigotry engendered by the events of 1204, Greeks of what may be called the ruling classes continued to marry Franks and Italians without troubling their consciences.

Pope Innocent III, the prime mover of the Fourth Crusade, had a keen eye for this sort of problem, and realised that, from his point of view, there were important issues of principle at stake. For Innocent looked upon the results of the Crusade and the establishment of a Latin Empire of Constantinople as God's plan for the healing of the schism and the union of Christendom under Rome. The first mixed marriage after the conquest of Constantinople was, strangely enough, between two Latins, one a Catholic, the other a convert to Orthodoxy. The partners were Boniface, marquis of Montferrat, and Margaret or Maria of Hungary, widow of the late emperor Isaac II Angelos. Boniface, as leader of the Fourth Crusade, wanted to improve his prospects of becoming the first Latin emperor by marrying the widow of the late Byzantine emperor. It was a rushed affair. But Pope Innocent took a personal interest in the marriage, not because he had much hope of saving the soul of Boniface, but because of Margaret. She had been born of Catholic parents, as a daughter of Béla III of Hungary, but had gone over to the Greek Church when she married Isaac II, at a tender age. Her marriage to Boniface in 1204 was performed according to the Latin rite, but for some time afterwards she remained a member of the Greek Church, until brought back to the fold by the combined efforts of her new husband and the papal legate to Constantinople. It was on the occasion of her reconversion that Innocent wrote to congratulate her most warmly on her good sense and took her under his protection.[1]

As it happened, Margaret of Hungary never lost her love for the Greek Church. In 1208, when she became a widow for a second time, and was left as queen-mother at Thessalonica, she appointed a Greek as governor of the city; and the Latin archbishop of Larissa complained to the pope that she was interfering in the affairs of his diocese and encouraging the Greek clergy not to obey their new Latin superiors.[2] Some at least of the ladies of western Europe who found their way to Byzantium preferred the civilised comforts of the Byzantine world, if not the Byzantine faith, to the colder and more austere conditions in their own countries. When the crusaders first entered Constantinople in 1203 they enquired for Agnes of France, a sister of King Philip Augustus, who had been living there for many years, first as the wife of the usurper Andronikos Komnenos and then of a Greek nobleman called Theodore Vranas. No doubt they expected that she would welcome them as long-lost compatriots and friends. But in fact she refused to have anything to do with them, pretended to have forgotten her French, and insisted on having an interpreter.[3]

Of course Margaret of Hungary had married Isaac II when she was 'of tender age,' and hence perhaps not accountable for her actions. But her elders knew what they were about. The canonical age for marriage in Byzantium was usually twelve for a girl (as it

[1] Letters of Innocent III, viii, 134 (1205); PL, ccxv, 714. Cf. R. L. Wolff, 'The organisation of the Latin Patriarchate of Constantinople, 1204-1261. Social and administrative consequences of the Latin Conquest,' *Traditio*, VI, (1948), 37-40.

[2] Letters of Innocent III, XI, 152 (1208); PL, ccxv, 1467. Demetrios Chomatianos, ed. by J. B. Pitra in *Analecta Sacra Spicilegio Solesmensi Parata*, Rome 1891, VII (VI), 447-62, n. 106; Wolff, art. cit.

[3] Robert of Clari, *La Conquête de Constantinople*, ed. P. Lauer, Paris 1924, 52-4, 81-90; Geoffrey of Villehardouin, *La Conquête de Constantinople*, ed E. Faral, Paris 1938, I, 186-96; J. Longnon, *L'Empire latin de Constantinople*, Paris 1949, 41; C. Diehl, *Impératrices de Byzance*, Paris 1959, 243-4.

still is in some places) and fourteen or sixteen for a boy.[1] Agnes of
France had married Andronikos Komnenos when she was twelve
and he was sixty. There were exceptions to this rule, but they were
rare. In 1299 Andronikos II Palaiologos married his daughter
Simonis to Stephen Milutin of Serbia when she was only five and
he about forty, though the patriarch raised all manner of objections.
Some years later, when she was about twenty-two, she tried to take
refuge from her husband in Constantinople, and had to be sent
back to Serbia in tears.[2]

The most celebrated Greco-Latin marriage in the thirteenth
century was that between the Byzantine emperor at Nicaea, John
III Vatatzes, and Constance of Hohenstaufen, or Anna as the
Greeks called her, the daughter of Frederick II. The wedding took
place at Brusa in 1244, when John was fifty-two and Constance
twelve. There was, of course, some doubt as to whether Frederick
was a Catholic or not; the doubt was especially strong in the mind
of Pope Innocent IV, who excommunicated him at the Council of
Lyons in 1245. But it is interesting to find that among the reasons
given for Frederick's excommunication was the very fact that he
had given his daughter in marriage to a schismatic and heretic
prince. Matthew Paris describes the shock that this marriage
caused in the West. 'It was regarded,' he says, by the pope and the
whole Roman Curia, 'as a serious offence, because it was through
the same John Vatatzes that the schism arose between the Roman
and Greek Churches, whence the Roman Church called him a
schismatic.' Innocent IV defined it as a heretical marriage, although
John Vatatzes was no more and no less of a heretic than the
emperors of the twelfth century who had married Catholic wives
without incurring papal disapproval. Heresy apart, the pope
considered it an undesirable union. The Byzantine emperor, on the
other hand, considered it desirable because it was highly diplomatic,
and calculated to enhance the prestige of the Greek Empire exiled
by the Latins from its capital to Nicaea. The patriarch seems to
have taken the same view, and overlooked the canonical objections

[1] Koukoules, op. cit. 76; H.-G. Beck, *Kirche und Theologische Literatur im Byzanti-
nischen Reich*, Munich 1959, 88.

[2] Nikephoros Gregoras, *Byzantina Historia*, ed. L. Schopen, Bonn 1829-55, I, 203,
287-8; George Pachymeres, *De Michaele et Andronico Palaeologis*, ed. I. Bekker, Bonn
1835, II, 278 ff.; Koukoules, op. cit., 128-9.

which in other circumstances he might have raised; what scandalised the patriarch far more than the marriage was the fact that John promptly forsook his young wife in favour of one of her ladies-in-waiting.[1]

At an earlier stage in the history of the Empire of Nicaea its founder, Theodore Laskaris, had taken as his third wife Maria of Courtenay, sister of the then Latin emperor, Robert.[2] There is no record of any protest being made about this marriage either by the pope or by the patriarch. Once again it was a diplomatic marriage: Laskaris hoped to secure the succession to Constantinople by marrying into the family of the Latin emperors. Two of his three daughters also married Latin husbands.[3] Not long afterwards, however, when he suggested that his daughter Eudokia should marry the Emperor Robert, the patriarch put his foot down.[4] He described the project as an 'athesmogamia.' The canonical impediments were certainly strong, owing to the degree of affinity already existing between the prospective partners. But objections of this nature could be overcome, and were overcome in other circumstances when it was thought convenient.[5] It would seem that in this case the patriarch was rather glad to have grounds for forbidding another marriage between Greeks and Latins. The emperor argued with him, as Byzantine emperors were wont to argue with their

---

[1] George Akropolites, *Historia*, ed. A. Heisenberg, Leipzig 1903, I, 104; Pachymeres, op. cit. I, 181; Matthew Paris, *Chronica Majora*, (RS) 1877, IV, (1240-7), 299, 357, 453; F. Dölger, *Regesten der Kaiserurkunden des Oströmischen Reiches*, Munich-Berlin 1932, III, nos. 1779-81; G. Schlumberger, 'Le tombeau d'une impératrice byzantine à Valence en Espagne,' *Byzance et Croisades*, Paris 1927, 57-86; Diehl, *Impératrices de Byzance*, 249-264; D. J. Geanakoplos, *Emperor Michael Palaeologus and the West*, Cambridge, Mass. 1959, 144-5.

[2] Akropolites, ed. Heisenberg, pp. 27, 31. Laskaris's second wife was an Armenian princess, but the marriage ended in divorce after only one year.

[3] Maria Laskarine married the son of King Andrew II of Hungary, the later Béla IV (1235-1270); Eudokia married the French baron of Constantinople, Anseau of Cahieu. Akropolites, ed. cit. 26, 41, 85; Pachymeres, op. cit. I, 317-18.

[4] Akropolites, ed. cit. 31; Skutariotes, *Additamenta*, ibid. 280.

[5] As, for example, in the case of Michael (Demetrios) Angelos, son of Michael II, despot of Epiros, who fled to Constantinople in 1278 and married Anna, second daughter of the Emperor Michael VIII. A sixth degree of affinity existed between the partners to this marriage, but a synod decided that the political advantages to be gained outweighed the canonical objections and granted a dispensation. Pachymeres, op. cit. I, 440-1; dispensation of November 1278 in A. Papadopoulos-Kerameus, 'Ιεροσολυμιτικὴ Βιβλιοθήκη, St Petersburg 1891-1915, IV, 382.

patriarchs. But on this occasion the patriarch won, for Laskaris died in the same year.

The Greeks seem to have assumed that the Orthodox partner in mixed marriages would retain the Greek rite and creed, and that the children would be brought up in the Orthodox faith.[1] Among the lower classes of Byzantine society the children of such marriages were thought to be slightly improper and contemptuously called 'gasmouli,' though some of them were said 'to combine the prudence and discipline of the Greeks with the daring and courage of the Italians.'[2] But among the upper classes the situation was different. For even after the Fourth Crusade Byzantium still retained some of its glamour in the eyes of foreigners. A Byzantine prince was still considered to be a good catch in the West; and, as John Cantacuzene points out, even in the fourteenth century members of the Italian and Latin aristocracy longed for the chance to be connected by marriage with the Byzantine imperial family.[3] When Andronikos II, for example, was looking for a wife for his son Michael in the 1290s, ambassadors from three Catholic countries were pressing their claims in Constantinople, although it was known that Andronikos was excommunicated by the pope. Some of the most illustrious families in Byzantium in the thirteenth century were in fact of Latin and Catholic origin, but their descendants had embraced the Orthodox faith through intermarriage. The families of Petraliphas and Raoul, for instance, both of Latin ancestry, provided many soldiers, administrators and champions of Orthodoxy in Byzantium. The Raouls were, indeed, among the most outspoken opponents of the Emperor Michael VIII's policy of union with Rome at the time of the Second Council of Lyons, while

---

[1] Cf. the ps.-Photian *Nomocanon*, t. xii, c. xiii: 'If one of the partners to the marriage be Orthodox, the other heretic, their children must become Orthodox'; *Nomocanon Photii Patriarchae Constantinopolitani*, ed. Christophorus Iustellus, Paris 1615, 133-4, 194-6 (Latin trans.); Rhalles and Potles, op. cit. i, 270-2. The scholiast on this passage marvels at the spectacle of perfectly Orthodox Spaniards marrying their daughters to Saracens, and wonders why their bishops, who are well aware of the law, do not forbid such unions.

[2] Pachymeres, op. cit. i, 188; Gregoras, op. cit. i, 98. Cf. Du Cange, *Glossarium ad scriptores mediae et infimae Graecitatis*, s.v. Βασμοῦλοι; and literature cited by Geanako-plos, op. cit. 127. Gregoras, op. cit. iii, 555, speaks rather scathingly of the 'children with Latin heads and Persian bodies' to be seen in Constantinople in the fourteenth century—advertisements for the torn and disjointed body of the Empire and its sick and suffering soul diseased by strange dogmas.

[3] John Cantacuzene, *Historiarum Libri*, ed. L. Schopen, i, Bonn 1828, 195-6.

the Petraliphas family added a saint to the Orthodox Church in the person of Theodora of Arta. Sometimes, it seems, certain conditions were written into the terms of the marriage contract regarding the faith of the Orthodox partner. When arrangements were being made for the marriage of Thamar, daughter of Nikephoros the Greek despot of Epiros, to Philip of Anjou, prince of Taranto, in 1294, it was agreed that Thamar should have complete freedom to practice her own religion.[1] Philip violated his pledge as soon as the wedding was over, forced his young wife to adopt the Catholic faith, and drove her to distraction before divorcing her for adultery in 1309.[2] Her sister Maria fared rather better. For she married John Orsini, son of the Italian count of Cephalonia, and apparently converted him to the Orthodox faith. He came to settle in Greece, and his sons inherited the despotate of Epiros.[3] His grandson Nikephoros married a daughter of the Emperor John Cantacuzene, while his grand-daughter Thomais married into the Serbian royal family and produced one of the most remarkable figures in the later history of the Byzantine Church—John Uroš Doukas Angelos Komnenos Palaiologos, second founder of the monastery of the Great Meteoron in Thessaly.[4]

During the years after 1204 it was the Greeks in Greece itself who suffered most of the burden of Latin occupation; and it was they who protested most vigorously against the overtures made to the papacy and the 'heretical' Latins by the Byzantine emperors at Nicaea. In their view Constantinople was to be recovered from the 'Latin dogs' by force and not by adulterating the faith of their fathers. One of their greatest spokesmen in this respect was Demetrios Chomatianos, archbishop of Ochrida, the most learned of all the thirteenth-century Byzantine canonists. He felt that no good could come of marriages between Greeks and Latins, and

[1] Pachymeres, op. cit. II, 202. See W. Miller, *The Latins in the Levant*, London 1908, 182-3; Longnon, *L'Empire latin*, 272-3.

[2] At least forty of his barons were cited as co-respondents, the chief among them being the count of Caserta; Ptolemy of Lucca, *Historia ecclesiastica*, in L. A. Muratori, *Rerum Italicarum Scriptores*, Bologna 1903, XI, 1232. Cf. R. Rodd, *The Princes of Achaia and the Chronicles of Morea*, London 1907, II, 60-1.

[3] Miller, op. cit., 179-82; Longnon, op. cit., 269.

[4] Gregoras, op. cit. III, 249, 557; Cantacuzene, op. cit. I, 503; II, Bonn 1831, 195. For John Uroš, the monk Joasaph, see, most recently, M. Lascaris, 'Deux Chartes de Jean Uroš, dernier Némanide,' *Byzantion*, XXV-XXVII (1955-7), 277-323, and D. M. Nicol, *Meteora. The Rock Monasteries of Thessaly*, London 1963, 64-5, 101-12.

ruled that the Orthodox partner in a mixed marriage celebrated by a Catholic priest should be excommunicated, and that any Greek priest who gave his blessing to such a union should be suspended.[1] The separatist rulers of Epiros and Thessaly, who had been encouraged by Demetrios Chomatianos, continued to protest, long after Constantinople and the Byzantine Empire had been restored by Michael VIII Palaiologos in 1261, against the policy of negotiation with the papacy and the Latins which Michael found it necessary to pursue in order to preserve his empire from its western enemies. In 1277, for example, three years after the Second Council of Lyons, at which the union of the Greek and Roman Churches had been proclaimed, John Doukas, the ruler of Thessaly, assembled a council of his own in Greece, at which the pope, the patriarch and the emperor were all anathematized as heretics.[2] Yet such fiercely anti-Catholic sentiments did not, apparently, prevent amicable relationships between Orthodox and Catholic at the personal level when they seemed convenient. John Doukas could set himself up as the defender of the purest Orthodox faith and yet at the same time, for reasons of policy, marry his daughter to the French Catholic duke of Athens.[3] It is a remarkable fact that eight of the eleven female members of the Greek ruling families in Greece in the thirteenth century married either Italian or Frankish husbands; though not a single male member married outside the Orthodox world.[4] Daughters, unlike sons, were thought to be expendable commodities for diplomatic purposes. The usurper

[1] Demetrios Chomatianos, ed. Pitra, 713.

[2] See V. Grumel, 'En Orient après le IIe Concile de Lyon,' *Echos d'Orient*, XXIV (1925), 321-4.

[3] Gregoras, op. cit. I, 114; Pachymeres, op. cit. I, 328; Marino Sanudo *Istoria del Regno di Romania*, ed. C. Hopf, *Chroniques gréco-romanes*, Berlin 1873, 136; *Livre de la Conqueste de la Princée de l'Amorée, Chronique de Morée*, ed. Longnon, Paris 1911, 4c8, 413.

[4] A daughter of Michael I of Epiros married Eustace of Flanders, brother of the Latin Emperor Henry; Michael's sister Anna married Maio Orsini of Cephalonia; of the two daughters of Michael II of Epiros, Anna married William of Villehardouin, prince of Achaia, and Helena married Manfred of Sicily (see D.M. Nicol, *The Despotate of Epiros*, Oxford 1957, 29, 107, 172-3, 177-8). Michael II's sister-in-law, Maria Sphrantzaina, married Manfred's admiral Philip Chinardo (Pachymeres, op.cit. I, 508; P. J. Alexander, 'A chrysobull of the Emperor Andronicus II in favor of the See of Kanina in Albania,' *Byzantion*, XV (1940-1), 197-201). Of the daughters of Nikephoros I of Epiros, Maria married John Orsini of Cephalonia, and Thamar married Philip of Taranto (see above), while Helena, daughter of John Doukas of Thessaly, married William de la Roche, duke of Athens and Thebes.

Michael Palaiologos established his position on the Byzantine throne in 1261 partly by blinding the legitimate Emperor John Laskaris, but partly also by marrying off John's three sisters to foreigners, two of them to Latins. It was a useful way of getting rid of them.[1]

The attitude of the papacy towards marriages between Greeks and Latins was based upon more rigid principles. The popes seem to have been unable to prevent Catholics already living in the Byzantine Empire from marrying Greeks when they felt like it; and there are cases of Catholics being converted to the Orthodox faith, in spite of the social embarrassments which such a conversion entailed. Pachymeres tells a cautionary tale about an Armenian Catholic in Constantinople who was converted to Orthodoxy, thereby dividing his family. In the course of one of the violent domestic arguments over the matter, the convert threatened to denounce them all to the patriarch, at which one of his relatives blasphemed against the Orthodox Church and said that the patriarch had no power in any case. Shortly afterwards the same man slipped and fell while crossing the street. The accident was taken to be a miracle wrought by the patriarch, although Pachymeres thought that it should rather be attributed to God and the faith.[2] However, when it was a question of a Catholic from western Europe going to Constantinople to marry a Greek, the popes seem to have insisted upon certain conditions. The Byzantine historians comment with interest upon the fact that Latins of the aristocracy, when contemplating marriage with Greeks, thought it necessary to seek a dispensation from the pope. It was this irksome formality which persuaded Andronikos II, when he was looking for a wife for his son Michael, to reject the offer of a daughter from Henry II, the Lusignan king of Cyprus. 'The king himself,' says Pachymeres, 'was willing enough; but there was one objection, namely that the marriage contract must be made with the consent and approval of the Roman Church.' Andronikos had rather hoped that Michael might marry Catherine of Courtenay, niece of Charles II of Anjou and claimant to the title of the defunct Latin Empire of Constanti-

---

[1] Pachymeres, op. cit. I, 180-1; Gregoras, op. cit. I, 92-3. Cf. V. Laurent, 'Les grandes crises religieuses à Byzance. La fin du schisme arsénite,' *Académie Roumaine: Bulletin de la section historique*, XXVI (1945), 230-1.

[2] Pachymeres, op. cit. III, 520-1.

nople. But the negotiations foundered on the same rock. The consent of the pope had first to be obtained. Andronikos, of course, was a schismatic and heretic in the eyes of the papacy, as being the emperor who had renounced the Union of Lyons. But he also offended the pope by failing to address him as 'hagiotatos' or *sanctissimus*, because he could not do so without feeling that he was lowering the status of his own Church. Finally, in the words of Pachymeres, 'suspecting the arrogance of the pope, he looked elsewhere for a daughter-in-law,' and picked on a sister of the king of Armenia, Hethoum II, who though himself a Catholic was obviously not so fussy.[1]

Andronikos should have known the difficulties involved in arranging mixed marriages, for he had himself married a daughter of Stephen V of Hungary. Stephen was officially a Catholic, though he was Greek on his mother's side, and his own wife had been a Cuman slave-girl who, though very lovely to look at, was a pagan.[2] No objections seem to have been raised to the marriage of his daughter Maria to Andronikos. But that was in 1271, at a time when Andronikos and his father Michael Palaiologos had both solemnly declared themselves obedient to the See of Rome prior to the Second Council of Lyons. Thirteen years later, in 1284, after Maria had died leaving Andronikos with two sons, Michael and Constantine, he married again. His second wife was also a Catholic—Yolanda or Eirene of Montferrat. She was a descendant of the Marquis Boniface, leader of the Fourth Crusade, and a grand-daughter of the king of Spain. It was regarded as a modest enough marriage for the Byzantine emperor, and Yolanda was only eleven years old. But the succession to the throne was already ensured, and the marriage was largely for diplomatic purposes. It was to Yolanda's grandfather that Andronikos applied; and Gregoras makes a point of saying that the Spanish king 'overruled the tradition of the Latins by sending his grand-daughter to Constantinople without the permission of the pope. For it is the custom among the Latin nobility not to contract marriages with Greeks without first

---

[1] Pachymeres, op. cit. II, 153-4, 202-6; Gregoras, op. cit. I, 193; F. Dölger, *Regesten*, IV, Munich-Berlin 1960, nos. 2156a-2157b; C. Marinescu, 'Tentatives de mariage de deux fils d'Andronic II Paléologue avec des princesses latines,' *Revue historique du sud-est européen*, I (1924), 139-43.

[2] Pachymeres, op. cit. I, 317-8; Gregoras, op. cit. I, 109.

obtaining a dispensation from the pope.' He remarks that the king of Spain was at this stage under papal anathema, so that he felt no doubt that he could act as a free agent. He might have added that in 1284 the Byzantine emperor was also excommunicated by the pope, so that from the papal point of view the marriage was hardly Christian at all.[1]

The question of relationships between Greeks and Latins in the Byzantine Empire is far too complex to be treated in a few words. But it may be fair to say that the latent prejudices on either side were reinforced by the events of the thirteenth century, which brought Greeks and Latins together in a way that had never occurred before. The Byzantine emperors, however, when thrown on to the defensive by the Latin conquest in 1204, tended to look upon intermarriage with their conquerors as a matter of policy, and set the interests of their empire above the possible restrictions of canon law. For so long as the Latin empire of Constantinople existed marriages between Greeks and Latins held out hope of a diplomatic settlement from the Greek point of view. The popes on the other hand were only disposed to approve such marriages if there was at the time some evident desire on the part of the emperor to bring the Byzantine Church into communion with Rome. After the restoration of the empire in 1261 Michael Palaiologos, overriding the hostility of his clergy and people, brought about the Union of Lyons in 1274, as a result of which he ceased to be a heretic in the eyes of the Latins, since he accepted the Roman creed. When the Union of Lyons collapsed, however, and he and his subjects were excommunicated by Pope Martin IV as schismatics and heretics, it was no longer canonical for Latins to marry Greeks without first seeking a dispensation from the papacy.[2]

In the western world people were content to regard as heretics those who were defined as such by the popes. But in the Byzantine world the matter was not so simple. For a definition of heresy

---

[1] Pachymeres, op. cit. II, 87-8; Gregoras, op. cit. I, 167-8 (and Du Cange's note thereon, in the Bonn ed., II, 1186); Dölger, *Regesten*, IV, no. 2098.

[2] Michael Palaiologos was denounced in the following terms: 'tanquam eorumdem Graecorum antiquorum schismaticorum, et in antiquo schismate constitutorum, et per hoc haereticorum; necnon et haeresis ipsorum ac schismatis antiqui fautorem . . . .' (O. Raynaldus, *Annales Ecclesiastici*, ed. A. Theiner, Bar-le-Duc, 1870, XXII, 490:s.a. 1281, § 25.) The excommunication was pronounced three times. Cf. Raynaldus, ed. cit. 495-6: s.a. 1282, §§ 8-10; Geanakoplos, op. cit. 342.

required the ruling of an oecumenical council; and the Latins, though perhaps technically heretics, had never been condemned as such by any council. They were, as the Chartophylax John Bekkos remarked in 1273, in the position of being but not being called heretics.[1] Demetrios Chomatianos indeed argued against the opinion of Theodore Balsamon, that Latins should not be given communion in Orthodox churches, on the ground that they had never been proscribed by a council, 'nor, like heretics, openly cast forth from the Church.'[2] The popes also were loth to brand the Greeks as heretics, and invoked the charge of heresy in mixed marriages only in very special cases such as that between John Vatatzes and Constance of Hohenstaufen, which was undesirable for other reasons. The popes were inclined to date the origin of the schism to the last Byzantine emperor who had given them trouble. Innocent IV, for example, claimed to believe that no schism existed between the Churches before his own time, and blamed the breach on John Vatatzes of Nicaea. In a sense he was right, even though he may have cast the blame in the wrong direction. For it was without doubt the Fourth Crusade and its consequences which split Christendom into two opposing camps and made the schism a reality.

[1] Pachymeres, op. cit. I, 376. Bekkos subsequently modified his views sufficiently to become the chief supporter of Michael VIII's unionist policy and was made patriarch of Constantinople (1275-82).

[2] Demetrios Chomatianos, in Rhalles and Potles, op. cit. V, 434-6, commenting on Balsamon, ibid. IV, 460. Balsamon divides heretics into two classes: those who accept the 'mystery' or sacrament of the Church and yet are in error on certain matters, and those who reject the sacrament and are infidels, 'namely Jews and Hellenes.' But he was inclined to feel that Latins wishing to marry Greek wives came into the second category. Rhalles and Potles, II, 253, on the fourteenth canon of the Council of Chalcedon.

Archbishop Pecham's Register

DECIMA L. DOUIE

Senior Lecturer in History, University of Hull

ARCHBISHOP Pecham's register is not only interesting as the first surviving Canterbury register, but also because an attempt has been made in it to abandon the older chronological arrangement for some sort of classification of documents in order to facilitate rapid consultation.[1] The scheme adopted is unique among English registers, being that used by the Curia, for the letters are divided into 'littere directe pape et cardinalibus,' 'littere regi,' 'littere episcopis' and 'littere communes.' This order, however, is not rigidly followed, for there is a special section of 'littere directe domino pape,' and many letters to bishops are included among the 'littere communes.' Nevertheless, the arrangement was probably due to John of Bologna, the Italian notary brought by Pecham to England. To make consultation even easier, each leaf on which they occur has the heading 'littere communes' followed by the year of the archiepiscopate. There is also a rough sub-classification, not very systematically followed.

The register begins with the heading 'littere temporalitatis,' under which comes the appointment of a steward of the lands, various other appointments and the records of homage paid by certain vassals.[2] Then come the 'littere directe domino pape'[3] and 'procurationes et commissiones,'[4] arranged chronologically and followed by 'collationes et institutiones,'[5] both the last two sections being interspersed with ordinary letters including the ordinance

---

[1] For details of Pecham's register published so far, cf. C. Trice-Martin, *Registrum epistolarum Iohannis Peckham, archiepiscopi Cantuariensis*, Rolls Series 1882-5, and Canterbury and York Society, 1908 and 1910.

[2] ff. 9^r-20^v.   [4] ff. 30^r-41^v.

[3] ff. 21^r-29^v, 142^r.   [5] ff. 34^v-55^v.

173

establishing the collegiate church at Wingham.[1] The next parts
contain the sequestrations,[2] letters directed to the king and bishops[3]
and the ordination lists,[4] which form one block broken by an
occasional letter, these being generally commissions to the archbishop's clerks to act as his proctors at the Curia or to contract loans
on his behalf.[5] The 'littere communes' which follow form the last
section of the register.[6] Most of these are headed with the name of
the recipient, with often a short description of the contents, as for
instance 'pro electo Wynton.'[7] or 'Episcopo London. pro villa de
Neuport.'[8] Important letters are indicated by a hand, and, either
at the time of registration or shortly afterwards, useful formularies
and precedents, generally connected with the archbishop's rights,
had marginal notes inserted beside them to draw attention to them.
One letter, ordering the publication of Cantilupe's excommunication, is annotated 'excommunicantes episcopum per civitatem
London.',[9] and another, threatening the barons of Sandwich with
excommunication for procuring a writ of prohibition, has a note to
show that it was issued at the wish and with the consent of the
archbishop, in the presence of the archdeacon of Canterbury,
brother William Bret and John de Leyk, clerk.[10] Injunctions to
religious houses,[11] documents connected with Pecham's unsuccessful
negotiations with the Welsh,[12] the papal bull relating to the foundation of Wingham, and the royal charter confirming this[13] are all
collected together at the end of the register.

One problem connected with the register is the paucity of
documents belonging to the second half of Pecham's archiepiscopate. No satisfactory explanation has been given for this, especially
as a few letters from that period have been found in other registers
and elsewhere.[14] It has been suggested that there was a decline in
efficiency due to Pecham's failing health. This, however, seems
unlikely as the same registrars were employed, with the exception
for a short time of John de Beccles, who quarrelled with the arch-

[1] ff. 56^r-64^v.

[2] ff. 70^r-101^v.

[3] ff. 103^v-141^v.

[4] ff. 139^r-141^v.

[5] ff. 156^r-216^v.

[6] f. 173^v.

[7] f. 173^v.

[8] f. 180^v.

[9] f. 182^r.

[10] ff. 223^r-239^v.

[11] ff. 242^r-249^v.

[12] ff. 221^r-222^v.

[13] Notably in the register of bishop Godfrey Giffard of Worcester; cf. J. W. Willis
Bund, *The Register of Bishop Godfrey Giffard of Worcester*, Oxford 1898-1902.

[14] Historical Manuscripts Commission *Various*, i, 252.

bishop and left his service but subsequently returned to it.[1] Since the present binding is a sixteenth-century one, it is possible that the second part was lost, but too few letters belonging to the latter part of Pecham's archiepiscopate have been found to make this more than a conjecture.

The most interesting part of the register was published by C. Trice-Martin in the Rolls Series between 1882 and 1885, but its value was somewhat diminished owing to the fact that the original arrangement was ignored in the text, though it and the headings were retained in the calendar at the end of the third volume. The Canterbury and York Society began the publication of the remainder in 1908, but only two instalments appeared, the second of which ends in the middle of the ordinations.[2] The most interesting documents in the unpublished part are those connected with administration, one of which is a good illustration of the lack of care in the custody of judicial records. The precentor of Wells, commissary of the bishop of Exeter, who was acting as papal judge delegate in an appeal, wrote to ask for a record of the case, which had originally been tried by two of the archbishop's clerks, Alan de Freston and Robert Lacy, neither of whom was at present with him. The answer was that the documents could not be found in the archbishop's archives but were believed to be in the custody of a certain notary, then absent on important business but likely soon to return. Pecham undertook to send them under his seal at Michaelmas provided that he first saw the bishop of Exeter's commission. In the last sentence of the letter, however, it is stated that another notary had made the useful suggestion that many of the documents sealed with the archbishop's seal and those of the two commissaries would be in the hands of the two parties, most probably in those of the appellee.[3] Another interesting document is connected with the will of a vicar-choral of Exeter Cathedral, whose executors in accounting mention certain of his possessions. These include £12 3s. 9d in cash collected by him for the projected Crusade, ten shillings of which was his own legacy for this purpose, a *Liber Sententiarum*, three *Summae*, the *incipits* of which are given, and various domestic articles, such as eight spoons, a dish and a basin, the value of which amounted to eight shillings.

[1] f. 131^v.   [3] f. 183^r.
[2] f. 188^r.

Ely Diocesan Records

DOROTHY M. OWEN

AUGUSTUS Jessopp, reporting in 1891 for the Historical Manuscripts Commission[1] on the records of the bishop of Ely,[2] found three stores of documents: Ely House, Dover Street; the consistory court in Great St Mary's church at Cambridge; and the palace at Ely.[3] This division seems to have been customary since the sixteenth century and ended only when the bishop of Ely, Bishop Lord Alwyne Compton, had the contents of all three repositories moved, first into Bishop Alcock's tower in the palace at Ely where Alfred Gibbons saw and listed them,[4] and then into the 'old prison,' now 4 Lynn Road, Ely,[5] where they remained until their transfer, in June 1962, to the Cambridge University Library. The consistory court had been a store of current records as long as the registrars or their deputies had their office in Cambridge; but about 1790 the diocesan registry seems to have been transferred to Ely, at which time began the long connection with the diocese of the firm of Evans and Son, solicitors, members of which firm acted as registrars almost without interruption from then until 1959. In Messrs. Evans's office, and also since 1902 in the 'old prison,' the registrars had accumulated a considerable store of documents. These, too, have come to the University Library, where the Church Commissioners have also deposited the records of the Ely episcopal estates which they have held since the mid-nineteenth century.

For a year before the records were moved to Cambridge the writer was engaged in cataloguing the contents of the registrar's

---

[1] References to the Ely Diocesan Records are prefaced by the letters EDR.

[2] HMC, *Report* XII, 1891, App. ix, 375-88.

[3] Tanner noted this division, *Notitia Monastica*, 1744, Cambs. 37.

[4] A. Gibbons, *Ely Episcopal Records*, Lincoln 1891.

[5] For an account of this building, see *VCH: County of Cambridge and the Isle of Ely*, ed. R.B. Pugh, IV, 1953, 31.

store for the present deputy registrar, Mr B. D. Boyd, and in checking and amending Gibbons's list. It is now proposed to do more detailed work on the earlier records so as to make them more accessible, but the time seems ripe for attempting a brief survey of the main classes of the whole collection.

Perhaps the best known of the Ely records are the registers,[1] which, with some gaps, cover the years 1337 to 1600. Jessopp described their contents fairly fully,[2] the Reverend J. H. Crosby printed detailed abstracts of their contents, up to 1586, in the *Diocesan Remembrancer* between the years 1889 and 1914,[3] and Gibbons published in his list some useful notes on the same registers. They contain a chronological section which includes records of *acta* such as probates, admissions to benefices, commissions to dedicate churches, licences to celebrate divine service in private chapels and an occasional inhibition from the official of Arches. This chronological section is followed by a *quaternus de brevibus*, containing royal writs, a *quaternus de emanentibus*, which includes a considerable variety of commissions and mandates on such topics as drainage and the conduct of the temporalities as well as the more usual purely ecclesiastical matters, and a *quaternus de ordinationibus*. There is so little visitation material, apart from brief memoranda in the chronological section, and an occasional quire bound in at the end of one of the larger sections, that it seems probable that, as in other dioceses,[4] separate visitation records were kept and have not survived. This may well be borne out by a reference in the consistory court book of 1374 to a *registrum correccionum* kept during the vacancy of the bishopric recently ended.[5] This consistory court book for the episcopate of Thomas

---

[1] The registers which survive are those of the following bishops: Montacute 1337-45, Lisle 1345-51, Arundel 1374-88, Fordham 1388-1412, Bourchier 1444-54, Gray 1454-78, Alcock 1486-95, West 1515-34, Goodrich 1534-54. There is also a volume of miscellaneous acts for the period 1540-1600. It is worth noting that Arundel seems not to have had access to the registers of his immediate predecessors: see EDR D2/1, f. 19, 'registra predecessorum nostrorum protunc ad manus non habuimus.'

[2] Op. cit., 382-86.

[3] *Ely Diocesan Remembrancer*, nos. 54-355, 1889-1914.

[4] There are numerous references to such records in the second volume of the register of Roger Martival, bishop of Salisbury 1315-30, e.g. ff. 309^{rv}, 331^v, '*in rotulis visitacionis.*' Cf. R.M.T. Hill, *Rolls and Register of Bishop Oliver Sutton*, iii, Lincoln Record Society XLVIII, 1954, xxviii-xxix.

[5] EDR. D2/1. The volume was rescued from a waste paper merchant in the mid-eighteenth century by Samuel Peck, fellow of Trinity (Gibbons, op. cit. 79).

Arundel is the sole survivor of what was evidently a series; it has no successor until the mid-sixteenth century. It is clear from this volume that the official of Ely, sitting in his consistory court, conducted and recorded a good deal of business which elsewhere would be found in the main registers. There are here sequestrations, probates, appointments of coadjutors, and records of diocesan synods in which proctors for convocation were elected and provincial constitutions enunciated. The synod of 1377, for example, received through the official the bishop's injunction to obey Archbishop Stratford's constitution *Humana concupiscentia* forbidding clandestine marriages.[1] It seems probable that in these acts the official was acting as commissary, but the subject is very involved and a study of diocesan administration comparable to Mr Morris's work on Lincoln[2] is necessary before any conclusion can be reached. The court book is also of great interest for its record of the types of case heard by the official in his regular sessions in court. There are prosecutions for failure to observe the provincial constitutions and the record of the 1377 synod is followed shortly by a case in which the Stratford constitution is the basis for prosecution.[3] Proctors attempt to recover fees from their clients,[4] a chaplain at Stow-next-Quy brings a case against his employers, the *confratres* of the gild of All Saints Stow, for subtraction of salary;[5] four parishioners of West Wickham bring a case against the prior of Colne who as rector of the parish was failing to provide proper services and had wasted the rectory buildings.[6] Much of the business seems to have been caused by the prolonged dispute between the bishop and archdeacon about the limits of their respective jurisdictions and this too requires further detailed study.[7]

[1] f. 72*v*. For the constitution see W. Lyndwood, *Provinciale*, Oxford 1679, lib. iv, tit. 3, c.2,275-7 and D. Wilkins, *Concilia Magnae Britanniae et Hiberniae*, 4 vols. 1737, ii, 707.

[2] C. Morris, 'The commissary of the bishop in the diocese of Lincoln,' *JEH*, x (1959), 50-65.

[3] ff. 82*v*-83.

[4] f. 52*v*: 'John Freborn de Fulbourn citatus ad instanciam Magistri Hugonis Caundelesby clerici domini archidiaconi Eliensis registrarii in causa salarii pro scriptura processus cause sue.....'

[5] f. 45*v*.

[6] f. 35.

[7] For a discussion of this dispute cf. C. L. Feltoe and E. H. Minns, *Vetus Liber Archidiaconi Eliensis*, Cambridge Antiquarian Society publications, XLVIII, 1917, xxiii-xxiv.

No seventeenth-century registers have survived and after 1702 the main records of the see are day-books of institution. In the sixteenth century, however, the registrars had begun to keep separate registers to record probates, ordinations and marriage licences and the separate registration of faculties began in 1724.[1] Each type of register had its supporting files, which survive as bundles of wills, administrations, inventories, testimonials, faculty papers, affidavits and bonds. This multiplication of register-making continued in the later eighteenth and nineteenth centuries when Parliament and later the Church Commissioners began to require from bishops and their registrars the registration of glebe mortgages, licences for non-residence and so on, and here too the natural accumulation of supporting documents in bundles has accompanied the register-keeping.

The sixteenth and seventeenth-century records of visitation and court books are unusually full and detailed. There is no need to specify the types of material to be found there: Gibbons has given a number of examples[2] and some full abstracts were printed by Dr W. M. Palmer.[3] It should perhaps be noted that Gibbons's descriptions should be used with great care, as Miss Midgley noted while reporting on the records for the Pilgrim Trust Survey.[4] The class described by Gibbons as 'visitation books' is in fact very heterogeneous and contains *libri cleri*, *comperta* books and court books of office, besides some seventeenth-century parochial visitations which appear to be archidiaconal.[5] Files of court papers, citations, depositions, certificates and confessions can be recognised in classes called correspondence and formularies by Gibbons, and a large uncatalogued box of seventeenth and eighteenth-century papers appears to contain similar material.[6] These papers and, apparently, the court and visitation books were kept in Great St

---

[1] W. M. Palmer, 'The faculty books of the diocese of Ely,' *Cambridge Antiquarian Society Proceedings*, XXXV, 1933-4, 54-86.

[2] Op cit. 36-45.

[3] W. M. Palmer, 'Episcopal visitation returns for Cambridgeshire,' *Transactions of the Cambridge and Huntingdonshire Archaeological Society*, IV, 1915-30, 313-411; 'Archdeaconries of Cambridge and Ely in 1599,' ibid. VI, 1938-47, 1-28.

[4] In conversation with the writer.

[5] EDR B3; Gibbons, op. cit. 45.

[6] EDR F5 passim, H2, K5.

Mary's, and losses were heavy from there, especially in the eighteenth century when the executors of a defaulting registrar allowed some of them to be sold as waste paper. Samuel Peck rescued a few of the court books, including Arundel's, and was reluctantly compelled to restore them to the bishop.[1] The *Vetus registrum sive liber niger*, which William Cole saw in Great St Mary's (and which is a register of the admissions of proctors in the consistory court 1372-1708), passed into the Heber and thence to the Phillipps collection and was acquired at Sotheby's in 1898 for the Cambridge University Library.[2] Several files of loose court papers also found their way into the University Library;[3] others are in the Bodleian Gough Eccles. MS 3[4]; and Henry Bradshaw reported in 1875 some in private hands in Northampton, which had been bought as waste paper at Market Harborough.[5]

The eighteenth-century visitation records are unusually informative about schools, fabric and buildings, and are accompanied by a series of diocesan surveys or *specula*, beginning as early as 1682 and full of material about services and clergy, recusants, nonconformists, parochial organisations and church buildings.[6] These are scattered in various classes by Gibbons but appear to form a recognisable series, resulting from a clearly defined diocesan practice.[7]

Mr Miller has described in some detail the materials for a study of the temporalities of the medieval bishops and there is no need to embroider on his theme.[8] It should however be reported that there was found in the registrar's office a good series of *compoti* and court rolls for the large manor of Downham and some missing

[1] P. 177 n. 5 above and W. M. Palmer, 'Churchwardens' bills . . . for the deanery of Barton, 1554,' *Tr. Cambs. and Hunts. Arch. Soc.* v, 1931-37, 257-75.

[2] Additional MS 3468. The particulars of its history and of its identification as the missing 'Black Book' by J. H. Crosby are entered on the fly-leaf of the manuscript.

[3] Additional MS 6605.

[4] F. Madan and W. M. Palmer, *Notes on Bodley manuscripts relating to Cambridgeshire*, Camb. Ant. Soc. Pub., LII, 1931; Palmer, art. cit.

[5] Henry Bradshaw, 'Notes on the episcopal visitation of the archdeaconry of Ely in 1685,' *Camb. Ant. Soc. Proc.*, III, 1864-76, 323-62.

[6] An example of this class of record, for the diocese of Lincoln was partially printed by R. E. G. Cole, *Speculum Dioeceseos*, Lincoln Record Society, IV, 1913.

[7] The earliest item in this series exists only in a copy in bishop Fleetwood's transcripts, Gibbons, op. cit. 13-14.

[8] E. Miller, *The Abbey and Bishopric of Ely*, Cambridge 1951, 4-7.

Chatteris court rolls.[1] It should also perhaps be noted that the charters by which the bishops acquired their temporalities no longer exist here; it is to be presumed that as in Canterbury and Lincoln[2] they had been held in the cathedral church of the diocese. There is very little in the way of central accounting records for the bishop and only a few household accounts, for Bishops Arundel and Goodrich,[3] survive before the late-seventeenth century. Two volumes of Bishop John Moore's personal accounts, which were among the records deposited by the Church Commissioners, have useful information about his expenditure on books and manuscripts, and the vouchers of Bishop Yorke's episcopate survive in some bulk.[4] The later history of the temporalities is best seen in the lease registers and estate papers of the Church Commissioners' deposit, in the plea and session rolls of the Ely liberty[5] and in the disappointingly scanty records of fen drainage.[6]

There is scarcely need to mention the remaining types of record which are common to most dioceses. Glebe terriers, parish register transcipts, faculty registers and papers are all to be found here as in other places.[7] There is a good source of biographical information in the subscription books which begin in the late sixteenth century and which seem in this diocese completely to have replaced the register of ordinations.[8] A less usual type of record is the material relating both to the university and to various colleges in Cambridge. The registers have been exhaustively used for all the materials they will yield on these matters [9] but less notice seems to have been taken

---

[1] These rolls were lost as long ago as 1809, Gibbons, op. cit. 78.

[2] R. M. T. Hill, op. cit. xxviii.

[3] EDR D5 and D6; Gibbons, op. cit. 92, 97. Some further rolls of Arundel's time were found among the Downham records.

[4] C.C.95579 and 95580. I owe this reference to my husband.

[5] EDR D1.

[6] Mr Miller has made some use of these in his paper, 'The Liberty of Ely,' *VCH : Cambridgeshire*, IV, 1953, 1-27; EDR E1-E14, F1-F4.

[7] EDR A8; Gibbons, op. cit. 18.

[8] EDR A5/1-25.

[9] Most writers on these topics (e.g. C. H. Cooper, *Annals of Cambridge*, 5 vols., 1842-1908) have used the transcripts made by the antiquary Thomas Baker (1656-1740) whose manuscripts are now partly in the British Museum (MSS Harl. 4115, 4116) and partly in the Cambridge University Library (Mm.1.35-1.53); *DNB.*, art. Baker, J. and J. A. Venn, *Alumni Cantabrigienses*, 8 vols. 1922-54 and A. B. Emden, *A Biographical Dictionary of the University of Cambridge to 1500*, 1963, have consulted the original registers.

of the appeals to the bishops' visitatorial powers made by Peter-house, St John's, Trinity and Jesus in the late seventeenth and eighteenth centuries.[1]

Some less official material among the records seems worthy of separate note. Keepers and students of episcopal records know how rarely the private papers of the bishops are to be found among them and Ely is no better off than most. Simon Patrick's papers are in the Cambridge University Library,[2] those of Francis Turner are among the Rawlinson manuscripts in the Bodleian Library[3] and Bishop Yorke's remain with his diocesan records.[4] They include much that is interesting about S.P.G. and S.P.C.K. schools and missions, and throw an interesting light on the bishop's concern for public safety during the French wars, in the shape of a series of returns to an enquiry about the political opinions of schoolmasters which elicited from the incumbent of March the following reply:

The seven church schools all regularly teach our church catechism and the different collects for each Sunday besides the Bible and other proper books. The two first masters are inrolled among our loyal military association. Besides the above we have another school consisting chiefly of boarders and taught by the two Miss Smiths. . . . They are of our dissenters but I consider them as pious good women. They teach about forty, both boys and girls, from five to fourteen . . .; they are attentive to the Bible and Testament and make it a point that their children shall be able to repeat the Ten Commandments. They never inculcate evil principles but wish our government may stand as long as the World. . . . On the whole the state of the schools, the morals, the civil and religious principles of the generality is such as the Bishop will much approve and such as I hope will be a source of comfort to myself both in this and the next world.

Abraham Jobson.[5]

The court papers and registrars' memoranda of the sixteenth century,[6] together with the large and important group of formularies

[1] EDR C4 and 5; Gibbons, op. cit. 58-66.

[2] Additional MSS 60, 71, 84 and various smaller items.

[3] S.C.14986-7, Rawlinson letters 95.

[4] Most of them were found in a trunk in the registrar's office but a few bundles had been listed by Gibbons, op. cit. 50-3 (B6).

[5] EDR B6, schools' bundle.

[6] This group, EDR K5, is completely unsorted but a brief survey shows that it includes much very interesting material on the practice, secular as well as ecclesiastical, of Cambridge lawyers in the reigns of Elizabeth I and James I and indicates clearly that the town clerk might very well be a proctor in the bishop's consistory court.

which are with the records,[1] throw some unexpected light on the training and peregrinations of ecclesiastical officials, and pose a series of questions which cannot be answered until the disjointed information we now have about the numbers and provenance of the surviving formularies in record repositories and manuscript collections has been properly collated. There are two medieval York formularies here, which, taken in conjunction with a book of similar provenance which in the early sixteenth century was owned by one of the Lincoln registrars and is now Cambridge University Library Add. MS 3115,[2] suggest a wide dispersal of the influence of ecclesiastical lawyers from York.

Although Mr Miller and the dean of Gloucester[3] have already collected, for their own purposes, a considerable amount of information about the dispersal of former Ely records and something has been said above about other straying Ely records, much remains to be done in this field. Meanwhile the task of making the records available for scholars is the first consideration. An interleaved copy of Gibbons's *List* has been prepared and annotated and with it is placed a duplicated handlist[4] in which the records described in it and those in the registrars' store are classified. It is hoped to produce a fuller list on this basis, with more detailed descriptions of such classes of records as cannot be easily used, and to prepare for use in the Cambridge University Library calendars and indexes of all classes, when time and opportunity make this possible.

[1] EDR F5 Gibbons, op. cit. 126-8.

[2] I owe this reference to my husband. The Lincoln antiquary and book-collector Thomas Pownal owned it in 1726; cf. R. W. Hunt, 'Thomas Pownal', *Lincolnshire Architectural and Archaeological Society, Reports and Papers*, IX, pt. 2, (1962).

[3] Miller, op. cit.; S. J. A. Evans, 'Ely Chapter Ordinances and Visitation records,' *Camden Miscellany*, XVII, Camden Society, 3rd series, LXIV, 1940, xvii-xix.

[4] Published by the Historical Manuscripts Commission, National Register of Archives.

Correspondence between England and the Council of Constance, 1414-18[1]

C. M. D. CROWDER

Lecturer in Palaeography and Diplomatic, The Queen's University of Belfast

T HE problem with which this paper is concerned is the present poverty of material to illustrate the policies which the English delegates to the Council of Constance were intended to carry out. The problem is one of particular interest in the case of the most important group among these delegates, the ambassadors of Henry V. There is no great difficulty in tracing their activity in the Council between the autumn of 1414 and the spring of 1418 since this is recorded in the official and unofficial records of its proceedings, but it is not always possible to identify and then establish with documents the motives behind their actions. Partly this is due to the absence of reports of the discussions within the separate nations into which the Council was divided[2]; partly it is due to the large gaps in the correspondence between principals in England and their representatives at Constance. It is only with this second aspect of the problem that the following pages attempt to deal.[3] Most of the manuscripts and collections related to the subject are well-known; in a number of cases they have been printed wholly or in part; but, so far as the writer is aware, they have not been

---

[1] Since this paper was read improvements have been made to it in the light of the discussion which followed, and in consequence of the observations which Dr A. L. Brown of Glasgow University kindly sent to the writer after reading the MS. Some of the suggestions made on these occasions have been adopted, others have not, and the writer alone is responsible for the published text.

[2] The Council's findings were promulgated in the general sessions in which a representative of each constituent nation (*nacio*) gave its *placet*. The discussions in the separate nations which preceded this stage are rarely recorded in the Council's *acta*.

[3] Some observations on the absence of reports of the meetings of the nations at Constance will be found in my article in *RHE*, lvii (1962), 472 ff.

considered consecutively in relation to the information which they contain about a single, limited topic.

To begin with it should perhaps be established that there is a problem at all. Is one entitled to expect more evidence than now exists? As the view taken of this question is closely related to the opinion which is maintained about the general trend of English policy during the Council, the argument is to some extent circular; but a number of considerations suggest that more might have been expected to survive than has done. It may be true that the Council of Constance did not take a very large place in the interests of contemporary Englishmen as a whole, whether they were clerks or laymen. As seen through the pages of English chronicles of the fifteenth century it was chiefly memorable for ending the long schism in the papacy, and this was indeed its most considerable achievement.[1] On the other hand in some quarters in England there was a lively interest in different aspects of the Council's progress. At Salisbury there was an established tradition of concern with ecclesiastical reform under the inspiration of Bishop Hallum.[2] Both universities were alert to the needs of their own graduates for benefices and to the necessity for defending doctrinal othodoxy. For a few weeks, at the time of Martin V's election and the restoration of unchallenged authority in the Catholic Church, the City of London showed a persistent interest in her bishop's contribution to this happy and long-deferred outcome.[3] In respect of the all-important

[1] The St Albans chronicle is held by common consent to give the most adequate narrative of events concerning England in the first two decades of the fifteenth century, and its most recent editor has commented on the attention which it pays to the general councils of that time, *St Albans Chronicle, 1406-20*, ed. V. H. Galbraith, Oxford 1937, xxii. This opinion may be justified by its report of developments leading to the Council of Pisa, op. cit., 31 ff. In the case of Constance the chronicler summarises the activity of the opening months, op. cit., 83-5, and only returns to it with Martin V's election two and a half years later, op. cit., 104-09. Nevertheless this is a much fuller account than that given by any other contemporary English chronicle.

[2] E. F. Jacob, *Essays in the Conciliar Epoch*, Manchester 1953, 78 ff. More light will be thrown on this interesting topic by the studies at present being undertaken by Miss Margaret Harvey.

[3] The main items in this correspondence are Bishop Clifford's letter of 8 December 1417, the City's reply on the following 18 January, and a further letter from the bishop, undated, nos. 21, 22, 24 in table below. The formulary in Cambridge University Library, MS Dd. III. 53, ff. 99, 99^v, 102^v contains three undated letters from the City to their bishop, two asking for news of him and one acknowledging a letter from him (nos. 16, 17 and 19). If these letters were ever sent, and their absence from the register

13

factor of royal policy the present writer has given his reasons elsewhere for believing that the Council of Constance had a prominent place in the development of Henry V's policy towards France.[1] At a less favourable stage of Anglo-French relations the Council of Basle figured in the calculations of Henry VI's advisers as they looked about for a way of accommodating their differences with the House of Valois, and on this later occasion the instructions from the King's Council to the royal delegates at the Council of the Church are preserved in several different instances as are the reports which those delegates sent home.[2]

The Council of Constance was not less vital to the interests of Christendom than the Council of Basle and it certainly did less to exhaust the patience of its supporters. A recent writer on the Council of Basle has succinctly indicated the scope of its predecessor: 'Autant qu'un assemblé de l'église, le concile de Constance était apparu comme un congrès des nations.'[3] The attendance from England was correspondingly comprehensive, and this is a further indication that the problem which is to be examined is not an illusory one. There were upwards of a hundred of Henry V's subjects at Constance during the three and a half years of the Council, and clearly it is not possible to attach the half of them to a definite proctorial position or delegation with certainty. The surviving evidence, whether it is the proctorial instrument itself, a letter containing instructions, or merely the actions of a particular Englishman in the Council, does, however, place beyond doubt that there were at Constance accredited representatives of the king, of the two Convocations of Canterbury and York embracing the secular clergy of the realm, of the archbishop of Canterbury individually and of some other single bishops.[4] The English

suggests they may not have been, their place in the sequence would probably be prior to the bishop's letter of 8 December 1417.

[1] See 'Henry V, Sigismund, and the Council of Constance, a Re-examination,' *Historical Studies*, IV (1963), 93-110.

[2] For the period 1433-4, see Dr Schofield's article 'The first English delegation at Basel,' *JEH*, XII (1961), 167-96. What would seem to be the privy seal office draft of the instructions of 14 August 1433 (Schofield, ibid. 193-94) is preserved among Ancient Correspondence at the P.R.O. S.C. 1/57, no. 70, (*Lists & Indexes*, London 1902, XV 260).

[3] P. Ourliac, 'Sociologie du concile de Bâle,' *RHE*, LVI (1961), 25.

[4] For the king's representation, T. Rymer, *Foedera &c.*, The Hague 1740, IV, pt ii, 91, 169; for the Convocation of Canterbury, *The Register of Henry Chichele*, ed. E. F.

Benedictine chapter sent its representatives and the Cistercians in England probably did the same.[1] If the English friars were represented, it must have been by the provincials of the different orders.[2] Both English universities were represented[3]; but it proves impossible to distinguish certainly between any who held a formal proctorial mandate and those who had journeyed to Constance on their own account. Finally, at least one, and perhaps two, English cathedral chapters sent their own representatives.[4]

These different groups of delegates, who with the other unattached Englishmen at the Council formed the English *nacio* and thus contributed to its decisions, would presumably have written and received a considerable number of letters. In fact for the three and a half years of the Council's duration it has so far proved possible to trace twenty-four letters certainly written either by or to Englishmen at Constance, while another dozen or so are indicated as having probably been written. Only nineteen of these letters are

Jacob, Oxford 1943, III, 11; and of York, *Records of the Northern Convocation*, ed. G. W. Kitching, Durham 1907, 135; for archbishop Chichele, *Reg. Chichele*, ed. E. F. Jacob, IV, 107-08; for the bishop of Exeter, *Register of Edmund Stafford*, ed. F. C. Hingeston-Randolph, London 1886, 67; and for other possible proxies see the list of oaths taken at Constance on 4 February 1416, H. von der Hardt, *Magnum oecumenicum concilium Constantiense &c.*, Frankfort 1697, IV, 586 ff. (cited hereafter as Hardt).

[1] *Chapters of the English Black Monks*, ed. W. A. Pantin, London 1931, III, 94-7. The representative capacity of the Cistercian abbots of Fountains, Jervaulx and Beaulieu for their order is less clear; cf. E. Martène & U. Durand, *Thesaurus novus Anecdotorum*, Paris 1717, IV, 1562-3.

[2] The provincial of the English Dominicans may have been present in the early weeks of the council, Hardt, IV, 385. Thomas Netter, the Carmelite provincial, is frequently said to have attended the Council, C. L. Kingsford, in *DNB*, XL, 232. William Butler, the Franciscan, was there after being removed from office, E. Déprez, *Etudes de diplomatique anglaise*, Paris 1903, 29-30. In none of these cases is there any indication of a representative capacity.

[3] Henry de Abendon, later warden of Merton, claimed to speak for Oxford, Hardt, IV, 595, and William Corffe is plainly called a proctor of the same university in the funeral oration by his colleague, Richard Flemming; G. Leidinger, *Andreas von Regensburg, Sämtliche Werke*, Munich 1903, 255. Constance was a natural magnet to aspiring graduates since it housed the papal curia as well as the Council.

[4] An entry in their chapter act-book makes it clear that Salisbury sent proctors; Salisbury, Dean and Chapter Muniments, Reg. Pounteny, f. iiij^v. A payment made by the Communar at Wells to Henry de Abendon, who was a canon of the cathedral, suggests the possibility of his having acted for the chapter there, W. H. P. Bird and W. P. Baildon, *Calendar of Manuscripts of the Dean and Chapter of Wells*, HMC, London 1907, II, 55. Cf. *The Register of Nicholas Bubwith*, ed. T. S. Holmes, Somerset Record Society XXIX, 1914, I, xxx.

extant and the contents of some of them are too trivial or too general to be of much assistance.[1]

It is true that not every question that cropped up in the Council could be referred to headquarters for a decision. The converse in fact would be nearer the truth: not many decisions could be taken in this way. Communications in the fifteenth century did not allow it.[2] Conditions obliged a principal to empower his proctor with a wide discretion. This and the general indifference of England as a whole towards the Council, which has been mentioned, are factors which reduced the volume of correspondence with those at Constance. Yet, when every allowance has been made, a principal was not obliged to drop his representatives into limbo indefinitely, and despite the uncertainty of communications views could be exchanged from time to time. Equal emphasis must be placed on the equally well-attested fact that no less a person than the king was concerned with what was done at Constance not only by his accredited envoys but by all members of the English nation. In July 1417 the king ordered the English bishops at Constance to prevail on all their countrymen attending the Council to accept whatever lead they decided to give and to direct any recalcitrant member to return home.[3] Nor did this authoritative command come out of the blue. As the king says at the beginning of his instructions, they were issued in response to a request from the English bishops at Constance. That original request, like other items to which the surviving

[1] See the table at the end of this article. In addition to the three letters from London to its bishop which may never have been sent (nos. 16, 17 and 19) and which in any case do nothing to illuminate the activity of the English delegates at Constance, the letter from Ixworth to Swan (no. 7) betrays only a general interest without any particular knowledge.

[2] The war with France was an added obstacle. Another correspondent of William Swan, probably writing early in 1417, refers to a ban imposed by the king on all traffic across the Channel, Bodleian Library, MS Arch. Seld. B. 23, f. 96^v. Probably there never was such a thing as an average journey, since local conditions were too variable; but such examples as there are make it reasonable to reckon three to four weeks for the passage of news between Constance and London. An interval of eight weeks was cause for complaint in the letter to Swan just cited. Martin V's election on 11 November 1417 was known in London by 26 November, *Reg. Chichele*, ed. Jacob, III, 33, and the chapter at Salisbury knew of Bishop Hallum's death at Constance three weeks after it occurred, Salisbury, D. & C. Mun., Reg. Pountney, f. xxx, although this does not appear from the corresponding letter asking the archbishop to name the official for the vacant see, *Reg. Chichele*, ed. Jacob, III, 426.

[3] No 15 in the table below. Cf. the royal mandates to Robert Appleton, proctor of the convocation of York and of archbishop Chichele, nos. 8 and 9.

correspondence refers, is lost and we are therefore left in doubt as to the precise circumstances which gave rise to it.

Together these facts are enough to establish that what now remains of the correspondence between England and Constance at the time of the Council is not all that there was once. The problem of what has happened to the remainder is therefore a real one. On this occasion it is not necessary to deal systematically with every group of correspondents, potential and actual. It is sufficient to sample the group of letters to and from the king which contributes most to the reconstruction of English policy at Constance. There are seven of these in addition to the letter of July 1417 which has just been mentioned.[1] Some of these seven also refer to letters which have not survived;[2] but even including the elements which are known to be missing, the whole group is still too small to have covered adequately three and a half years of Henry's correspondence upon the Council's business at a time of active diplomacy. What has happened to the rest?

An indication of what has happened is given by a brief glance at the sources from which these eight surviving letters have been obtained.[3] Only three are found on the rolls of chancery: two letters close (nos. 8 and 9) and the letter of July 1417 (no. 15), which is taken from the Treaty rolls. The latter is undoubtedly the most important extant document for illuminating Henry's relations with his representatives at the Council, but the reason that it was sent under the great seal rather than the privy seal or signet is probably untypical. The English bishops at Constance might need to display this authority from the king to enforce obedience on their countrymen. A similar document of less general interest is the king's instructions to the two leading bishops of his delegation for the settlement of the long dispute over the abbacy at Fountains (no. 10). It is preserved in the letter book of William Swan who was curial proctor of one of the contending claimants. Two reports to Henry from different periods of the Council survive. The earlier was printed from a manuscript in private hands by C. Munro in 1863 (no. 4). This manuscript was the commonplace book of John Edwards, receiver of Chirkland in the reign of Henry VII, and is now Additional MS 46846 of the British Museum; but the contents

---

[1] Nos 4, 8-10, 12, 20 and 23 in the table.   [2] Nos 4 and 15 in the table.
[3] The numbers in the text refer to the table.

of the letterbook which it contains has suggested that this part of it is due to a clerk of the signet office in the reign of Henry VI.[1] The later report (no. 12) is one of the two Constance pieces in Cleopatra F. VII of the Cotton collection.[2] This is a compilation put together in Sir Robert Cotton's library later than 1602 to illustrate the protocol for deciding questions of national precedence in international gatherings. The two remaining communications to the king report on the negotiations with Genoa which Henry's envoys in Constance had been empowered to undertake (nos. 20 and 23). They are in another Cotton manuscript, Vespasian F. I, which is also a composite collection, mainly of original papers in Sir Robert's library. The rest of its contents chiefly concern other aspects of Anglo-Genoese relations or deal with the diplomacy of Eastern Europe in the sixteenth century.

Such a list represents a characteristic feature of the evidence for the Council of Constance as a whole. It is widely scattered. With more particular regard to the fate of the correspondence between England and the Council it reflects the vicissitudes which have befallen documents issued under the privy seal or signet, and it is therefore a reminder of an important aspect of the king's administration in this period. It has been established for a long time that the diplomatic correspondence of the English crown in the last two centuries of the Middle Ages was conducted mainly through the small seals.[3] Chancery and exchequer preserve valuable information about who was sent on an embassy and where they were sent to, how long they were absent and how much they were paid. They give the powers with which the envoys were accredited and there may be a clue as to the route they travelled in the records which are disarmingly called *perticule compoti*. For the political content of the mission, for the instructions which guided its course in the delicate business of negotiation, the historian of this period looks

---

[1] J. Otway-Ruthven, *The King's Secretary*, Cambridge 1939, 119-20. I have to thank the Superintendent of the British Museum Reading Room for my knowledge of the manuscript's present location, but I have not yet been able to see it myself.

[2] The other is no 13, and not a royal communication.

[3] T. F. Tout, *Chapters in the Administrative History of Medieval England*, Manchester 1930, III, 15; E. Perroy, *The Diplomatic Correspondence of Richard II*, London 1933, xi; Otway-Ruthven, op. cit. 50-4, 122-23; G. P. Cuttino, *English Diplomatic Administration, 1259-1339*, Oxford 1940, 136-37; J. G. Dickinson, *The Congress of Arras, 1435*, Oxford 1955, xx-xxi.

to the offices of privy seal and signet.[1] Even there he is apt to be disappointed of evidence for anything more than the passage of information. For much was left to the oral reports of confidential messengers who required nothing more than a letter of credence, and presumably only needed that if they were accredited to a foreign power.

This is well established. It has been affirmed for even longer that the condition of the records of these small seals is lamentable.[2] By the beginning of the fifteenth century it is not easy to detect any attempt at the keeping of systematic records.[3] In the case of warrants for the great seal and for the exchequer this does not matter since those departments kept adequate records of their own; but for the products of the small seals which had original force, which led to executive action without any further intermediary, there is no opportunity for similar mitigations. Such documents have vanished, at least so far as the official records of the Crown take us.

Fortunately it does not follow that the record has been entirely obliterated. Original letters under the small seals, letters that were directly effective, do survive. They survive in formularies, among manuscripts and papers preserved privately or in the public archives of those who received them; and Professor Perroy's collection of the diplomatic correspondence of Richard II has shown that, with a measure of good fortune, they can be reassembled in considerable number. The limitation is that preservation in this manner is haphazard. For this reason one specialised group of documents may not provide a satisfactory standard; at the same time there may be some value in giving even a summary account of the experience gained in probing this undefined, perhaps indefinable, territory just because of its unpredictability, and despite the fact

[1] The reason why no. 15 is preserved on a chancery roll has been suggested above. The sealing clause is omitted in the existing record of the other royal instructions, no. 10; but their nature and form and the absence of any chancery registration make it likely that they were issued under the privy seal or signet.

[2] M. Giuseppi, *Guide to Public Records*, London 1924, II, 131, 133; H. C. Maxwell-Lyte, *The Great Seal*, London 1926, 26 ff.; Tout, op. cit. v, 64-5, 115; Otway-Ruthven, op. cit. 2, 114 ff.

[3] The privy seal office had made a promising start in keeping its records, Déprez, *Etudes de diplomatique anglaise*, 70-2; Tout, op. cit. I, 55; Maxwell-Lyte, loc. cit.; P. Chaplais, 'Privy Seal Drafts, Rolls and Registers,' *EHR*, LXXIII (1958), 270-3, cf. LXXVII (1962), 79. In the opinion of Dr A. L. Brown, who has made a special study of the small seals, the records of the privy seal continued to be preserved with care.

that the findings in this instance prove disappointingly negative. As with other sciences the presentation of negative findings may save other workers disproportionate effort—or challenge them to a successful rebuttal. Of the categories for the survival of privy seal and signet letters which have just been instanced I do not intend to discuss the possibility of foreign archive collections, because I have no direct experience of them.[1] I shall confine myself to formularies or letterbooks and collections of occasional papers.

These have been seen to be the resting-place of most of King Henry's correspondence with the Council that survives, and the early-fifteenth century is well provided in both instances. This, perhaps, is a result of the poverty of official records under the small seals. Two formularies indeed are based altogether on the correspondence of these small seals: John Prophet's letter-book, Harleian MS 431, and Thomas Hoccleve's Additional MS 24062 of the British Museum.[2] Prophet was successively Henry IV's secretary and keeper of the privy seal and his collection of precedents contains a large quantity of valuable material concerning the earlier Council of Pisa; but his period of office ended in 1415 before the Council of Constance was nine months old, and he died the following year.[3] Hoccleve had an even longer spell of service, as a clerk in the privy seal office. His formulary, which was on an altogether more ambitious scale than Prophet's letter-book, was

[1] The correspondence brought together by H. Finke in *Acta Concilii Constanciensis*, Munster 1896-1928, I, III and IV is a very handsome compensation. Nevertheless these volumes, based on collections of archives from Madrid to Leningrad, do not contain one unambiguous case of correspondence between England and English delegates at Constance. These delegates were empowered to act in the Council, an impermanent body with no archive of its own. The Vatican archives are the most likely place for traces of their activity to have lodged. The city archives at Constance are of no help in this connection.

[2] Taken together with John Rylands Library, Latin MS 404, Cambridge University Library, MS Dd. III. 53. and Edinburgh University Library, MS Laing 351a, the three formularies described by Perroy, op. cit. xvii ff., they provide a cross-section of the activity of the small seals spanning the best part of a century. The collections made by Bekynton continue the series after an interval.

[3] Prophet's collection was added to after his death, which must have occurred soon after he made his will on 8 April 1416; J. H. Wylie, *History of England under Henry IV*, London 1884, ii. 484, *n*.4; Otway-Ruthven, op. cit. 165. F.113ᵛ contains a letter dated 14 May 1416 and this is followed on f.114 by a group of documents associated with an embassy undertaken in July 1421. All of these are an integral part of the MS in its present form. Cf. *Catalogue of Harleian Manuscripts*, London 1808, I, 252-5, arts. 44, 46, 75, 79, 106, though some of these, like 106, may be artificial compositions. Thomas

classified and it includes a section headed 'Missives,' a section which is valuable for Henry V's relations with the empire. Nevertheless it has nothing about Constance, again possibly because of the personal fortunes of the compiler: Hoccleve went out of his mind and was on sick leave for a time between 1415 and 1422.[1] The handsome collection of models of dictamen in Royal MS 10 B. IX contains a number of signet letters from the early part of the fifteenth century, but none bears on Constance. On the other hand the proceedings of the Council are represented in this collection more than once. It contains decrees from its second session, an address in praise of Bishop Hallum and a number of letters directed to recipients at Constance. Two of these are also to Hallum, but only one is from an English correspondent.[2] In this Archbishop Chichele tells the bishop of Salisbury, who represented the province of Canterbury at the Council as well as the king, his views on reform and other relevant matters (no. 2).[3] Two other manuscripts containing evidence for the activity of the small seals at the time of the Council are something of a lucky dip because of the heavy damage which they sustained in the Cottonian fire. Tiberius B. VI of the Cotton collection is a manuscript of similar type to Royal 10 B. IX, where diplomatic papers are followed by a section containing models of humanistic Latin. Arranged less systematically than the previous manuscripts, and nowhere adequately described to my knowledge,[4] it can still be used and

Field, Prophet's nephew, is probably responsible for a number of the additions after inheriting his uncle's collection of precedents. Field's career was closely associated with his uncle's: he succeeded him in the deanery of Hereford and was appointed *secundarius* in the privy seal office two days after Prophet was made keeper; A. B. Emden, *A Biographical Register of the University of Oxford*, Oxford 1957, II, 683, III, 1522-3. There may be another trace of his activity in Harleian MS 431, art. 41. As Field died in 1419 a later owner must be responsible for the entries on f. 114, and so for the present form of the MS.

[1] Tout, *Chapters*, v, 109. Dr A. L. Brown tells me that Hoccleve was not absent from the privy seal office for as long as Tout suggests.

[2] The other is from the king of the Romans commending members of his entourage, B.M., MS Royal 10 B. IX, f. 201. There is another letter of recommendation addressed to a prelate at the council, but there is nothing to show that it has an English connection, ibid. f. 58*v*.

[3] Cf. Jacob, *Essays in the Conciliar Epoch*, 58-9, 75-6, where brief extracts from the letter are printed.

[4] Scholars can still differ, for example, about Wharton's suggestion that the MS was part of Bekynton's collection. G. Williams, *The official correspondence of Thomas Bekynton*, London 1872, i. xi, says that there is no basis for the suggestion. R. Weiss, *Humanism in England during the fifteenth century*, Oxford 1941, 75, *n*. 1, repeats it, but offers no argument.

much of it had been incorporated by Rymer into his *Foedera* before the manuscript was damaged. Its diplomatic contents are devoted primarily to Anglo-French relations in the reign of Henry V, but a number of items from Constance are included. There are letters to Henry from Pope Martin V notifying the king of his election, which took place in the closing months of the Council, and recommending Richard Flemming to the king's notice for his contribution to the Council's successful conclusion—an equivocal measure of praise *sub specie aeternitatis*, but one with which Henry agreed for his own reasons.[1] Several decrees from the Council's final session are included and, from a date shortly after its close, a sheaf of privileges granted at Henry's request and a copy of the concordat on reform agreed with the English delegates; but as for correspondence or reports passing between these delegates and their principals during the council—the volume has none.[2] MS Caligula D. V, a victim of the same fire, is also concerned with Anglo-French relations in Henry's time. Its contents come nearest to the Council in the highly secret instructions which Henry sent on 25 January 1417 under his signet of the eagle to his envoy to Sigismund.[3] Sigismund was in Constance before the end of the month, but these instructions are wholly concerned with negotiations with France and say nothing overtly about the conduct of the English delegates in the Council. MSS Cleopatra E. II and E. III escaped harm in the Cottonian fire and hold out the more promise since they have been put together to illustrate ecclesiastical history. They prove disappointing. Cleopatra E. II is valuable for reconstructing English policy during the Schism,[4] but for Constance the two manuscripts together contribute only a copy of Aragon's withdrawal of obedience from Benedict XIII and three sermons, all of them known elsewhere; and in the earlier manuscript a letter from Cardinal Orsini to Henry V,

[1] Flemming was provided to the vacant see of Lincoln in November 1419. Martin's attempt to raise Bishop Henry Beaufort to the cardinalate, a month earlier than his recommendation of Flemming, is also recorded in this MS. This, of course, was a failure; K. B. McFarlane, 'Henry V, Bishop Beaufort and the Red Hat,' *EHR*, LX (1945), 316 ff.

[2] The dictaminal section includes a funeral oration in memory of Manuel Chrysoloras, the Greek humanist who died at Constance in 1415, B.M., MS Cotton Tiberius B. VI, f. 172ᵛ.

[3] They are printed in Rymer, IV, pt ii, 190-1.

[4] See E. Perroy, *L'Angleterre et le grand Schisme d'occident*, Paris 1933. M. Perroy assigned the documents which the catalogue represents as originating in the discussions about reform at Constance to their correct date in 1381, pp. 160-2.

written the day after Hallum's death, urging that John Catterick, bishop of Coventry and Lichfield, deserved promotion to the vacant see on account of his loyal service in the Council.[1]

Consideration has been given so far to those manuscripts which in greater or lesser degree retain traces of official correspondence of the Crown. It would be going far afield to take account of the possible resting-places of correspondence concerning the other coherent groups among the English delegates.[2] It is worth mentioning only two other groups of manuscripts which retain collections of letters made in the first half of the fifteenth century. The first is connected with the diocese of Exeter, and Professor Jacob has drawn attention to the two most prominent members of it in his essay on 'Verborum Florida Venustas.'[3] These are MS Bodley 859, the first part of which is a collection of letters made by Gilbert Stone who was registrar to a succession of bishops in the west country,[4] and All Souls MS 182. Unhappily Stone's working life, so far as it is represented in Bodley 859, is a decade too early to be of use for the Council of Constance. All Souls MS 182, on the other hand, contains a little material that is contemporary with the Council. It falls into two main divisions, one in Latin, one in French. Both contain collections of letters. The letters in French which can be connected with the career of John Stevens, canon of

---

[1] Orsini's letter is printed by Rymer, IV, pt iii, 14. Rymer also printed Polton's reckoning of the cost of obtaining the privileges preserved in MS Tiberius B. VI (IV, pt iii, 88-9) and Catterick's confidential report to the king on his talks with Martin V (IV, pt iii, 88) in the course of which he later obtained a copy of the concordat which is likewise preserved in Tiberius B. VI. Cf. E. F. Jacob, 'A note on the English concordat of 1418,' *Medieval Studies presented to Aubrey Gwynn, S.J.*, Dublin 1961, 349.

[2] The heterogeneous collection of Oxford papers included in Cotton MS Faustina C. VII runs into the period of the Council of Constance but has no reports of its activity: H. E. Salter, *Snappe's Formulary*, Oxford 1924, 90-4. Nor is the material brought together by H. G. Richardson in 'Letters of the Oxford *Dictatores*,' *Formularies which bear on the history of Oxford*, ed. H. E. Salter, W. A. Pantin, H. G. Richardson, Oxford 1942, II, 331 ff. of any value in this respect, although it does reproduce Eugenius IV's letter of 16 February 1432 urging Oxford university to send its delegates to the Council of Basle and a draft of the university's reply, pp. 446-7. This is not to deny, of course, that the present collections of Oxford and Cambridge libraries contain a number of *acta*, sermons, and treatises originating in the Council of Constance, either separately or included in collections which embrace the whole period of the Great Schism, like Balliol College, Oxford, MS 165B or Emmanuel College, Cambridge, MS 9; but that is not the point under discussion.

[3] *Essays in the Conciliar Epoch*, 200 ff.

[4] Harleian MS 431 contains letters by Stone, *Catalogue of Harleian MSS*, I, 252-5, arts. 53, 54, 125, 128, 130, 131. Cf. arts. 49, 50, 52.

Exeter (died 1460),[1] are all of an earlier date; but the Latin section
has two letters from Sigismund, one of which clearly demonstrates
his haste to establish cordial relations with Henry V. Between these
dates there is an account of a conference with the duke of Burgundy
at Calais which must refer to 1416, although the dates are wrong in
detail. There is no mention of Constance.[2] Harleian MS 862 may be
joined to this group for, although it draws on more widely dispersed
sources than Bodley 859, the main part of the collection is due to
Robert Stephyn, a clerk who served as notary in the diocese of
Exeter as well as elsewhere.[3] Included in Stephyn's collection are
letters written by Walter Medford after his return from Constance
with the appointment of papal collector[4]; but the manuscript is not
for this reason of any more value in the present context than the
others of this group.

The second group of manuscripts is composed of the official and
semi-official papers which were accumulated by Bishop Bekynton
when he held the office of king's secretary and keeper of the privy
seal in the two central decades of Henry VI's reign. Like MS
Tiberius B. VI which has sometimes been associated with them, and
like Harleian MS 431 and Additional MS 24062 which virtually are
their predecessors, these manuscripts are stuffed with diplomatic
and ecclesiastical business. Lambeth MS 211, in fact, includes
letters concerning Constance; but they illustrate the part taken by
Frenchmen in the Council and not by the English.[5] This is all the

[1] M. D. Legge, *Anglo-Norman Letters and Petitions*, Oxford 1941, xi-xviii. Miss
Legge prints the letters in the French section. Dr A. L. Brown has prepared a catalogue
of the unpublished letters in All Souls MS 182.

[2] If John Stevens assembled the Latin letters as well as the French, there is an irony
for the student of Constance in Professor Jacob's observation that the notarial exemplification of the Anglo-French agreement of 1412, with which Henry sought to
demonstrate his rights in France, to the assembled Fathers in July 1415 was prepared
by Stevens himself when a royal chaplain and notary, Legge, op. cit. xiv, *n.* 1.

[3] *Reg. Chichele*, ed. Jacob, I, xxiii-xxiv. It is this MS, no doubt, which Dr Jacob
notes as the book of a diocesan *officialis* in *Essays in the Conciliar Epoch*, 198.

[4] Stephyn had probably served Walter Medford earlier when he was chancellor of
Salisbury, *Reg. Chichele*, ed. Jacob, loc. cit. Medford returned from Constance with the
letter (no. 21) in which Bishop Clifford described for the mayor and aldermen of London
the events of Martin V's election and coronation in November 1417, according to the
text of London's acknowledgement (no. 22).

[5] There is a copy of John XXIII's bull of summons to the university of Paris and the
reminder which he found necessary to send them; there are also two letters from the
university deploring John's flight from Constance, and one from Cardinal d'Ailly and
Gerson jointly urging Benedict XIII to resign. Respectively, Williams, *Official Correspondence of T. Bekynton*, II, 115-121, 134-8, 106-8.

more galling when these are the collections which contribute an extremely valuable insight on English policy at the Council of Basle. MS Ashmole 789 of the Bodleian Library again provides an excellent example of the kind of document which has already been noted as surviving from the later Council, and which one supposes must also have been issued for Constance, in the instructions of May 1434 for the second English delegation.[1] It is to be expected, of course, that Bekynton's papers should be concerned with the contemporary council rather than with its predecessor[2]; but in general the English delegations to Basle are well-documented in comparison with Constance, and the available evidence is in exactly the class of manuscript which one explores, so often unavailingly, for evidence of the earlier Council. This is surprising when the part of the English delegates at Basle was less spectacular and on the whole less successful than at Constance. Yet it is hardly an exaggeration to say that two substantial manuscripts of occasional documents Harleian MS 836 and Emmanuel College, Cambridge, MS 142, are devoted to the Council of Basle.[3]

Letters of instruction and ambassadors' reports are practical documents with an immediate and temporary purpose. Normally it is only the historian who is interested in them after the event. They called for no fine flourishes of style and consequently were not adapted to the needs of dictaminal collection. For this purpose the personal letter or the public testimonial, often less significant for the historian, are much more suitable. Formularies were compiled, however, not only to provide the standards for a correct style but also as a guide to appropriate diplomatic forms in situations of common occurrence. It is for this reason that they contain so much official correspondence. This resumé has indicated that a single collection frequently served both purposes, but it has concentrated on the materials which offer the best opportunity to compensate for

[1] Williams, op. cit. ii, 260-9. Bekynton's collection of documents to illustrate the English claim to the French throne, preserved in the damaged MS Cotton Tiberius B. XII and in MS Harley 861 and others, does not require consideration in the present context.

[2] At the same time MS Ashmole 789, f. 228^v carries a report to the English Council from the bishops of Lincoln and Rochester who led the delegation to the Council of Siena, the direct successor to Constance, in 1423. They relate the difficulties which they are encountering and ask for instructions.

[3] The recent article in *JEH*, XII (1961), 167-96, by Dr Schofield, cited above, is a reminder of their value.

the dispersal of the official records containing Henry V's correspondence with his envoys at the Council. In the hope of adding to the present meagre stock many less promising sources have been explored without success.[1] A negative result of this kind can hardly be satisfactory. Besides its inherently disappointing nature, it is vulnerable to succeeding studies which may be more intelligent, more pertinacious or more fortunate. Yet in view of what can be said about the fate of the records of the privy seal and signet in general, it does not seem likely that substantial additions to the king's correspondence with Constance remain to be discovered.

The contents of many of the formularies that have been considered are a reminder that if the records of documents of original force issued in Henry V's reign under the small seals are no longer extant, this was not always the case. The privy seal and signet offices may not have kept systematic records after the manner of the chancery, but they had records of some sort. There were documents to be deposited with the keeper of the rolls in the reign of Richard II.[2] There were more documents to be used by Prophet and Hoccleve and others in the compilation of their formularies in the first half of the fifteenth century. Henry V even more than Richard II was a king with an active diplomatic programme, and as Professor Jacob has reminded us he was a king who valued the record of past negotiations.[3] These facts predicate a substantial body of material contemporary with the Council of Constance; and one asks why it has not reached the Public Record Office for careful analysis and systematic arrangement.

The accepted explanation is to point to the combined effect of antiquarian curiosity and the ravages of fire. Antiquarian curiosity

[1] The register of Prior John Wyche of Llanthony secunda by Gloucester (1408-36) was one of the most generally rewarding, London, P.R.O. C. 115/A.3. It contains letters relating to both the Councils of Pisa and Basle. There are brief descriptions of the register by W. A. Pantin in *Essays to James Tait*, ed. J. G. Edwards, V. H. Galbraith and E. F. Jacob, Manchester 1933, 218 and by W. Holtzmann, *Papsturkunden in England*, Berlin 1930, I, 60 ff. Also in the P.R.O. is the precedent book of the curial proctor, Thomas Hope, (E. 36/195). It is of too late a date to be of use; cf. Emden, *Biographical Register*, II, 959. I have not seen the formulary in the Diocesan Registry at Rochester to which Dr Emden refers, op. cit. I, xli.

[2] Maxwell-Lyte, *The Great Seal*, 29. This amounted to a transfer of their safe-keeping to the chancery.

[3] Jacob, 'Wilkins' *Concilia* and the fifteenth century,' *TRHS*, 4th Ser. xv (1932), 112; also *Henry V and the Invasion of France*, London 1947, 13 ff. Cf. *Gesta Henrici Quinti*, ed. B. Williams, London 1850, 8, 10.

came chiefly in the guise of Sir Robert Cotton, whom it is hard to know whether to blame or praise in the matter of the survival of official materials. Fire did its destructive work on several occasions. Not the least was the damage done to Cotton's own collection in 1731. Earlier, in 1619, the privy seal and signet records suffered heavily in a fire in the official repository at Whitehall. Each of these hazards, together with the activity of eighteenth-century officials who re-sorted the records in their care, has been mentioned recently in an aside by Mr J. R. Lander.[1] There was another occasion when fire damaged a small part of Sir Robert Cotton's collection, which has attracted less notice but which is particularly relevant to the records of Henry V's reign.[2] This fire occurred in 1623 and destroyed the library of Ben Jonson. Jonson characteristically wrote a poem to mock his misfortune in which he says that the almost completed manuscript of his history of Henry V, on which he was then working, had been destroyed. Jonson numbered the historical *illuminati* of the time among his many acquaintances and in the poem he acknowledges the debt which he owes to some of them for help in compiling his biography. Sir Robert Cotton is one whom he names.[3] Jonson never returned to this task and probably could not have done so, since it seems very likely that the materials for his study perished at the same time. For in a catalogue of Cotton's manuscripts there is a list of some which had been borrowed before April 1621. Every entry has been cancelled, as if those volumes had been returned, save in one case: the loan to Benjamin Jonson of a copy of Titus Livy's *Vita Henrici Quinti* and of 'a great bundle of original things of Henry V, unbound.'[4] To bring this loan and the fire of 1623 together and to conclude for the destruction of much that had survived from the activity of Henry V's privy seal and

---

[1] J. R. Lander, 'The Yorkist Council and Administration,' *EHR*, LXXIII (1958), 34, n. 1. Recording the serious damage done by the fire of 1619 a contemporary wrote: 'Nothing is left but the walls and these not fit to build on again. All the records of the signet and privy seal offices are burnt. . . .', Otway-Ruthven, *King's Secretary*, 115. Those, that is, that had not been removed earlier.

[2] It is noted by Miss Hope Mirrlees, *A Fly in Amber*, London 1962, 64.

[3] In the poem called 'An execration upon Vulcan':

. . . and in storie there
Of our fift Henry, eight of his nine yeare;
Where was oyle, beside the succour spent
Which noble Carew, Cotton, Selden lent:

Ben Jonson, ed. C. H. Herford & P. Simpson, Oxford 1925, VIII, 207. Cf. I, 73-4, 261.

[4] Op. cit., ed. Herford & Simpson, XI, 78.

signet is only a guess; but the guess is made more probable by the fact that Sir Robert's collection still witnesses to his appropriation of many of the records of the small seals; and by the knowledge that Jonson, when he wanted to borrow from Cotton's library on a later occasion, promised to return the book on the very same day.[1] When guesses of this order are being made it is only a degree more hypothetical to suppose that evidence about the activity of the English at Constance was destroyed at this time. It serves to explain what is otherwise a surprising poverty of evidence.

Thus in the case of the king's correspondence the failure to discover more than the extant letters to and from the Council is condoned with some degree of probability by the history of the records of the small seals. The possibility of coming upon the correspondence of another group of delegates still remains; but it is safe to assume that it will be less valuable for reconstructing the English nation's policy than the king's own letters, and it must be admitted that the nature of episcopal registers, the condition of university archives for this period, the confusion in most chapter and monastic records, together with the poverty of contemporary English chronicles hold out little encouragement. The fact has to be acknowledged that as the volume of medieval records increases, it is often more difficult to probe the motives of public policy than in an earlier age when records are fewer but have been preserved more systematically. This is true particularly of the royal administration and the advance of the privy seal. The consequence is that in explaining English policy at Constance the historian has to rely more upon deductions and less upon documentary evidence than he would choose.

[1] Op. cit., ed. Herford & Simpson, I, 215.

Correspondence between England and the Council of Constance

Extant correspondence between England and Constance, 1414-18.

The following table includes only letters sent by Englishmen at home to Englishmen in Constance or *vice-versa* while the Council was in session between November 1414 and April 1418. A number of letters sent either by the pope, cardinals or the Council to the king or other authorities in England are therefore not included; nor are letters from England if they are not addressed to Englishmen in Constance. Also I am not sure that I have exhausted the contents of Bodleian Library, MS Arch. Seld. B. 23, containing William Swan's correspondence.

Dates in square brackets have been supplied.

Five letters no longer extant have been included, in italics, since an extant item unambiguously indicates that they were written. In addition there is a strong presumption that circumstances will have called for other items of correspondence of which all trace has vanished. Instructions from Henry V to his envoys are implied on at least two occasions:

(a) In July 1415 Henry V sent to Constance an exemplification of the treaty of 18 May 1412 between his father and the French princes as justification for his own attack on France. (*Gesta Henrici Quinti*, ed. Williams, 10; P.R.O., Exchequer, Diplomatic Documents, E.30/Dipl. Doc. 1695; *Lists and Indexes*, XLIX, London 1923, 39). It is likely that corresponding instructions were sent to his delegates.

(b) Martin V's recommendation of Walter Medford, newly appointed as papal collector in England, to the goodwill of the mayor and citizens of London in December 1417 notes that the appointment had been made in compliance with the wishes of the royal ambassadors as well as in recognition of Medford's own services. (Corporation of London, Records Office, Letter Book I, f. ccviii; R. R. Sharpe, *Calendar of Letter Books preserved among the archives of the City of London, Letter Book I*, London 1909, 193). The royal delegates must have been notified of the king's wishes.

Other circumstances indicate the existence of a report to the king:

(c) The presence of the Council's decree on the election of a pope (29 May 1415) among the diplomatic documents deposited in the exchequer (Dipl. Doc. 1662, *Lists and Indexes*, XLIX, 39) suggests an accompanying report.

(d) A similar indication may be given by the copy of the Aragonese withdrawal of obedience from Benedict XIII (6 January 1416) now preserved in B.M., MS Cotton Cleopatra E. II, f. 315 (old foliation).

(e) On 7 May 1416 Charles VI of France appears to have written a somewhat surprising letter to the English nation at Constance, inviting their co-operation in a satisfactory solution to the dispute over the doctrines of Jean Petit (St John's College, Cambridge, MS 210, f. 15v-f. 19v). This unforeseen development calls for a report to Henry V and consequent instructions.

(f) No. 10 in the table below instructs the two bishops to reach a conclusion on the Fountains case after taking advice in the curia and to report the result to the king.

(g) When Hallum died at the Council on 4 September 1417, it will have been necessary to notify Henry V of the death of his most prominent delegate. At all events the chapter at Salisbury had the news promptly, as has been mentioned.

Serial No. (a)	Date (b)	Correspondents (c)	Description of Contents (d)	Reference (e)
1	2 Feb. [1415]	Bishop Hallum to Archbishop Chichele	General report	As in 2
2	[May 1415][1]	[Archbishop Chichele to Bishop Hallum]	Reply to 1. Views on reform, payment of delegates, general information.	B. M. Royal MS 10 B. IX, f. 59. Jacob, Essays in the Conciliar Epoch, 58, 75-6.
3	19 Aug. [1415]	Unknown to king	Report, sent by John Hervey, antecedent to 4.	As in 4
4	[Jan. 1416][2]	Unknown to king	General report	Monro, Letters of Margaret of Anjou, 9
5	[Earlier than 20 Jan. 1416]	Simon Northewe and John Forster to unknown.	Repudiation of bulls obtained by Roger Frank in dispute over Fountains abbey.	As in 6
6	20 Jan. [1416]	Roger Frank to William Swan	Frank briefs his curial proctor in dispute over Fountains abbey.	Bodleian MS Arch. Seld. B. 23. f. 64v. Jacob in Medieval Studies presented to Rose Graham, ed. V. Ruffer & A. U. Taylor, Oxford 1950, 90-1, 96-7.
7	[1416, first half]	John Ixworth to William Swan	Client's letter to his curial proctor. Notes rumours from Constance.	Bodleian MS Arch. Seld. B. 23. f. 139v.
8	27 Jan. 1416	King to Robert Appilton and others	Orders their speedy return to England.	Calendar of Close Rolls, 1413-19, London 1929, 265.

(a)	(b)	(c)	(d)	(e)
9	29 April 1416	King to Robert Appilton	Cancels recall from Constance.	*Calendar of Close Rolls,* 1413–19, 303; Rymer, IV, pt ii, 158.
10	[late 1416]	King to Bishops Bubwith and Hallum	Instructions, relating to dispute over Fountains abbey.	Bodleian MS Arch. Seld. B. 23, f. 61v; Jacob, op. cit., ed. Ruffer & Taylor, 91–2, 97.
11	[c. 20 Jan. 1417][3]	Unknown to unnamed prelate, probably Archbishop Chichele	General report. Progress to-wards reunion.	Bodleian MS Arch. Seld. B. 23, f. 62v.
12	2 Feb. 1417	John Forester (or Forster) to king	General report. Sigismund's return to Constance.	B. M. MS Cotton Cleopatra F. VII, f. 19; Rymer, IV, pt ii, 192–3.[4]
13	14 March 1417	R[obert] A[ppilton] to T[homas Langley], bishop of Durham	Report on French attack on English right to be a *nacio.*	B. M. MS Cotton Cleopatra F. VII, f. 17; Rymer, IV, pt ii, 194–5.[5]
14	[*before 18 July 1417*]	*English bishops to king*	*Report on divisions within English nacio.*	As in 15.
15	18 July 1417	King to bishops of London, Bath & Wells, Salisbury, Coventry & Lichfield, and Norwich	Instructions on unity within English *nacio.*	Treaty (French) Rolls, Rymer, IV, pt iii, 6.[6]
16	[Spring or summer 1417][7]	Mayor and aldermen of Lon-don to Richard Clifford, bishop of London	Assurances of respect.	Cambridge University Library, MS. Dd. III. 53, f. 99.
17	[Spring or summer 1417]	London to Clifford	Request for news.	Cambridge University Library, MS Dd. III. 53, f. 99v.

(a)	(b)	(c)	(d)	(e)
18	*[Spring or summer 1417]*	*Clifford to London*	*Report of some kind*	*As in 19.*
19	[Spring or summer 1417]	London to Clifford	Acknowledgement of letter with news.	Cambridge University Library, MS Dd. III. 53, f. 102ᵛ.
20	[Sept–Oct. 1417]	Bishops Bubwith and Catterick to king	Report on negotiations with Genoese (fragmentary).	B. M., MS Cotton Vespasian F.I, f. 93.[8] H. Nicholas, *Proceedings & Ordinances of the Privy Council of England*, 1834, II, 236.
21	8 Dec. 1417	Clifford to London	Report on Martin V's election and coronation.	Corporation of London, Records Office, Letter Book I, f. ccviiiᵛ; (Sharpe, *Calendar, Letter Book I*, 193).
22	18 Jan. 1418	London to Clifford	Acknowledgement of 21.	Corporation of London, Records Office, Letter Book I, f. ccix. Sharpe, loc. cit.
23	25 Jan. 1418	Unknown to unknown, probably bishop Bubwith to king[9]	Report on negotiations with Genoese ambassador (fragmentary).	B. M., MS Cotton Vespasian F.I, f. 96.
24	[Later than 18 Feb. 1418][10]	Clifford to London	Acknowledgement to letter, probably 22, and comments on reunion (incomplete).	Corporation of London, Records Office, Letter Book I, f. ccxᵛ; Sharpe, op. cit., 194–5.

Apart from the king's correspondence, one or two other additions seem probable.

(h) In no. 13 Appilton undertakes to send on the text of the English answer to the French attack once the terms of it have been agreed.

(i) No. 11 refers to the writer's repeated letters (*meas repetitas litteras*) which he has written since his arrival at Constance giving news of events there.

It seems probable that the chapter at Salisbury would have been in regular correspondence with the Council and there is a hint to this effect in Richard Ullerston's sermon before the chapter in May 1416, when he refers to the canonisation of St Bridget which had taken place at Constance in the previous year (Salisbury, D. & C. Mun., Reg. Pountney, f. xxvii; cf. Jacob, *Essays in the Conciliar Epoch*, 80); but the chapter act-book preserves no incoming letters. When one finds in the St Albans chronicles a number of decrees from Constance (*St Albans Chronicle*, 1406-20, ed. Galbraith, 104-07; *Historia Anglicana*, ed. H. T. Riley, London 1863, II, 303-04) it may indicate an accompanying letter or report, but it is well to reflect that the chronicles were not written contemporaneously with events and that it may have been possible to purchase documents on the schism and conciliar periods (Jacob, op. cit. 69, *n.* 2).

[1] The identities of the writer and of the recipient of this letter are generally agreed, but opinions have differed over its date. The month is clear as the writer mentions St George's day (23 April) and 30 April as events of the recent past. It is not clear whether the year is 1415 or 1417. Gilson favoured the former when he catalogued the MS (Sir G. F. Warner & J. P. Gilson, *Catalogue of Western MSS in the Old Royal & King's Collections*, British Museum 1921, 317). This was supported by E. F. Jacob, 'Some English Documents of the Conciliar Movement,' *Bulletin of John Rylands Library*, xv (1931), 360, *n.* 2, and again *Henry Chichele and the Ecclesiastical Politics of his age*, London 1952, 8. In the second edition of his *Essays in the Conciliar Epoch* (1953), 58, Dr Jacob changed his mind to 1417. This had been the date given to the letter earlier by L. R. Loomis, 'Nationality at the Council of Constance,' *AHR*, XLIV (1939), 523, although erring over the month, and by Mr Hodgkiss in his Manchester University M.A. thesis on Bishop Hallum (unpublished), 191-3. The references in the text of the letter are numerous but thoroughly indecisive between the alternative years: the arrival of Sigismund gives hope of peace in Church and state; French malice against the English and their ambition to control the papacy must be resisted; monastic exemptions, as instanced by St Augustine's, Canterbury, are prominent among the abuses to be reformed; the king is on the point of personally leading his army overseas, after a meeting of his council which cannot be traced elsewhere (for the references given by Dr Jacob in 1953 are inconclusive); the writer looks for the co-operation of the bishop of Lichfield with the recipient at Constance; he notes the difficulty in raising the subsidy promised by the clergy of the province for maintaining their delegates. All these references indicate Chichele writing to Hallum, but could apply equally to May 1415 or 1417. The references to Sigismund and the French fit more obviously into the later context, but in that event they are surprisingly general; and the reference to St Augustine's might well be inspired by Chichele's visitation of his diocese in January 1415. Chichele refers to a *consanguineus* at Constance. This may be his cousin, William Chichele, but while William is known to have been there in November 1417 it is not known when he arrived. Several times Hallum's attitudes are referred to as habitual; but the bishop had been at Pisa earlier. The question could hardly be more open. I have preferred the earlier date until decisive reasons can be found to support the later.

[2] Monro (op. cit. 8) dates this letter to December 1415. I have preferred the following month since the report of events at Naples in the letter is probably due to the Neapolitan representatives who presented their credentials to the Council on 9 January 1416.

[3] The letter refers to the arrival of a Scottish Dominican at Constance on 18 January; but it says nothing about the reception given to Sigismund on his return on

27 January, in which the English took a prominent part, nor about the banquet to which the English invited the citizens of Constance on 24 January.

[4] The Hague edition of Rymer's *Foedera* wrongly ascribes the letter to MS Cotton Caligula D. VII. The original edition (IX, 434) is correct in its ascription.

[5] Rymer mistakenly ascribes the letter to MS Cotton Cleopatra F. IV in the original (IX, 439) as well as in the Hague edition of the *Foedera*.

[6] The warrant for this letter is preserved, P.R.O. C.49/48, no. 15.

[7] As already observed there is some doubt whether this letter and nos. 17-19 were ever sent. There is no trace of them in the City of London's register.

[8] The most recent foliation is used here and in no. 23.

[9] The letter is dated at Constance *in domo habitacionis prefati reverendi domini Bathoniensis episcopi.*

[10] The date on which Clifford received the letter to which he was replying.

The Beginnings
of English Sabbatarianism

PATRICK COLLINSON

Lecturer in Ecclesiastical History, University of London King's College

---

THIS communication summarises the findings of an enquiry into the origins of English Sabbatarianism at the turn of the sixteenth and seventeenth centuries.[1] Two aspects of this movement have seemed to merit fresh investigation: the sources of English Sabbatarian notions and the circumstances in which the Sabbath became a major controversial issue in the Church of England, dividing the puritan Nonconformists from the representatives of authority.

Sabbatarianism, for the purpose of this discussion, is defined as something more than a certain ethical and social attitude to the use of Sunday: it implies the doctrinal assertion that the fourth commandment is not an obsolete ceremonial law of the Jews but a perpetual, moral law, binding on Christians; in other words, that the Christian observance of Sunday has its basis not in ecclesiastical tradition but in the decalogue. The more important propositions of the Sabbatarians are that the Sabbath derives from the creation and so antedates both man's fall and the Mosaic law, although its use was defined in the decalogue; that the hallowing of the Lord's day in place of the Sabbath was of apostolic or even divine appointment, and more than an ecclesiastical convention; so that the Sabbath is still in force in this altered form, commemorating the second creation in Christ's resurrection, and robbed only of some of its ceremonial detail; that the whole day should be kept holy and devoted to the public and private exercise of religion; and that this

[1] I am indebted to Mr Ian Breward of Manchester University who has read this communication since it was delivered at Cambridge and has made some useful suggestions which I have incorporated. I have also benefitted from the comments of Mr Basil Hall on the occasion when the communication was read.

precludes all otherwise lawful recreations and pastimes as well as the work of one's calling, unlawful games and mere idleness.

This doctrine had long been as it were assumed in much that was indignantly said about the misuse of Sunday in sermons and tracts in the style of Philip Stubbes's *Anatomy of abuses.* Among the more notable complaints were the sermons preached at Paul's Cross by John Stockwood and Thomas White,[1] Humphrey Roberts's *An earnest complaint of divers vain, wicked and abused exercises practised on the Saboth day* (1572) and John Northbrooke's *A treatise wherein dicing, dancing, vain plays or enterludes with other idle pastimes etc. commonly used on the Sabbath are reproved* (1577?). The dogma was implied by the Sabbatarian bye-laws enacted by many corporate towns[2] and by the attempts of the House of Commons to legislate against Sabbath-breakers.[3] As early as 1573 one hears reported from the Kentish weald the kind of saying which would be a stereotype of anti-puritan satire thirty years later: 'It is said crediblelly in the countrie that he hathe preched that it is no greater a sinne to steal a horse on Munday then to sell him in fayre on the Sunday; that it is as ill to play at games as shoutinge, bowlinge on Sundaye as to lye with your neyghbor's wiffe on Munday.'[4] But the biblical authority for these attempts to regulate the Englishman's Sunday was uncertain, and it was only in the last fifteen years of the century that this practical Sabbatarianism received a dogmatic rationale, when English divines began to discuss the fourth commandment with some theological detachment and to publish whole works on its doctrine. The attention they paid to the Sabbath reflected a growing interest among puritan preachers and theologians with questions of ethics, which is suggested by the increased attention paid to the ten commandments both in catechisms and sermons, a trend discernible equally on the continent and in this country. It was in the course of catechising or delivering catechising sermons on the

---

[1] Stockwood, *A sermon preached at Paules Crosse on Barthelmew day, being the 24 of August 1578* and *A very fruitefull sermon preached at Paules Cross the tenth of May last,* 1579; White, *A sermon preached at Pawles Crosse on Sunday the thirde of November in the time of the plague,* 1578.

[2] W. B. Whitaker, *Sunday in Tudor and Stuart Times,* 1933, 37-44, collects some of the evidence.

[3] J. E. Neale, *Elizabeth I and her Parliaments, 1584-1601,* 1957, 58-60.

[4] The writer is Richard Fletcher (later bishop of London and father of the dramatist) attacking John Stroud, schoolmaster, hedge-priest and printer of Cranbrook; (Dr Williams's Library, MS Morrice B II, f. 9ᵛ).

doctrine of the decalogue that preachers were forced to examine their conception of the Sabbath.

The rigorism of the Sabbath doctrine might seem to make it a natural emphasis of puritan religion. But it was originally no part of protestant teaching, even in its more radical forms, to bind Christians to the literal observance of the fourth commandment. Tyndale taught that 'we be lords over the Saboth; and may yet change it into the Monday, or any other day, as we see need. Neither needed we any holy day at all, if the people might be taught without it.' [1] And when the official 'Homily of the Place and Time of Prayer' threatened Sabbath-breakers with the dire penalty of the Hebrew who gathered sticks on that day, it was a Puritan who protested that this was to confound 'our Sunday with the Jewes' Sabaoth . . . which doctrine is superstitious.' [2]

The first extensively argued, dogmatic assertion that the fourth commandment is morally and perpetually binding was published in 1595, *The doctrine of the Sabbath*[1] by the Suffolk puritan divine, sometime fellow of Peterhouse and rector of Norton, Dr Nicholas Bownd.[3] Within twelve years at least seven further treatments of the topic appeared from the press.[4] Perhaps the most extreme view was that expressed in Dod and Cleaver's *Exposition upon the ten commandments* which had nineteen editions between 1603 and 1635; 'For goe through the whole commandement, what one word in all of it hath any note of ceremony, what reason savours of any special thing to the Jewes, that the commandement should be tyed onely to them?' Mary Magdalene did well not to buy ointment for anointing the body of Christ on the Sabbath. Those who break the

---

[1] *An answer to Sir Thomas More's dialogue, the supper of the Lord*, Parker Soc. Cambridge 1850, 97-8.

[2] Dr Williams's Library, MS Morrice B I, p. 339.

[3] A second, expanded edition appeared in 1606 under the title *Sabbathum veteris et novi testamenti ; or the true doctrine of the Sabbath*.

[4] Richard Greenham, *A treatise of the Sabbath*, first printed 1599; George Estey, *An exposition uppon the tenne commaundements*, 1603; John Dod and Robert Cleaver, *A treatise or exposition upon the ten commandements*, 1603; George Widley, *The doctrine of the Sabbath*, 1604; *Three posicions concerninge the aucthoritie of the Lordes daye*, printed 1606 but not extant, see Arber's *Stationers' Register*, III, 146; John Sprint, *Propositions tending to proove the necessarie use of the christian Sabbaoth or Lords day*, 1607; *Master Bonner upon the Sabaoth*, 1608 but not extant, see Arber, III, 172. In the same period a more conservative point of view was represented by Robert Lowe's *Effigatio veri Sabbathismi*, 1605.

Sabbath will suffer 'all curses and wretchedneses.' Those who observe it 'shall thrive in the Lord's house and in religion and in other worldlie matters, so farre as may stand with true prosperitie.' [1] These publications presumably reflect much attention paid to the Sabbath in the pulpits. But what survives from the press suggests that there was a lull in controversy before the topic was revived by James I's *Book of Sports* in 1618.

It has been thought that this fairly novel teaching, so much in vogue in the early seventeenth century, was an original invention of the English puritan divines. We learn from the *Oxford Dictionary of the Christian Church* that 'in its more rigorous form [Sabbatarianism] is a peculiar development of the English and Scottish Reformation, being unknown on the Continent even among Calvinists.' And M. M. Knappen hazarded the statement that the doctrine was 'the first and perhaps the only important English contribution to the development of Reformed theology in the first century of its history.'[2] These assumptions require some qualification, at least with respect to the theology of Sabbatarianism.

Certainly Sabbatarianism was no part of the teaching of the proto-reformers, if one excepts the eccentric Andreas Karlstadt.[3] The earliest protestant teaching, equally in its Lutheran and Reformed expressions, relegated a literal Sabbath to the obsolete ceremonial law of the Jews and subjected the fourth commandment to a tropological exegesis.[4] It is also true that the Sabbath received an emphasis in English protestant religion which was unknown on the continent except in the Netherlands; and that the Sabbatarianism of Dutch Calvinists owed something to English influence. But to describe English Sabbatarianism as a wholly insular phenomenon is to ignore the probable influence of a number of continental Reformed theologians of the second generation who were well-known to Bownd and other English Sabbatarians. One might add that this question of the Sabbath seems to exemplify the insularity of puritan studies, the general failure to place English puritan

---

[1] Edition of 1603, ff. 62^v, 78^v, 90^v, 91^r.

[2] *Tudor Puritanism*, Chicago 1939, 442.

[3] See his *Von dem Sabbat und gebotten Feyertagen*, Jena 1524; discussed by Professor Gordon Rupp in 'Andreas Karlstadt and Reformation Puritanism,' *JTS*, n.s. X (1959), 308-26.

[4] There are useful extracts and summaries of the teaching of the reformers in Robert Cox, *The Literature of the Sabbath Question*, 2 vols. Edinburgh 1865.

theology in its European Reformed setting. The doctrine of the Sabbath, with its emphasis on obligation, was consistent with the theology of the covenant, teaching the necessity in the economy of salvation for faithfulness on either side of the compact between God and man. Covenant theology was not, as it has been represented, the independent fabrication of English puritan theologians but derived from the theological tradition of the Zwinglian reformation in Zurich, transmitted in part to the whole family of Reformed churches in the doctrinal *consensus* of the mid-sixteenth century.[1]

Among continental Reformed theologians of what may be loosely called the second generation one finds the view rather widely expressed that the fourth commandment is partly moral, partly ceremonial, and that an essential part of its moral content is that one set day—some would say, one day in seven—is to be reserved for God's worship and service. This belief is joined logically to the view that the Sabbath is older than Moses and belongs to the natural law, observed by man in his innocence. This teaching amounts to the recognition of a literal Sabbath and it represents an important modification of the purely figurative treatment of the Sabbath in the earliest Reformation writings. The way was prepared not only in Zurich but by both Melancthon and Calvin when they emphasised the third use of the law, to instruct the Christian in a life of virtue. The teaching that the Sabbath is natural, universal and moral occurs in Bullinger[2] and hence in the Anglo-Zuricher, John Hooper[3]; embedded in Bullinger's *Decades*, which from 1587 were required reading for all clergy below the status of Master of Arts,[4] it must have been familiar in late Elizabethan England. A positive view of the Sabbath, understood as the reservation of one day in seven for the service of God, received equal emphasis in Strasbourg, or so one gathers from Martin Bucer's later, English writings. In the *De regno Christi* Bucer taught that 'nos unum in septimana diem consecrare religionibus debemus' and that 'dies

[1] Jens G. Møller, 'The Beginnings of Puritan Covenant Theology,' in *JEH*, XIV (1963), 46-67.

[2] *Decades*, Parker Soc. Cambridge 1849, I, 253-67.

[3] 'A declaration of the x holie commaundements' in *Early Writings*, Parker Soc. Cambridge 1843, 337-51.

[4] Lambeth Palace, Registrum Whitgift, I, f. 131.

dominicus ab apostolis creditur in locum sabbati esse substitutus.' [1]
As in so many other matters, Bucer's thought here seems to have
been seminal. The same doctrine was upheld by Peter Martyr in his
Commonplaces and in his lectures on Genesis given at Strasbourg
and heard by many exiles from Marian England.[2] Similar views
were evidently entertained by Theodore Beza[3] and by Zacaharias
Ursinus of Heidelberg, although in his *Summe of christian religion*
Ursinus denies that the Sabbath was pre-Mosaic or that it possesses
predominantly the characteristics of a moral law.[4] Ursinus's view
was propagated in England by the master of Tonbridge School,
John Stockwood,[5] and it also became known through the Heidelberg Catechism composed by Ursinus and Caspar Olevianus.[6]

In the 1580s the Reformed theologians of what can best be
called in the usage of the time 'high Germany' were thus enlarging
on a well-established tradition when they emphasised the perpetual,
moral attributes of the Sabbath rather than its significance as a type
or figure. Their doctrine, if not identical with English Sabbatarianism, approximated to it and provided it with a dogmatic springboard.
It would appear significant that all these divines were Hebraists.
Two founders of the Reformed orthodoxy of the Palatinate,
Emmanuel Tremellius and Hieronymus Zanchius (Giralomo
Zanchi) of Heidelberg and Neustadt, both by origin Italians, were
disciples of Peter Martyr, but more narrowly biblicist and not so
well-grounded in patristics as their master.[7] Both, incidentally, had
strong English connections: Tremellius was Hebrew professor at
Cambridge in Edward's reign and Zanchius was a close friend of
Archbishop Grindal. The sense given to a number of texts, together
with the critical notes supplied in Tremellius's translation of the

[1] *De Regno Christi*, lib. I cap. xi; in *Opera Latina*, xv, ed. François Wendel, Paris
1955, 80-4.
[2] *The common places of the most famous and renowned divine Doctor Peter Martyr*, tr.
Anthony Marten, 1583, 374-7; *In primum librum Mosis . . . commentarii*, Zurich 1569,
ff. 8ᵛ-9. For a contrary, anti-Sabbatarian point of view, see the *Common places* of
Wolfgang Musculus, tr. John Man, 1563, ff. 60-70.
[3] See the annotations to his New Testament. These notes (for example on such texts
as 1 Cor. xvi, 2 and Rev. i, 10) were familiar to English Puritans in Laurence Tomson's
translation and were cited by Bownd.
[4] *The summe of christian religion*, 1645, 575-81.
[5] *A verie profitable and necessarie discourse concerning the observation and keeping of
the Sabboth day*, 1584.
[6] See A. S. Thelwall's 1850 edn., 86.
[7] Joseph C. McLelland, *The Visible Words of God*, Edinburgh 1957, 267-71.

Old Testament from the Hebrew and of the New Testament from the Syriac, tended to encourage a serious attitude to the Sabbath, while the whole great project fostered a more sympathetic understanding of the old law and of the judaic roots of the Christian religion. The influence of the Tremellius Bible was extensive for, when Henry Middleton printed a London edition in 1580,[1] it supplied a need in England, as elsewhere, for a Latin Bible of unimpeachable Reformed orthodoxy. In the following year a pious and cultured Suffolk gentlewoman, Frances Jermyn, bequeathed copies to a group of neighbouring preachers in this county where the intellectual system of Sabbatarianism was soon to make its first controversial appearance.[2] Within two years a Suffolk minister was referring to Tremellius's note on a text in Exodus in debating the Sabbath with his fellow-ministers,[3] and Nicholas Bownd on several occasions refers to his renderings of the text.

Franciscus Junius of Heidelberg and later of Leyden—François du Jon the elder—co-editor of the Tremellius Bible, taught in his sermons on Genesis, printed in 1589, that the substance of the fourth commandment was natural, and that for this reason it found itself in the decalogue. The Lord's day was substituted for the Jewish Sabbath 'Christi facto, exemplo institutoque Apostolorum et Ecclesiae veteris observatione constantissima et Scriptura teste. . . . Inepte faciunt qui observationem diei dominici ex traditione, non ex Scriptura sacra in Ecclesia perdurare asserunt, ut hominum traditiones his adminiculis (si Deo placet) statuminent.'[4] Zanchius expounded the fourth commandment at great length[5] in a systematic exegesis of the decalogue, emphasising the perpetual and moral character of the law that there should be one certain day in the week set aside for God's service: 'Secunda causa, ob quam Sabbatum institutum fuit, est: ut status dies esset, quo ad legem audiendam et

---

[1] *Testamenti veteris Biblia Sacra sive libri canonici . . . Latini recens ex Hebraeo facti . . . quibus etiam adjunximus novi Testamenti libros ex sermone Syriaco . . . in Latinum conversos.*

[2] Will of Frances Jermyn, Bury and West Suffolk Record Office, Register of Sudbury Wills, vol. 34.

[3] John Rylands Library, Rylands English MS 874 (papers of the Dedham puritan conference) f. 240: 'Therefore the word here doth not signify anie type but a common signe as Tremellius also speaketh of it, Exodus 31.'

[4] Πρωτοκτισια, *seu creationis a Deo factae . . . praelectiones Francisci Iunii*, Heidelberg 1589, 64; in *Opera theologica Francisci Iunii Biturigis*, Geneva 1613, I, col. 28.

[5] The fourth commandment takes up 206 of the 641 columns devoted to the decalogue in the Geneva edition of the *Opera*.

ceremonias peragendas conveniret populus. . . . Et propter hanc causam; quia non est umbra aut figura, sicut prima, non est abrogatum Sabbatum.'¹ The same doctrine is stated more emphatically by a Zürich theologian, Joannes Wolphius. In his *Chronologia*, printed in 1585, he asserted that the Sabbath was 'in paradyso ante hominis lapsum institutum ad cultum Dei, et in decalogo, qua nihil ceremoniale, nihil typicum et abrogandum continet, praeceptum est.' As for the new Sabbath, it was appointed by Christ and the apostles.² Here, in the orthodoxy of Heidelberg and Zürich, defined in the last quarter of the sixteenth century, there was a perceptible development towards Sabbatarianism, in dogma if not in homiletical application, at the same time as the question came under agitation in England.

In Geneva in the same years there seems to have been a slight trend in the same direction, although its strength is not easy to determine. Beza related the observance of Sunday to the decalogue and beyond that to the seventh day of the creation in the annotations to his New Testament, but I am not aware that he laid any emphasis on the Sabbath in his systematic expositions of doctrine; while Lambert Daneau (Danaeus) treated the Sabbath figuratively in an analysis of the decalogue in his influential treatise on Christian ethics.³ But among the *Propositions and principles of divinitie* propounded by students of the Geneva Academy, which were translated by the Welsh puritan extremist, John Penry, and printed in Edinburgh in 1591 by Robert Waldegrave, there are a number of strong Sabbatarian propositions, defended, it is interesting to note, by a Netherlander—none other than Jan Utenbogaert.⁴

¹ '*De decalogo*' in *Operum theologicorum D. Hieronymi Zanchii, tomus quartus*, Geneva 1613, col. 855. See also a number of passages tending to confirm the pre-Mosaic status of the sabbath in Zanchius's voluminous *De operibus Dei intra spacium sex dierum creatis opus*, 2nd. ed., Hanover 1597.

² *Chronologia, sive de tempore et eius mutationibus ecclesiasticis tractatio theologica*, Zurich 1585, 91-7.

³ *Ethices christianae libri tres: in quibus . . . atque etiam legis divinae sive decalogi explicatio*, Geneva 1577; see Paul de Félice, *Lambert Daneau*, Paris 1881, 173 ff. I have been unable to consult the *Ethices* at first hand, but I have deduced its teaching on the Sabbath from the English Sabbatarian writers.

⁴ These 'principles upon the fourth commandement' include the statements that the fourth commandment was established 'in the verie creation of the world'; that it was placed by our Lord Himself among the number of those that are moral and perpetual and that the apostles appointed the new Sabbath in place of the old in memory of the resurrection; 'the observance therefore of this Lord's day is not to be accounted as an

English Sabbatarianism was elaborated in full awareness of the progress of the question in learned circles overseas. When the Sabbath was debated in the Dedham conference in 1584,[1] reference was made to Bullinger, Martyr, Tremellius, Beza and Danaeus. Bownd made extensive use of Junius and Wolphius as well as of Bullinger and Martyr in the first edition of his *Doctrine of the Sabbath* (1595). By 1606, when the official onslaught on his teaching demanded some learned reinforcement of the argument, Bownd had become acquainted with Zanchius's voluminous lectures, and included in his second edition lengthy quotations from *De decalogo* and *De operibus Dei*. These authors were not necessarily unknown to other Sabbatarians who wrote more economically, or whose doctrine is known only from notes taken from their sermons by their hearers. Indeed, a Gloucestershire minister, John Sprint, in his *Propositions tending to proove the necessarie use of the christian Sabbaoth* is another English writer who claims to be in agreement with Martyr, Beza, Ursinus, Junius, Zanchius and Wolphius.

It would not be helpful to suggest that English Sabbatarianism was entirely derived from these continental sources, and there is certainly insufficient evidence to support such a contention. The use which the Sabbatarian divines made of their learned contemporaries was as opportunist as their pillaging of the Fathers for proof-texts: a speaker in the Dedham conference in 1584, and Bownd in 1595, both made use of an argument from Danaeus's *Ethices* that the fourth commandment should be placed first in the table 'because it is most ancient,' although Danaeus was not in other respects a Sabbatarian. The present writer would be the first to grant that theology was only one component of Sabbatarianism. Social factors characteristic of the English—and Scottish— scene must account for the widespread application of doctrines which were stated in Germany but never greatly emphasised or formative of social behaviour. But the familiarity of many of the Elizabethan country clergymen with theological works printed in Germany and Switzerland in the last twenty years of the sixteenth century and never printed in this country is in itself notable. It is clear that the theological climate in which the English Sabbatarian

indifferent thing, but as an Apostolical tradition to be perpetually observed.' (*Propositions and principles*, 78-82.)

[1] See 217, below.

doctrines were elaborated was anything but insular. Renewed investigation of the reception of continental Reformed theology in this country seems to be called for if we are to relate the definition of English puritan orthodoxy—not merely on the Sabbath question, but over the whole concept of the covenant to which it was related—to European theological development as a whole.

It is only possible here to outline the circumstances in which the Sabbath became a controversial issue in the English Church. The Sabbath was energetically discussed in Cambridge and in the conferences of preaching ministers in the neighbouring county of Suffolk from the early 'eighties onwards. The Suffolk ministry, insofar as it was learned, was a Cambridge ministry. Of some eighty or so Suffolk ministers of this generation who for one reason or another may be reckoned Puritans, more than fifty were resident in the university in the decade 1565-75, thirty of them at one college, St John's.[1] In Cambridge, early in 1586, John Smith, a graduate of Christ's who was soon to be beneficed in Suffolk, was examined by the vice-chancellor for implying in a sermon that the Christian Sabbath was of twenty-four hours' duration and that it was violated by any activity which was neither of religion nor of necessity. No more than a year before this, Lancelot Andrewes, still in his puritan phase,[2] had asserted the essentials of Sabbatarianism in his catechising sermons on the decalogue preached in Pembroke Hall on Saturday and Sunday afternoons.[3] We are told that these sermons were heard by 'divers,' not only out of other colleges in the university but also out of the country, and that 'many hundreds of copies passed from hand to hand.'[4] Rather earlier Andrewes had taken part in weekly conferences with other puritan students of his generation,[5] including at least three who were later celebrated preachers in East Anglia, Ezekiel Culverwell, John Knewstub and

[1] See my unpublished London Ph.D. thesis 'The Puritan Classical Movement in the Reign of Elizabeth I', 1957, 126.

[2] John Strype, *Annals*, Oxford 1824, III, pt i. 496-7.

[3] M. M. Knappen, 'The Early Puritanism of Lancelot Andrewes,' *Church History*, II, (1933), 95-104.

[4] Printed in garbled form in *The pattern of catechisticall doctrine*, 1630; in John Jackson's improved ed., *The morall law expounded*, 1642; and in a further ed. under that title prepared from Andrewes's own notes but 'doctored' to conform to Laudian doctrine, 1650.

[5] Isaacson's 'Life of Andrewes' in *Two Answers to Cardinal Perron*, ed. J. Bliss, Lib. of Anglo-Catholic Theology, Oxford 1854, vi; Jackson's preface to *The morall law expounded*, Sig. A 3ᵛ.

John Carter.[1] Another of Andrewes's puritan friends was the famous Richard Greenham of Dry Drayton. Greenham was a fellow of Pembroke Hall when Andrewes matriculated in 1571, and Thomas Fuller, whose father knew Greenham, tells us that 'if Greenham gained any learning by Andrews, Andrews lost no religion by Greenham.' [2] Greenham was Bownd's step-father,[3] and he himself had written a treatise on the Sabbath which circulated in manuscript and was known to Bownd before he embarked on his own work on the subject.[4] It was printed posthumously in 1599 and Fuller says that 'no book in that age made greater impression on people's practice.' [5] Perhaps Greenham was the original source of the doctrine of the Christian Sabbath in this country; his famous household at Dry Drayton was certainly a nursery of English Reformed casuistry.

As we know from the minutes and other papers of a conference of preaching ministers which met monthly in the neighbourhood of Dedham on the Essex-Suffolk borders,[6] the Sabbath was under debate among the Suffolk ministers as early as 1582—in fact the question was raised at the first meeting of the Dedham conference on 3 December of that year, and discussion went on sporadically until 1585.[7] As in other districts, the problem tended to rear its head when sermons were delivered on the decalogue. It was while filling his place in a series of sermons devoted to the ten commandments in 1586 that Bownd made known his views on the subject and was persuaded by his brethren to put them into print.[8]

Bownd wrote of the Sabbath that 'I doe not thinke that there is any one poynt of our religion that is so in controversie among the

[1] Life of Carter in Samuel Clarke, *A collection of the lives of ten eminent divines*, 1662.

[2] *Church History of Britain*, ed. J. S. Brewer, Oxford 1845, v, 191.

[3] Knappen, *Tudor Puritanism*, 450.

[4] See Bownd's preface (1595), Sig. A 3.

[5] *Church History of Britain*, v, 193.

[6] John Rylands Library, Rylands English MS 874; the minutes and some of the other papers were edited by R. G. Usher, *The Presbyterian Movement in the Reign of Queen Elizabeth*, Camden Soc. 3rd. ser. VIII, 1905.

[7] *Presbyterian Movement*, 27-8, 30-3, 35, 47.

[8] In a dedicatory epistle to his 'Christian Readers', dated 27 June 1595, Bownd explained that 'about nine yeeres since I was solicited to publish my sermons upon the tenne commaundements by certaine of my godly brethren, auditors then of the same.' (Sig. A 3.) Other references in the work suggest that the whole course of sermons was not handled by Bownd: e.g. 'surely to speake of the true manner of worship-

15

learned of all sortes . . . wherein many friendes doe disagree.'[1] The papers of the Dedham conference confirm that the Sabbath was a question which divided those who otherwise regarded themselves as brethren. The early debates on the subject were left unconcluded 'till further conference of brethren in other places might be required.' In June 1583 it was agreed to 'crave the judgementes of some godly men in Cambridge,' while members of the conference were invited to dispute the matter scholastically, giving in their reasons to Dr Richard Crick, the preacher at East Bergholt. Crick was not a Sabbatarian, and during the ensuing twelve months he conducted a vigorous and sophisticated debate with the chief defender of the Sabbath in the conference, Henry Sandes, pastor of Boxford. Boxford was on the way to Bury St Edmunds from Dedham, and Sandes combined membership of the Dedham conference with attendance at a meeting of ministers in West Suffolk which probably included Nicholas Bownd. He argued that the Church had no liberty to alter the Christian Sabbath; that it was 'a natural day' since 'the busynes of the Sabboth . . . will take up all the tyme'; and that the breaking of the Sabbath would be requited with the same punishment as blaspheming the name of God. Crick opposed these arguments with assertions that 'to thinke one tyme more holie then another is to observe tymes'; that if the Sabbath were moral, the day could not have been changed or the rest in any way relaxed, since 'nothing prohibited in the morall lawe is dispensed with by God'; and that 'if any writer affirmeth yt necessarie to have the resurrection of our Savyour only remembered by a daie, it is more then I knowe'; he believed that Bullinger and Martyr and all other writers taught that the observance of Sunday was an ecclesiastical convention.[2]

The Sabbath was not an issue which united all the forward ministry or which could serve to identify them as a party, any more than the presbyterian doctrine of church order had served that function. How then did Sabbatarianism establish itself as one of the main planks of the seventeenth-century puritan platform? Largely, no doubt, through the growing success of the Sabbatarian doctrine,

ing God doth not properly belong to this place, it was sufficiently opened unto us in the second commandement' (165).

[1] *Doctrine of the Sabbath*, 30.

[2] Sandes's and Crick's arguments are lengthy and occupy ff. 15 (237)-25 (247) of Rylands English MS 874; they have not been printed.

which seems to have carried all before it in puritan circles in the reign of James I. But initially the identification of Sabbatarianism with presbyterian Puritanism was effected in an attack from the opposite camp akin to the literary 'smear campaign' by which Richard Bancroft had implicated the whole cause of further reformation with presbyterian extremism.[1] This campaign was conducted by one of Bancroft's chaplains, Thomas Rogers, rector of Horringer in Suffolk, a neighbour of Bownd but an Oxford man, and perhaps for that reason isolated from the godly fellowship of the preaching ministers. In 1590 Rogers complained in a letter to the archdeacon of Sudbury, John Still,[2] of his 'shameful seclusion' from the regular Monday 'exercise'[3] of preachers at Bury. This seems to have been the penalty for a sermon against Laurence Chaderton's notorious presbyterian sermon on the twelfth chapter of Romans which Roger had preached in the exercise and at once printed.[4] He was also blamed for a provocative attack on a fellow-minister, Miles Moss,[5] a Bury preacher and later rector of Combs. Moss had published what Rogers took to be defamatory words against himself in the preface to a catechism which had commented unfavourably on the excessive quantity of books published in their own time and 'such as disturbe the Church.' It was not surprising that Rogers was sensitive to an attack of this nature. The *Short-Title Catalogue* and Anthony à Wood between them list twelve of his original works and eleven translations,[6] eighteen of which had been published by 1590.

[1] See his *Daungerous positions* and *Survay of the pretended holy discipline*, 1593.

[2] The letter, dated 8 June (1590 ?) survives on the fly-leaf of Roger's own annotated copy of his pamphlet against Miles Moss, *Miles Christianus*, 1590 (B.M., press-mark 4103.bbb.26).

[3] The catalogue of Dawson Turner's MSS, sold by Messrs Puttick and Simpson on 6 June 1859, describes (p. 61) a volume of 'Ecclesiastical Miscellanies' (originally a Selden MS) which included 'articles drawen according to the verie thoughts of the classical brethren for the wel-managing of theire Mondaie exercise at Burie' and 'a Narrative of an Exercise or Disputation, held, apparently, amongst certain ministers assembled at Bury St. Edmunds, 1st April 1590.' I am indebted to Dr A. H. Smith of Homerton Training College for this reference.

[4] *A sermon upon the 6.7. and 8. verses of the 12 chapter of S. Paules Epistle unto the Romanes . . . made to the confutation of another sermon*, 1590.

[5] *Miles Christianus, or a just apologie of all necessarie writings and writers*, 1590.

[6] Roger's translation of the *Imitatio Christi* had fourteen editions between 1580 and 1640. He translated mystical works ascribed to St Augustine and several works by contemporary Lutheran divines.

They are the product of a learned, diverse but ambitious church-man, an inveterate controversialist who had already ranged himself with the opponents of the godly preachers in the preface to his commentary on the thirty-nine articles, *The English Creed*.[1] Few divines of his generation had so strong a conviction of the catholicity of the reformed Church of England[2] or such loyalty to the implications of the Act of Supremacy. But neither this, nor a sedulous approach to numerous influential patrons[3] and the enjoyment of Sir Christopher Hatton's and Bancroft's active patronage brought the preferment he sought, and he died rector of Horringer.

When Bowle published his Sabbatarian doctrines in 1595, Rogers sensed an opportunity to uphold Anglican orthodoxy against a new-fangled notion and at the same time to avenge himself on the Suffolk ministers and recommend himself to those in authority. 'It is a comfort unto my soul,' he wrote 'and will be till my dying hour, that I have been the man and the means that these sabbatarian errors and impieties are brought into light and knowledge of the state.'[4] He preached a sermon in Bury on 10 December 1599 in which the doctrine that 'we Christians of the Church of England ar bound to keepe the Sabbath day' was described as 'antichristian and unsound.' With characteristic Erastianism he preferred to call Sundays 'the Queen's dayes.' 'Those which hold that opinion against which he himself preched he called Sabatarians and dominicans.'[5] I know of no earlier use of the label 'Sabbatarian' to describe those of Bownd's persuasion. At this time Archbishop Whitgift called in the remaining copies of Bownd's book and Lord Chief Justice Popham at the Bury assizes in 1600 forbade any more copies to be published. Rogers claimed the credit

[1] *The English Creede, consenting with the true, auncient, catholique and apostolique Church*, 1585.

[2] Norman F. Sykes, *Old Priest, New Presbyter*, Cambridge 1956, 59-60.

[3] Besides his acknowledged patrons, Hatton and Bancroft, Rogers dedicated his works at various times to the queen, Dr Thomas Wilson, Sir Francis Walsingham, Sir Thomas Bromley, the countess of Sussex, Archbishop Grindal, Bishops Aylmer and Ravis of London, Bishop Scambler of Norwich and Henry Blagge and Thomas Poley esquires, two Suffolk justices.

[4] *The faith, doctrine and religion . . . of England*, 1607, edited by the Parker Society as *The Catholic Doctrine of the Church of England*, Cambridge 1854, 20.

[5] Brief notes of the sermon survive among the papers of Sir Edward Lewkenor of Denham, Suffolk; B.M. Add. MS 38492, f. 104.

for both these actions.[1] Later he announced in the preface to a new edition of his *English Creed* that the Sabbatarian teaching represented a new and subtle manoeuvre by the Presbyterians: in their efforts to supplant episcopal government with the presbyterian discipline, 'from an odd corner and after a new fashion' they had assaulted the Church with 'their sabbath speculations' which Rogers calls presbyterian 'more than either kingly or popely,'[2] ignoring, if he was aware of it, that there were Presbyterians in Suffolk, like Dr Crick, who shared his own anti-Sabbatarian views. Anthony à Wood reports that Rogers's attacks provoked the puritan party 'so far to be enraged as maliciously to asperse and blemish him. Whereupon he wrote a vindication of himself in MS., now in the hands of a near relation of his'.[3]

Thomas Fuller records that the suppression of Bownd's book increased its sale and stimulated a market for the second edition; 'and scarce any comment, catechism, or controversy was set forth by the stricter divines, wherein this doctrine (the diamond in this ring) was not largely pressed and proved; so that, as one saith, "the sabbath itself had no rest".'[4] But Rogers's ingenious insinuation that Sabbatarianism was a new and cunning attempt at subversion of the established order by the Presbyterians was exploited by Peter Heylyn and repeated by Fuller and Jeremy Collier in their church histories,[5] and so established itself as a plausible if not a sufficient account of the origins of English Sabbatarianism.

[1] *The Catholic Doctrine*, 20.

[2] Ibid. 18.

[3] Ibid. ix.

[4] *Church History of Britain*, V, 218-19.

[5] Ibid. V, 216-17; Heylyn, *History of the Sabbath*, 1636, II, 249-56; Collier, *An Ecclesiastical History of Great Britain*, ed. Thomas Lathbury, 1852, VII, 190-2.

Peter Gunning, 1613-84 :
Scholar, Churchman, Controversialist

H. A. LLOYD JUKES

Vicar of Dullingham, Newmarket, Suffolk

THE architects of the Restoration Church Settlement were, it is alleged, those divines whose loyalty and High Church opinions had driven them into long and bitter exile with their sovereign. Considerable attention has been focused upon these men by recent research.[1] A number of the younger divines, however, did not go into exile, but laboured diligently in the cause of king and Church throughout the period of the Commonwealth. Their influence upon the eventual settlement of ecclesiastical affairs, if settlement it may be called, was considerable and merits further attention from historians. Among those who remained in this country throughout this period was Peter Gunning, whose consistent loyalty to the crown and devotion to the Church of England was rewarded after the king's restoration by his appointment successively to the sees of Chichester and of Ely.

'I was born,' Gunning tells us, 'in the year of our Lord according to the style of the Church of England 1613, January 11, on Tuesday at five of the clock in the afternoon, and was baptised by the mercy of God January 16, being Sunday, as appears by the register of the parish of Hoo in Kent, near Rochester.' Two years later the family removed to Gravesend where his father died.[2] Having little or no fortune the future bishop had to rely upon the favour of influential patrons whose interest he won by his own merit and ability. By his will proved at Rochester on 31 March 1616 Gunning received a legacy of £40 from his father, who charged his mother to 'have a

[1] R. S. Bosher, *The Making of the Restoration Settlement*, 1951, 88.

[2] Cambridge University Library, Add. MS 41, ff. 125-8; cf. Thomas Baker, *The History of the College of St John the Divine*, Cambridge 1869, I, 234.

222

special care'[1] in respect of his education. In 1626 he left the private school which he had been attending at Lenham in Kent and, being then about twelve years old, was elected a king's scholar at the King's School, Canterbury. He owed much to the influence of Dr Bargrave the dean and the competent care of Mr Ludd the master.[2] Among his school friends was William Somner, later to become a celebrated antiquary.[3] An able, even brilliant scholar, Gunning was chosen 'upper victor' of his school and was said to be 'remarkably ripe' for the university when he went up to Clare Hall as a sizar at the age of fifteen. He did not remain very long in this lowly position for, says he, 'I soon had a double scholarship: one of the foundation, and another of my lord of Exeter.'[4] He later enjoyed the patronage of the Cecils as chaplain at Exeter House, their London residence.

The years which Gunning was to spend at Cambridge were turbulent and critical both for the university and for the nation, as the late Dr J. B. Mullinger has so ably shown.[5] Gunning showed an honesty of purpose and, aided no doubt by his tutor, Barnabas Oley, an integrity of opinion which accorded with the times. Naturally he sought the company of those who shared his sturdy Anglican[6] views, Isaac Barrow at Peterhouse and John Barwick of St John's. He was also friendly with the simple, pious and kindly Nicholas Farrar, who later was to attempt a form of Anglican community life at Little Gidding.[7]

In 1632 Gunning commenced Bachelor of Arts and was made senior brother.[8] This was an expensive honour. The senior brother was expected 'to feaste the Doctors and Masters of Houses . . . and to give the Father of the Acte a Satten Suyt, or the value thereof.' In 1611 this had cost £18 for the banquet alone, a very large sum for those days. 'In the yeare of our Lord 1632 . . . I was chosen fellow of the college when I was nineteen years old. . . . At the same year I was made "tripus".' In 1634 he became 'moderator of the bachelors' and having commenced Master of Arts in 1635 was

[1] Baker, op. cit. II, 647.

[2] Ibid.

[3] W. Kennett, 'Life of Somner,' prefixed to W. Somner, *Ports and Forts*, Oxford 1693.

[4] Camb. Univ. Lib., Add. MS 41, ff. 125-8.

[5] *History of the University of Cambridge*, Cambridge 1873-1911, III, 98-288.

[6] For my use of this term, see Bosher, op. cit. 4.

[7] J. R. Wardale, *History of Clare College*, Cambridge 1903, 102.

[8] Camb. Univ. Lib., Add. MS 41, ff. 125-8; cf. Baker, op. cit., I, 234.

chosen praevaricator or varier. This official had to make 'a jacose or satyrical speech' at the commencement ceremony. Soon after this he received the cure of St Mary the Less on the presentation of the master and fellows of Peterhouse. It is strange that Gunning makes no reference to his ordination nor to the bishop who ordained him.[1] He became a licensed preacher to the university in 1641 and was very much in the eye of the university 'and looked upon as one whose extraordinary parts and indefatigable industry and study promised great things.' [2] Gunning tells us that he should have commenced Bachelor of Divinity the same year but 'the heads of the university being caryed away by Cromwell' he refused it.[3]

Gunning became deeply involved in the religious and political controversy which was soon to reach its climax in the university and the nation concerning the alliance with Scotland and the imposition of the Solemn League and Covenant. The Westminster divines, the lords and commons had taken the oath in the presence of the Scots commissioners in St Margaret's, Westminster, on 15 September 1643. The earl of Manchester was not entrusted with the task of imposing the oath upon the university until 5 February 1644. Gunning saw the shape of things to come and preached against the Solemn League and Covenant from the pulpit of St Mary's. The text of his sermon has not survived.

By this time the royalist party in the associated counties although in the minority, alarmed at the turn events were taking and fearing for the eclipse of their cause in East Anglia, resolved to send an urgent 'Remonstrance' to the heads of colleges and fellows urging them to use their influence to see that the university rejected the Covenant. The Remonstrance did not achieve the desired result. Gunning however took up the implied challenge and together with six other distinguished Cambridge men, Barwick and Lacy of St John's, Barrow of Peterhouse, Ward of Sidney, Edmund Boldero and William Quarles of Pembroke Hall, drew up a treatise against the Covenant. It was somewhat cumbrously entitled *Certain Disquisitions and Considerations Representing to the Conscience the Unlawfulness of the Oath Entitled A Solemn League and Covenant for*

[1] No ordination books or bishops' registers exist for this period for the diocese of Ely.

[2] Anthony à Wood, *Athenae Oxonienses*, Oxford 1820, IV, 140.

[3] Camb. Univ. Lib., Add. MS 41, ff. 125-8; cf. Baker, op. cit. I, 235.

Reformation etc.[1] John Walker describes this pamphlet as 'well penned and resolute.'[2]

A significant portion of the *Disquisitions* may be assigned to Gunning's hand, in spite of the attempt made to eradicate divergences of style. Of its major importance as an historical document there can be no possible doubt. 'It is the most important manifesto written at Cambridge during the Civil War, and with the "Querela Cantabrigiensis" of 1646 forms the weightiest appeal made by the still Royalist University to the sympathy "of the world outside".'[3] That the university was 'still Royalist' is an overstatement. Dr Browrigg, the vice-chancellor, refused to allow the *Disquisitions* to be published, but Dr Madan has proved conclusively that the eventual publication was made in London. Gunning's hand in the production of this pamphlet is said to have contributed more than anything else to his favour with Charles II at his restoration.

Gunning was deprived of his fellowship and expelled from the university on 1 May 1643. In the same year he went to Oxford, which was held strongly for the king, accompanied by his friend Isaac Barrow.

The Cambridge exiles were hospitably received by Dr Pink, warden of New College, who appointed them both as chaplains of the college. Gunning incorporated Master of Arts on 10 July 1644. He was appointed curate of Cassington under Dr Jasper Maine. While engaged in his pastoral ministry he received many indignities from the soldiers of the rebel garrison at Abingdon.

Oxford capitulated in June 1646. Gunning tells us that he 'came out with articles for freedom of my conscience.'[4] He went to London where he held various private chaplaincies and was tutor to the young Lord Hatton and his friend Sir Francis Compton. The ultimate contribution towards the success of the royalist cause made by these chaplaincies held by the loyal clergy was considerable.[5] Gunning throughout his stay in London lost no opportunity of furthering the Anglican cause by preaching and public disputation.

[1] Printed at Oxford, 1644, according to the title-page. But see Dr F. Madan's essay arguing that the place of publication was in fact London, appended to the copy of *Certain disquisitions* in Camb. Univ. Lib., press-mark Cam.d.644.3.

[2] *Sufferings of the Clergy*, 1713, 142; cf. J. Bentham, *History of the Conventual Church of Ely*, Norwich 1812, 202.

[3] Dr Madan's essay cited above.

[4] Camb. Univ. Lib., Add. MS 41, ff. 125-8.

[5] Bosher, op. cit. 40.

So impressed was Sir Robert Sherley with his performance against two Roman Catholics that he gave him an annuity of £100. It is possible that these were Spencer and Lenthall, who subsequently published an account of their discussion with Gunning under the title *Schism Unmaskt*. It was printed in Paris without Gunning's knowledge or consent.

In 1657 Gunning became chaplain at Exeter House, London residence of the earl of Exeter.[1] He attracted a large congregation and became the acknowledged leader of Anglican thought and practice. He was not the only Anglican divine to use the Book of Common Prayer in London during the Protector's rule; Sir John Bramston records 'I had usually frequented St. Gregories, Dr. Mossoms [St Peter's, Paul's Wharf] Dr. Wild's [St Bride's, Fleet Street] Dr. Gunning's or some other congregations where the orthodox clergie preacht and administered the sacraments; but the soldiers often disturbing those congregations, it was not so convenient for my father to appear there.'[2] John Evelyn the diarist was a regular member of Gunning's congregation and held him in the highest esteem. Gunning's ministry at Exeter House inevitably brought him into conflict with authority. A resolution was passed by the council when it met on the Tuesday and Friday of the week beginning 21 December 1657 requiring the authorities in London and Westminster to see that the ordinance for taking away festivals was observed, and to prevent the solemnities heretofore used in their celebration taking place.[3] One result of this was the creation of a great disturbance at Exeter House chapel on Christmas morning.[4] 'In addition the Protector was advised to send for Mr Gunning and Dr Taylor and require an account of the frequent meeting of multitudes of people held with them, and cause the ordinance for taking away the Book of Common Prayer to be observed.'[5]

About this time occurred the interview between Gunning and Cromwell which was noted in the "Day-book" of Dr Henry Sampson.[6] Cromwell spoke of the great number of people who follow-

[1] Camb. Univ. Lib., Add. MS 41, ff. 125-8; Baker, op. cit. I, 235.

[2] Sir John Bramston, *Autobiography*, Camden Soc. 1845, 91-2.

[3] W. C. Abbott, *Letters and Speeches of Oliver Cromwell*, Cambridge Mass. 1937, IV, 681.

[4] John Evelyn, *Diary*, ed. E. S. de Beer, Oxford 1955, III, 203-04, (entry for 25 December 1657).

[5] Abbott, op. cit. IV, 691.

[6] *Gentleman's Magazine*, n.s. I, no. xxxv, April 1851, 386-7.

ed him and asked him if he were a minister of Jesus. Gunning replied 'yes'; whereupon the Protector asked how he could prove this. Gunning replied that his ministry was derived from our Lord through his ordination by a bishop who had been consecrated by another bishop 'and he by another up to Cranmer, and he up to St Augustine, and he up to St Peter the Apostle, and so from Jesus Christ.' 'Can you take your oath of this?' said Cromwell, 'Was there no incision, no interruption of this succession, or have you any authentic records of all this?' He said he would not take his oath of it, neither could it be expected records should last so long. 'Then,' said Cromwell, 'it is but by uncertain tradition and your credulity.' To this Gunning made no reply, whereupon the Proctector continued: 'I'll set you,' said he, 'how you may make proof of it a nearer and surer way. Do you be qualified as St. Paul requires in Timothy and Titus; let the good people call you to the work, begin it with fasting and prayer and the approbation of judicious ministers, then you may call yourself their minister, and of Jesus Christ. As for your meetings, it is against my principle to persecute any for their religion, but if they be still affronting the government under which they have protection, I must and will look to it.' Gunning paid little attention to this rebuke and continued to draw large congregations at Exeter House.

It was in this same year that he corresponded at length with Dr Cosin on several theological issues. Among these was the question of the right of presbyters to ordain and that of the canon of holy scripture. Gunning at first approved of Cosin's work on the canon but later raised several questions connected with it. A copy of a letter from Cosin is preserved in the British Museum to which is appended a note regarding the rest of the correspondence.[1]

Gunning continued to defend Anglican doctrine against 'all sorts of sectaries.' 'He would dispute with them openly on the weekdays in their own congregations. Nor was there any considerable Sect whether Presbyterian, Independent, Anabaptist, Quaker, Brownist, Socinian etc. but that he held with them at some time or other set and Public Disputation in Defence of the Church of England.'[2]

---

[1] B.M. MS Harley 7033, ff. 185-9.

[2] Walker, op. cit. 141-3; quoted Bosher, op. cit. 39.

The baptism of Raghep Dandulo, son of a Turkish silk merchant of the isle of Tzio near Smyrna, to whose conversion to the faith at Exeter House chapel, on Sunday 8 November 1657, Gunning made a considerable contribution, attracted a great deal of attention at a date at which the missionary activity of the Church of England was not great.[1]

As early as 1653 Gunning began his long and acrimonious controversy with Richard Baxter, who provides a great deal of evidence from his point of view, while there is little or none from Gunning's. There was a 'passage of arms' between them over the Worcestershire Agreement, some disputation at the Worcester House Conference which was renewed at the Savoy Conference and continued many years afterwards through the pamphleteering activity of Gunning's chaplain, Dr William Saywell.[2] Gunning himself never wrote against Baxter, but he refers to his views on episcopacy in a letter to Archbishop Sancroft.[3]

Charles II was proclaimed in London on 8 May 1660. Consecrations to the episcopate and the restoration of ejected ministers and fellows of colleges proceeded slowly but steadily. Gunning was restored to his fellowship at Clare by an order dated 20 June 1660. He also became a royal chaplain, Doctor of Divinity and prebendary of Canterbury. Lord Hatton presented him to the benefice of Stoke Bruerne in Northamptonshire and Sir Edward Heath presented him to Cottesmore in Rutlandshire. In these he was non-resident but kept curates.[4] An order made in July 1660 directs that the vice-chancellor of Cambridge admit Gunning at once to the Lady Margaret professorship, 'notwithstanding any statute to the contrary.' [5] He was, after some demur, elected master of Corpus Christi College but became master of St John's College on 25 June 1661. He surrendered the Lady Margaret professorship to Pearson on appointment to the Regius professorship of divinity. As master of St John's he made a few serious mistakes but his government of the college was on the whole good. He sat as proctor for the chapter

---

[1] T. Warmstry, *The Baptised Turk*, London 1658.

[2] W. Saywell, *Vindication of the Rt. Revd. Father in God, Peter Lord Bishop of Ely*, 1682.

[3] B.M. Add. MS 29546. ff. 96-102.

[4] 1662 and 1664 visitations of the diocese of Peterborough: Peterborough diocesan records, Northamptonshire County Record Office, Lamport.

[5] *Calendar of State Papers Domestic, 1660-1661*, 145.

of Canterbury and for the clergy of the diocese of Peterborough in the convocation of 1661. He was one of the commissioners appointed to revise the Book of Common Prayer, but is not likely to have composed the 'Prayer for all conditions of men' which has been attributed to him. He certainly did not produce the prayer in its present form.[1]

Gunning was one of the divines appointed as 'assistant' at the Savoy Conference. As the late Charles Hole observed in 1910 he was 'the man of all others to have been selected if it was meant that the conference should not succeed.' [2] Here he again encountered his old adversary Richard Baxter who states that his discussions with Gunning were long and bitter. In the formal debate at the end of the conference Gunning was declared the victor. There is good evidence for concluding that the conference was in fact a duel between these two devoted but misguided divines. It has been said that the bishops sincerely desired agreement. Had they done so they would, it is suggested, have secured the appointment of anyone but Gunning. He received their support and therefore it seems reasonable to conclude that the desire for victory over their opponents was the determining factor in this conference. Gunning's real attitude towards Nonconformists showed itself in his inflexible opposition to Baxter and in his harsh treatment and acrimonious debate with them when he became bishop of Chichester.[3]

Gunning was consecrated to that see on 6 March 1670.[4] He resigned his prebend but retained his mastership of St John's until 25 March 1670 and his Regius professorship until 1674, to compensate for his payment of first-fruits. He also resigned both of his rectories. During the five years of his episcopate at Chichester his main concerns were to check the spread of Nonconformity and to promote pastoral reorganisation within the boundary of the city of Chichester. In neither of these was he completely successful.

In respect of his treatment of Nonconformists one example must suffice.[5] 'Bishop Gunning . . . had long disturbed the meetings at Chichester in person. Once, finding the doors shut against him and

---

[1] See my article in *Cambridge Antiquarian Society Proceedings* for 1962.
[2] C. Hole, *Manual of English Church History*, London 1910, 312.
[3] Matthew Sylvester, *Reliquia Baxteriana*, 1696, II, 337-63.
[4] William Stubbs, *Registrum Sacrum Anglicanum*, Oxford 1856, 125.
[5] Edmund Calamy, *Account*, London 1713, II, 692; cf. Baker, op. cit. II, 650.

ordering the constable to break them open with a sledge, one in the crowd cried out 'What, has Peter lost his keys?' and upon his firing hotly another called him Peter Gunning. But not being discouraged he sat as justice on the bench at quarter sessions at Lewes. A counsellor in the Commission who us'd to give the Charge desired the Bishop to do it,[1] but he refused and took the offer for an affront. The Bishop thought himself sure of Sir T—— N——'s[2] Assistance who had over acted himself before. But he plainly told him that he found they who would have good neighbours must be such themselves.' This is a colourful story and is in keeping with Gunning's reputation for intolerance. Barwick describes him as that 'incomparable hammer of the schismatics.'[3]

Gunning's scheme for pastoral reorganisation within the city boundary is outlined in a letter to Archbishop Sheldon dated 14 August 1670.[4] The city of Chichester was with certain exceptions the peculiar of the dean and chapter. The exceptions were the liberty of the Pallant and the church of All Saints therein. Gunning proposed among other things to unite the benefice of All Saints in the archbishop's gift with that of St Andrew Oxmarket which was in the gift of the dean and chapter. This was disallowed, but the two benefices were in fact united in 1878.[5] The problems which Gunning desired to solve were the ever-present ones of manpower, adequate stipends and the due performance of divine service. He contemplated a visitation of the diocese in September 1670, but no evidence concerning this has survived. Three years later (30 June 1673) he held a searching visitation of the cathedral. The text of this, in nine folios, is extant.[6]

In 1675 Gunning was translated to Ely. Information as to his episcopal acts and his tenure of the bishop's temporal jurisdiction within the Isle of Ely is either exasperatingly scarce or non-existent. All that is known is that he held regular triennial visitations. The printed schedule of articles for the visitation held in 1679 has

---

[1] See 5 and 6 Ed. VI caps. 17-23 for the statutory authority for this. See also Burn, *Ecclesiastical Law*, III, 406-07.

[2] This was Sir Thomas Nott; see P.R.O. C 193/12/3.

[3] *DNB*, xxxiii, 347, art. Gunning.

[4] B.M. MS Birch 4274, f. 159.

[5] *VCH: Sussex*, III, 164-6.

[6] West Sussex County Record Office, Chichester, EPI/18/43.

survived.[1] It comprises twenty-two octavo pages and is a most interesting document. Unfortunately the returns made by the churchwardens cannot be found. Hence its value as an historical document is not as great as it would have been if it were possible to collate it with the replies of those to whom it was addressed. It is clear from study of these articles that the influence of ecclesiastical law upon every individual was potentially very great. It is equally clear that Bishop Gunning was concerned to maintain and extend that influence. Formal proceedings in the bishop's court in so far as records exist do not suggest that there was either personal intervention by Gunning or undue harshness in his administration at Ely.

Gunning showed some considerable interest in Ely Cathedral and left among other bequests (including one to augment poor livings) a sum of money for paving the choir with marble. He also desired to move the choir further to the east.[2] Neither of these proposals was carried out.

It seems that Gunning was a frequent attender at the House of Lords and was a member of several of its committees. He was concerned with the popish plot but easily cleared himself of complicity therein.[3] He opposed the foundation of the Royal Society and refused his licence for the publication of Dr Mulin's *Parerga* because it contained some lines in praise of the Society. The *Parerga* was published and Gunning's name was added to the list of 'censors' in his 'absence.' Gunning objected to the Royal Society on the ground that too much study of natural science was detrimental to revealed religion.

Gunning died on 16 July 1684 and was buried in Ely Cathedral on Thursday 17 July. A monument with the usual fulsome inscription is in the south aisle. Gunning's recumbent effigy is a curious piece of sculpture. He is robed in rochet and mitre, which is strange vesture indeed.

In conclusion, then, Gunning was an uncompromising High Churchman of the school of thought which is usually described as Laudian. His sturdy royalist opinions, which emerged during his residence at Cambridge and developed during his 'exile' at Oxford,

---

[1] *Articles of visitation and enquiry within the diocese of Ely*, 1679.
[2] Bentham, op. cit. 204.
[3] *Journals of the House of Lords*, XIII, 512; *HMC, 11th Report*, 121-35.

grew and bore fruit during his residence in London during the Protectorate. His work as tutor to the young Lord Hatton and the phenomenal success of his ministry at Exeter House showed him to be a brave and determined Anglican. If he cannot be numbered amongst the architects of the building of the Restoration Church he at least deserves notice as one of the principal pioneers who prepared the site for its erection. He left his mark, also, upon the theological speculation of his age.

Oxford and the Origins of Liberal Catholicism in the Church of England

W. R. WARD

Senior Lecturer in History, University of Manchester

THE publication of *Lux Mundi* in 1889 has long been regarded as an important moment in the development of Anglican thought. Equally familiar is the distress which the new turn gave to H. P. Liddon, who could only regard the effort made by the *Lux Mundi* group to set the Catholic faith in its right relation to modern knowledge as capitulation to the snares of liberalism, and as ultimately fatal to the close coherence of Christian truth. The book represented a new grafting upon the stock of the English Catholic party, and no satisfactory explanation has ever been offered of the reasons why such a theology was produced within the post-Tractarian circle at Oxford. The new outlook involved a wholesale change from the deductive theology of the Tractarians with its imperatives against the world and all those things which liberalism accepted in the world, to an inductive theology which appealed to men for Christ by showing how the best and truest things led up to Him and found fulfilment in Him. At the same time religion appeared now as an interpretation of the world as well as of the Church, and the intense conservatism of Pusey and Keble was replaced by the radicalism of Scott Holland and Gore. The question is first why these new attitudes grew up amongst men who more than any others were conditioned against them by intense religious training, and, secondly, a question regarded by Prestige as inexplicable, how it came about that Liddon was so shocked by a publication which embodied tendencies which had been notorious for twenty years and of which, in a letter to Scott Holland in 1884, he had seemed quite clearly aware.[1] The archbishop of Canterbury's

[1] *Henry Scott Holland, Memoir and letters*, ed. Stephen Paget, London 1921, 112.

recent reference to the influence of Westcott upon Gore when the former was a master at Harrow, will hardly explain the new departures, still less his allusion to the influence of F. D. Maurice,[1] for no one had been more hostile to Maurice than the older Tractarians, even those, such as J. B. Mozley, most amenable to other points of view. In his life of Dean Church, B.A. Smith has lately suggested that the link between the old Catholicism and the new is provided by Church, or at any rate by the alliance of Church and Gladstone; but for the crucial years in the 'fifties and 'sixties he has to admit that he cannot trace their influence upon each other and contents himself with the statement that their 'intellectual transformation . . . ran parallel.' [2] The truth is that in those years the two men had no direct connection. Yet Gladstone and Church undoubtedly had a good deal to do with the story, and it is the purpose of this paper to suggest that the middle term between them and between the old Catholicism and the new is to be found in the political circumstances of the Catholic group in Oxford, and of the uncomfortable adjustments to which it was forced from its earliest days by virtue of being in opposition.

Although Newman kept the anniversary of Keble's Assize sermon of 1833 as the starting-point of the Oxford Movement, it is evident that the regrouping of forces which it was to bring into the open had begun during the crisis of Roman Catholic emancipation and the bitterly contested bye-election which cost Peel his seat for the university. It was in this battle that the crucial division in Oriel College took place, and Keble took with him the younger members of the college in defence of the Protestant ascendancy, and in defiance of the liberal traditions of his college for thirty years past. Newman gained his first experience of conspiracy with a wildly indignant body of juniors, and, still more important, the idea was first put about that all the troubles of the university, whether with her burgesses or with her examination statutes, were due to one hydra-headed monster, namely liberalism or the march of mind. Peel's supporters, who included most of the talent in the university, though Newman would not admit it, were abused as 'men of mind,' and 'philistines of literature,' and the all-pervading spirit of liberalism was seen as animating Peel and the emancipators,

---

[1] A. M. Ramsey, *From Gore to Temple*, London 1960, 2.

[2] B. A. Smith, *Dean Church: the Anglican response to Newman*, London 1958, 103.

compassing the overthrow of the Anglican ascendancy, and even permitting examination candidates to illustrate ancient with modern authors, a prospect which struck Newman cold.[1]

Here already are the atmosphere and the slogans of the campaign for Church defence as it developed after the Reform Bill, and the same coalition of High Churchmen, the greater part of the Oxford evangelicals, together with men averse to all change, which in 1834 and 1835 Newman managed to manoeuvre in defence of the university tests, and in 1836 to bring about the famous censure upon Professor Hampden. The same attitude was carried over into the defence of the university's archaic statutes. In the 'thirties great pressure was put on the universities by liberals, by radicals, and on some matters by evangelicals, to put an end to the abuses by which oaths were exacted to college and university statutes which often were not and sometimes could not be observed. When Sir William Hamilton impeached the current university constitutions as an illegal usurpation by the colleges, the Tractarians could give no ground, for they were then transforming the old idea that the university was a political oracle into the view that it was an ecclesiastical oracle, that it was the conscience of the Church, though a conscience not bound to comply with a Church lapsed into error.[2] The heads, however, knew, as the governors of universities know in every generation, that if there was an outright conflict between the government and the university, the university would lose. Moreover, it is clear from the papers at Apsley House that the heads had come under the strongest possible pressure from an unexpected quarter. The duke of Wellington who had been elected chancellor in 1834 as a prop to the old order, turned out to be a most obstinate university reformer, convinced that there was no hope of defending the university in Parliament unless she put right what plain men could clearly see to be abuses.[3] He it was who had pressed the heads to get rid of the matriculation subscription, and in 1837

---

[1] *An address to members of the lower division of the house of Convocation on the proposed examination statute*, Oxford 1830; *Letters and Correspondence of John Henry Newman*, ed. Anne Mozley, London 1891, I, 200–03, 220; *Reply to an expostulatory letter*, Oxford 1829; καλοῖς κἀγαθοῖς, Oxford 1829.

[2] *Quarterly Review*, LIX, 474–5.

[3] The duke's programme from which he never swerved was set out shortly after he had been installed in office as chancellor; Apsley House MSS; duke of Wellington to vice-chancellor, 27 August 1834.

he drove them to begin a systematic revision of the university statutes. The Tractarian machine was now set in motion against them in defence of the indefensible. This moment was an important one for the Tractarians, for not only did they suffer their first defeats, but they set themselves to argue that though under the Laudian statutes the Hebdomadal Board had the exclusive right to initiate legislation, they had no right to initiate a general revision; the Laudian constitution must be interpreted in the light of the pre-Laudian constitution and, on this view, the right of general revision belonged to Convocation alone and should be executed by a delegacy of Convocation. In other words, the Tractarians were saying for the first time that the heads were exercising a usurped power, and agreeing with Sir William Hamilton and the liberal critics that the practical operation of the university constitution was illegal. They ought, of course, to have put the legally respectable argument that under the Laudian code it was *ultra vires* for the university to alter statutes without a royal licence, but this argument had been abandoned to abridge the statutory powers of Professor Hampden.

Moreover, the Tractarians found, like others before them, that however ideological their motives in declaring war, when once the combat had begun they were very strongly subject to the tactics of battle, the more so as from 1837 the tide ran powerfully against them. Their power as coalition leaders had been based on the sense that they were the dedicated defenders of a persecuted Church. But the anti-Church coalition was now in full disarray. As the external threat to the Church relaxed, so the clerical coalition headed by the Tractarians began to fall apart, its dissolution hastened by the reaction of other Church parties to the logic of Tractarian development. As the Tory party revived, their fortunes further deteriorated. The Tractarians had begun with the defeat of Peel in 1829, they had sulked at the election of Wellington as chancellor, and they appeared to the heads of the triumphant ministry of 1841 as men bent on overthrowing settled academic government, and on obstructing that prudent reform which the university owed to public opinion. The Whigs had neglected Oxford men in their Church patronage, but now Peel set out to use every agency of preferment in favour of the enemies of Tractarianism. Pusey and Keble, both rigid-minded men who moved with the years perhaps less than any of the party, never forgot the lesson which they learned at this time, which was that modern conservatism had no principles.

If the Tories were damned, the younger set were beginning to lose confidence in a Church which no longer needed their defence, and the university also was conspicuously failing to live up to the role of Catholic conscience of the Church for which the Tractarians had cast it. There is no need to recount the long agony of the party between the publication of Tract XC and the secessions of 1845, an agony later transformed by the literary skill of Newman and Church into one of the most one-sided legends of English history. But the outcome was plain enough. The Tractarians began as unyielding defenders of the tests, but they found that the tests were a double-edged weapon and were ready to join with the liberals against new tests. Furthermore, when Pusey and Hampden, the Regius Professors of Hebrew and Divinity, were under suspension for breach of their undertakings, of what use was it to apply tests to the rest? The university constitution which had seemed so splendid as long as the Tractarian juniors were in the ascendant looked even worse. The Tractarians came to believe that both the executive and the judicial organs of the university had been twisted against them, and the wildest of radicals could not exceed the vehemence of their denunciations of the illegality of university government. Their struggles, moreover, had discredited the machinery of the university and almost brought it to a standstill.

The desperate conflicts into which they plunged not only prepared moderate opinion for the view that some public action would soon have to be taken about the universities, but brought the diehard Tractarian juniors to at least one common platform with the liberals, the view that the university would get nowhere without constitutional reform. Moreover they had driven a reforming wedge into the mind of another young reactionary, W. E. Gladstone, and drawn him to the side of the Tractarian remnant. Gladstone claimed never to have read the Tracts, but his doctrine of the Church was as high as that of Keble, and his confidence in the Anglican position as unwavering. Gladstone had been thoroughly soured by the behaviour of the heads, and on 21 June 1845 he wrote a long letter to Peel, bitterly denouncing his old chief's support of the *status quo* in Oxford, and accusing the Hebdomadal Board of driving men to Rome, and doing nothing to enable the university to meet the needs of the day.[1] One of these needs was a larger flow of ordinands for the new parishes, a flow which Gladstone and the Tractarian remnant were convinced could only be established by the provision of special cheap education in Oxford. This plan never came to anything and the steadfast resistance of the Hebdomadal Board, though based upon very strong financial grounds, exposed them to charges of wantonly obstructing any efforts to satisfy the critics of the university, and gave the Tractarians another push in the direction of the liberal opposition.

The rapprochement of the Tractarians with Gladstone and with a section of the liberals was taken a stage further at the general election of 1847. The heads promoted Edward Cardwell, the celebrated Peelite, and nephew to the principal of St Alban Hall, and showed again that their politics was less the bigoted Toryism of which they have often been accused, than the ministerial conservatism which had infuriated the Tractarians. Cardwell was supported by protestant High Churchmen and Evangelicals, and by the bulk of the Oxford liberals. Gladstone's cause was taken up by the Tractarian juniors on their own, and was championed week in and week out by their new party organ the *Guardian*. Not a single head appeared on his committee, and his only committee man of liberal inclinations was Frederick Temple. Both Cardwell and Gladstone affronted the ancient Oxford orthodoxies. Each advocated free trade which was expected to reduce tithes by a quarter; each had favoured the Maynooth grant, and in the famous phrase of *The Times* the anti-popery fire engine played on both candidates with absolute impartiality. It was clear that the orthodoxies were now less dear to residents, whether senior or junior, than to the clerical mob in convocation, but for them a candidate was found in Charles Gray Round, member for North Essex. Behind him were the bulk of the protestant High Churchmen, the main body of the Evangelicals and the more rabid evangelical journals, the Tractarian fellow-traveller William Sewell, and six heads. The position thus was that the protestant High Churchmen were divided among the three candidates, the liberals between Cardwell and Gladstone with a preponderance to the former, and while the majority of Evangelicals

---

[1] B.M. MS Add. 40470, ff. 305-08; printed in C. D. Lathbury, *Correspondence on church and religion of W. E. Gladstone*, London 1910, I, 342-7.

favoured Round, the more intelligent came out for Cardwell or Gladstone. In the ferocious contest which followed there proved to be little room for Cardwell, who appeared like Gladstone but on every count inferior, and a creature of the Hebdomadal Board to boot. Before the poll he had to be withdrawn, and the pattern at once became simpler. The liberals mostly came over to Gladstone and those heads who did not abstain mostly voted for Round.

Gladstone's victory in the poll proved therefore to be the biggest drubbing the heads had received since the Hampden affair of 1836. Equally striking was the distribution of talent. Gladstone polled 157 firsts against Round's 46, 45 Chancellor's prizemen against Round's 12, 218 foundationers against Round's 128. These statistics vividly illustrated the changes in the university since the great election of 1829. Then Peel had been defeated, but he had polled almost half the heads, and the great preponderance of talent; his friends had been reviled by Newman's party as intellectual philistines. The Peelite candidate still attracted the talent among the voters, but he was now the choice not only of the majority but also of the Tractarians. The men who denounced the march of mind in 1829 were now in alliance with it and with liberals who were its most self-conscious champions. Moreover the political evolution of Gladstone was to have a profound influence on their development as a party. In 1829 Keble had insisted that the university should not swerve by a hair's breadth from its old constitutional doctrine. In 1847 he declared that Gladstone (who avowedly expected a revision of the ascendancy) was 'Pusey in a blue coat: and what can be said more for any layman? . . . I am so sure of him that I don't at all mind here and there a speech or a vote which I can't explain.' [1] The older leader's personal trust in Gladstone was often tried, but Keble's loyalty was lifelong, and the enthusiasm of the younger men, nourished weekly by the *Guardian* took them with him gradually into liberalism and enabled them to transform the rigid orthodoxy and high tory politics of the early apostolicals.

The alliance between liberal and Catholic which was adumbrated in 1847 was very far from cemented. Liberal power in Oxford after 1846 owed less to the great accessions of strength imagined in many of the books than to the fact that the talented liberal minority had the ear of Lord John Russell and were doing their best to push

[1] Keble College MSS, Letters of J. Keble to T. Keble, 9 June 1847.

him towards intervention in Oxford under statutory or prerogative powers. The Catholic party had no greater bugbear than Lord John Russell. They regarded him as committed to undermining the independence of Church and university. His tepid liberal rationalism was all that they deplored, and his elevation of Dr Hampden to the see of Hereford in 1847, followed as it was by the consecration of Prince Lee, Samuel Hinds and John Graham, suggested that he would use the royal prerogative to save the day for the whole connection of Whately and Arnold. The commotion created by these appointments revealed again how deep was the theological gulf between the liberals and the Catholics. To Stanley and his friends the loss of faith of men like H. H. Vaughan, Froude and Pattison was evidence that without the liberal insights the Church would fail the age altogether; to Pusey the loss of faith of Clough and Goldwin Smith, and the increasingly impoverished religion of Jowett, showed that liberal reconstruction was a device for the destruction of faith, and that hope lay solely in the full catholic programme. Suspicion of each side towards the other was embittered by the fact that neither could foresee the movement of theological opinion away from both entrenched positions. Yet this theological development was one of the consequences of the fact that the alliance of liberal and Catholic was finally clinched, to the consternation of the sterner spirits on both sides, and it was clinched on the issue against which the early Tractarians had fought hardest, that of university reform.

By 1850, when the first royal commission on Oxford was appointed, the junior members of the university of whatever shade in theology or politics had wearied of the difficulty of securing their nostrums through the Laudian constitution, but the appointment of the commission seemed likely to revive all their differences. Failing to obtain any co-operation from the university,[1] Russell packed his commission with disciples of Dr Arnold, and the *Guardian* discounted their report in advance on the ground that no-one but liberals would voluntarily tender evidence before so partisan a body.[2] Gladstone also declared against any interference with chartered liberties. When the report appeared in the early summer

[1] Apsley House MSS, F. C. Plumptre to duke of Wellington, 16 Aug. 1850; B.M. MS Add. 34578, ff. 123-5; Bodleian Library MS Top Oxon. e 80, ff. 15-19.

[2] *Guardian*, 1852, 45.

of 1852 it proved to contain the full liberal programme, not only free trade in fellowships and scholarships, but a professorial system on the lines of that latest cynosure of liberals and Unitarians, Owens College, Manchester.

The reception of the Blue Book in the press and in influential society marked its publication as a point of no return, and it was very significant that the *Guardian* recanted its calumnies, took the report seriously, and in the course of developing a reform plan of its own showed that if the tutorial system and college independence could be maintained, the alliance between Catholics and liberals towards which both sides were being driven against their dearest theological prejudices was a real possibility.[1] By the beginning of the following session the *Guardian* was calling for a parliamentary combination of liberal-conservatives and liberals to liberate the universities from their shackles, while the other Tractarian organ, the *Christian Remembrancer*, was also calling for state intervention.[2] The bulk of the party, however, still preferred the grant of enabling powers to state intervention to remodel the university, but this gap separating them from the liberals was sharply narrowed by three acrimonious contests between July 1852 and January 1853. In July 1852 Gladstone found that the faction which had supported Round against him in 1847 was going to make another assault upon his seat, in defiance of the old university tradition that sitting members should not be disturbed. The final result was much as in 1847. Most of the heads opposed Gladstone and were soundly beaten. Much of the liberal party again went with him and this more than compensated for his losses among High Churchmen like Charles Wordsworth who denounced him for advocating 'the political equality of all religions.' Gladstone's juniors still shrank from the liberal plan of state intervention, but they were incensed at the heads' conspiracies against Gladstone, and, if the Hebdomadal Board (which could not be reformed from within) continued to behave as at present, the gap which separated them from the liberals would certainly narrow.

This was in fact what happened. Towards the end of the long vacation the chancellor of the university, the duke of Wellington, died, and at once the heads of houses staked their survival on

[1] Ibid., 1852, 384, 401, 424, 441, 489, 521, 569.
[2] Ibid., 1852, 696; *Christian Remembrancer*, XXV, 192-212.

securing the earl of Derby who, as prime minister, might stave off unpleasant legislation, and who was a decided anti-Puseyite. Gladstone's friends favoured the duke of Newcastle, but were outmanoeuvred in some characteristically slippery diplomacy by the bishop of Oxford, Samuel Wilberforce.[1] The heads for once outwitted their critics, but the embarrassments of their political gamble came home the following December when Lord Derby's government was defeated on its budget proposals after a powerful speech by Gladstone. Relations between Gladstone and the Derbyite Tories were now extremely bitter, and a few nights later a group of drunken Tories came across Gladstone in the reading room at the Carlton, and threatened to throw him out of the window into the Reform. Instead, a few days later, when Gladstone had created another sensation by joining the coalition government of Aberdeen and had to face a bye-election in the university, they made a desperate and unscrupulous effort to throw him out of Oxford. In this election as in the last a group of High Churchmen, now led by Archdeacon Denison who could not stomach the idea of Gladstone's entering the same government as Russell and Molesworth (the editor of Hobbes), broke away, but to Gladstone's friends their manoeuvres were the ultimate in political immorality. The main body of High Churchmen were still behind him, and so were all the liberals except extremists like Jowett. J. B. Mozley noted how the battle had 'a tendency to increase a sort of Liberalism even in quarters most sacred from such intrusion, and a High Church liberalism bids fair to be the order of the day. . . . It is certainly surprising and shows great power in Gladstone, the way in which he contrives to retain two large parties, who hate each other, both supporting him.' [2] Gladstone was seen to be liberalising his Catholic friends, and this was the more important because it was perfectly apparent to him that his enemies in the university would leave no stone unturned to drive him from his seat. Gladstone already began seriously to consider whether he ought not to retire, but always he was implored by his friends to stay on. Given the animosity of his enemies, however, his liberal and Catholic friends

---

[1] A. R. Ashwell and R. G. Wilberforce, *Life of Samuel Wilberforce*, London 1880-2, II, 150; bishop of Oxford to lord Derby, 17 Sept. 1852. MS Knowsley Papers, 156/3.

[2] *Letters of J. B. Mozley*, London 1885, 217.

would have a very long haul in their uncomfortable harness if he was to remain their member.

The election of January 1853 was also important in that it convinced Gladstone that the crux of the question of university reform was the constitutional issue, that the power of the heads must be broken and that this must mean state action.[1] With his encouragement Russell early in 1853 pledged the government to take action unless the university met its requirements promptly. State intervention under the aegis of Lord John Russell was an acid test of the new found liberalism of the Catholic party, and it was not surprising that Pusey finally threw in his lot with the heads and backed a scheme to preserve their constitutional power. The basic conservatism of the old Tractarian position triumphed in Pusey over all the more recent developments. But he was quite unable to check the leftward movement of his own party. The High Church residents helped to form a tutors' association and worked out schemes of their own. Although the tutors' schemes were much more favourable to the college and tutorial system than those of the Blue Book, they made it quite clear that they were out for the destruction of the Hebdomadal Board, and as through Gladstone they possessed the ear of the government, and were in touch with him at every stage, it seemed likely that they would have the decisive influence in legislation. This influence with Gladstone, and the success of Gladstone's machine in capturing the second Oxford seat for Sir William Heathcote in January 1854, brought the bulk of the Oxford liberals to make their contribution to the consummation of the liberal-Catholic coalition. They agreed to yield much more to college influence and claim much less for professors.[2] In its turn the explicit establishment of the alliance between liberal and Catholic was an enormous advantage to Gladstone when he came to introduce his university reform bill in the spring of 1854. This bill, which was in the main a compromise between the tutors' plan and a scheme of Jowett's, the whole revised in the light of an enormous correspondence with the Oxford residents, he could

[1] *Pages from the diary of an Oxford lady*, ed. M. J. Gifford, Oxford 1932, 20; *Correspondence of Arthur Hugh Clough*, ed. F. L. Mulhauser, Oxford 1957, II, 373. Cf. B.M. MS Add. 44183 f. 57.

[2] B.M. MSS Add. 44376, f. 246; 44377, ff. 193, 199; 44230, ff. 278, 283-4, 288: *Guardian*, 1854, 136.

present as carrying the consent of the great body of the working members of the university.

It is worth noting that the strains created in the Catholic party by their reconciliation with the liberals were exactly reproduced on the liberal side. H. H. Vaughan would yield no ground on behalf of the professors, while Liddell, the liberal dean of Christ Church, conspired with a phalanx of radicals to play havoc with Gladstone's relatively conservative bill in the Commons. In later life Gladstone declared that he had never had so bad a time with a bill as Liddell now gave him, and the wound was slow to heal.[1] But in the end, much modified, the bill got through both houses, the university began a new lease of life, and the parties were left to try their fate in the new circumstances.

The striking fact about Oxford history in the next dozen years is the way in which liberalism was contained and conservative sentiments regained lost ground. This unforseen development was due partly to the defects of the liberals; liberal reconstruction in theology proved to be a damp squib, and the liberal theologians of Oxford became more obviously unproductive as time passed; they were moreover a singularly unpleasant lot of men, they hated each other at least as much as their enemies hated them, while Jowett and Mark Pattison would have been distasteful in almost any company. Once their most personable character, A. P. Stanley, had been removed to the deanery of Westminster in 1864, their recruiting power flagged altogether, even while H. P. Liddon was developing the art of personal propaganda to an unrivalled pitch on the High Church side. Indeed, the growth of High Church sentiments was one of the things which held the liberals back. Lord Derby's political machine re-established itself in Oxford in the 1860s, and Lord Robert Cecil came down to the university propagating the notion that every good conservative must be a good Churchman and every good Churchman a good conservative. His doctrine was given added cogency by the Liberation Society which gave currency to the idea that every good dissenter was a good liberal and every good liberal a liberationist. By the middle 'sixties it was clear not only that Gladstone had given up the Irish Church but that the first instalment of disestablishment in England was only awaiting a

---

[1] Bodleian Library, MS Acland d.68, ff. 8-11. Cf. MS Acland d.69, ff. 30-3.

liberal majority in parliament, and that was the abolition of the university tests.

In short, on the Catholic side the alliance with the liberals was imperilled by the increasing seductions of conservatism, to which almost all the High Churchmen admitted they were emotionally subject,[1] and by fears for the Establishment especially in Oxford itself. Furthermore, according to any ordinary reckoning of probability, the alliance was bound to collapse under the vicious series of campaigns and counter-campaigns produced by the *Essays and Reviews*. Pusey's counter-attack drove the Oxford liberals to a desperate struggle to get rid of the tests, if not in the Church as a whole then at least in the university. In Oxford, unlike Cambridge, the struggle was all the sharper because the question of the concessions to Dissenters was of no importance. On the liberal side it was the relief of the Anglican conscience that was at stake; on the High Church side the maintenance of orthodoxy.

At this point there is not much doubt that the Catholic alliance with the liberals would have broken up altogether but for the personal standing of Gladstone. The extremer liberals in Oxford never liked or trusted him, but it was abundantly clear that the liberal party in Oxford had no hope whatever of carrying any other candidate, and after 1859 they became steadily more attached to him. Moreover he was becoming increasingly liberal. He took office under Palmerston, and fought another bitter bye-election in Oxford. His coalition however held firm, and the only ominous signs were that he lost a small group of High Churchmen of Exeter College, and that he was plainly losing ground among the youngest voters of all. In the next few years Gladstone continued to move to the left, and his High Church friends were subject not only to the mortifications of the *Essays and Reviews*, but also to that of the sight of Palmerston, unrestrained by Gladstone, handing over his Church patronage to Shaftesbury. The time was obviously ripe for High Churchmen to succumb again to their conservative instincts; Archdeacon Denison and Montagu Burrows founded the *Church and State Review* to drive the point home, and the institution of a postal vote by an act of 1861 opened the prospect of polling the country clergy against Gladstone on an unprecedented scale. In an

---

[1] *Life and Letters of Dean Church*, ed. Mary C. Church, London 1895, 171.

elaborate conspiracy Denison began grooming Gathorne-Hardy as a candidate to oppose Gladstone at the next election.[1]

To maintain his cause among the High Churchmen Gladstone now depended heavily upon the pleading of the *Guardian*, pre-eminent among whose correspondents were R. W. Church and J. B. Mozley. The *Guardian* spared no pains to plead Gladstone's personal merits to be an Oxford representative, it stressed over and over again the soundness of his Church views, and argued that he must be left to fight his battle for the Church in his own way. The strength of the Church did not lie in its privileges as an establishment.[2] That there was much truth in all this did not alter the fact that the *Guardian's* single-minded Gladstonianism did its hero a good deal of harm. It was obviously special pleading, and the recital of Gladstone's surpassing merits did not obscure his equally portentous defects. Where the privileges of the Establishment were concerned he was always urging the Church to concentrate on essentials and not to defend the indefensible; but, as even Keble was moved on occasion to point out, it was often impossible to tell in advance of an engagement what positions could be held and what could not. Moreover when the *Guardian* urged the university to return the best candidate irrespective of all other considerations, it was arguing rather absurdly for that constitutional freak, an unpolitical election, and exposed itself to a cunning article by Lord Robert Cecil in the *Quarterly* which sought to identify the Church and the conservative interest. According to this view the basic issue in English politics since the Solemn League and Covenant was the issue between the Church and a body of Dissenters who were helpless except in alliance with the liberal rationalising party within the Church. On one side or other of this crux all politicians must ultimately fall. The liberal Catholics in the *Guardian* might urge that the Church should not ally herself with a particular political party, and that the Church's representative at Oxford ought not to be challenged for affronting the party shibboleths, but this was an ideology produced by the schism of the Peelites, who, in ceasing

[1] G. A. Denison, *Notes of my life, 1805-78*, Oxford & London 1878, 334-7; *Guardian*, 1864, 684; Keble College MSS, Corr. of E. B. Pusey with J. Keble [1864, soon after 27 July].

[2] E.g. *Guardian*, 1865, 460, 498, 716-7.

to be conservatives, obstinately refused to admit that they were becoming liberals.[1]

At the poll Gladstone was soundly defeated by Gathorne-Hardy, even though, to the general surprise, the postal vote had no influence on the result.[2] His defeat was due to a large secession of High Churchmen who had supported him as recently as 1859, and the margin of defeat was increased by a factor which had begun to operate even in the last election, his failure to hold the young. Many of these were of course High Churchmen who had gone conservative with their elders. Liddon wept at the result.

> That our friends should have enabled [the Carlton Club and the *Record*] to carry out their wishes is one of the saddest episodes in the history of the Church Movement.[3]

Pusey concluded that 'the High Church are broken to bits.' [4] The accuracy of this diagnosis was borne out in an open split in the Oxford Church Union the following year. (1866 was of course the year in which Pusey joined the English Church Union and began to defend the ritualists.) A meeting under the chairmanship of the Tory Montagu Burrows gathered to hear a paper advocating advances in ritual. To this paper Burrows made a hostile reply, and his 'sentiment was hissed, and his whole speech interrupted by cries of "no" &c.'[5] Burrows thereupon resigned from the Union, and with others bought the *English Churchman* and tried to run it against the *Guardian*. It is well-known that R. W. Church and others associated with the *Guardian* had no instinctive sympathy with ritualism, but in the realignment of the party at this date they were more willing than the conservatives to recognise the ritualists as the genuine offspring of the Catholic movement, and to organise in their defence. And in due course the ritual prosecutions added point to the *Guardian's* constant Gladstonian pleas that the independence of the Church was worth far more than its privileges.

[1] *Quarterly Review*, CXVIII, 193 ff. Cf. *Is Mr. Gladstone the right man for Oxford?* (n.pl. 1865).

[2] E. W. Urquhart, *The late Oxford University election*, London 1865.

[3] J. O. Johnston, *The life and letters of Henry Parry Liddon*, 2nd ed. London 1904, 99; Liddon House MSS, Liddon Diary, 18 July 1865.

[4] H. P. Liddon, *Life of E. B. Pusey*, London 1893-7, IV, 199-200.

[5] *Guardian*, 1866, 1203: *Autobiography of Montagu Burrows*, ed. S. M. Burrows, London 1908, 209-227.

In other words, the position after Gladstone's defeat in Oxford in 1865, was no longer that a naturally conservative High Church party had been uncomfortably edged into liberal policies, but that in one wing of the party innate conservatism had triumphed, while the other wing had, under pressure, remained attached to Gladstone and the liberal connexions to which successive crises had driven the party for twenty years past. The High Church liberalism which had delighted J. B. Mozley in 1853 was now a badge of a section of the party only, and as the years went by important issues of policy were to separate them from the rest. The liberals and liberal Catholics were almost alone amongst the clergy in accepting the disestablishment of the Irish Church, the only considerable group of clerical disestablishers was in the Oxford diocese, and the *Record* was able to treat Irish disestablishment as an Anglo-Catholic ramp. Again, the shape of things to come was revealed in the final stages of the struggle for the repeal of the university tests. Conservative churchmen fought as long as they could for the maintenance of the tests, claiming that the interests of religion were at stake; the liberal Catholic side was for concession, but there was a significant rift in opinion as to the form which concession should take. The *Guardian* had now come to the conclusion that the tests were useless as they plainly did not prevent the discussion and propagation of infidelity in the university, and only annoyed the Nonconformists outside. The tests should be surrendered therefore in return for guarantees that religious instruction and worship should be maintained for Anglicans. Liddon and Pusey, however, still wished to maintain the principle of unmixed education. It seems at first sight absurd to class so reactionary a man as Pusey as a liberal Catholic, yet, in fact, he still was. Pusey had opposed every new turn in Gladstone's career as blasphemy, and yet followed him in the end. And now, in 1868, he took up a hint dropped by Gladstone,[1] and made a proposal to the Wesleyan Conference that instead of secularising Oxford by simply abandoning the tests, college property should be divided among the denominations according to their strength, so that each religious body might receive its own sons in Oxford uncontaminated by the rest. Moreover, this operation should be a pilot scheme for disestablishment without secularisation on the Irish pattern. No conservative Catholic could yet face disestablishment

[1] Liddon House MSS, Liddon Diary, 4 Sept. 1866.

in this cold-blooded way. Nevertheless the differences between Pusey and the *Guardian* were sufficient to suggest that the liberal Catholics would again be shorn of their conservative wing when the time was ripe. In 1869 the moment arrived for Pusey, and he parted with Gladstone for ever when Temple was raised to the see of Exeter. As recently as 1865 he had written that 'all must be right in the end where there is that single-hearted loyal love of God and His Church, of his Faith and Truth, which there is in Gladstone.' Now he wrote to Gladstone his sorrowful farewell.[1] But for Liddon the magic in Gladstone persisted.

It was into this world that the *Lux Mundi* group came to complete their education and polish their churchmanship. E. S. Talbot matriculated in 1862, R. C. Moberly in 1863, Walter Lock in 1865, Scott Holland in 1866, Illingworth in 1867, Francis Paget in 1869 and Charles Gore in 1871. They came up from a country in which the Catholic cause was prospering to find that in the head-quarters of the movement there were irreconcilable differences. Moreover, the reigning deities in the schools exercised them considerably. Talbot as the first up was faced above all by John Stuart Mill, whose inductive lines of thought and immense range had to be reckoned with in every quarter of the Greats School. Scott Holland and Gore were faced with Balliol Hegelianism as mediated by T. H. Green. In the 'thirties and 'forties it could be said that the liberals believed in progress while the Tractarians believed in the Church. To those young Catholics who still saw this as the crux, and it is clear that they were many, the great object was to maintain the fences of the Church and university, and in the purely academic sphere to displace the present authorities in the schools by the works of H. L. Mansel.[2] But the long reluctant association of the Catholic party with liberal causes, the hold which an increasingly liberal Gladstone had upon a portion of it, and the open split in the Catholic ranks meant that this was no longer an automatic choice. If for any reason a young Catholic felt indisposed to go with the conservative side, and E. S. Talbot admitted candidly that they would not listen to Mansel because of his Derbyite politics,[3] the possibility was open to him of running Catholicism in a

---

[1] Liddon, *Life of Pusey*, IV, 198; B.M. MS Add. 44281, ff. 352-3.

[2] Cf. M. Burrows, *Pass and Class*, Oxford 1860, 143.

[3] E. S. Talbot, *Memories of my early life*, London 1924, 45.

liberal political harness, and of bringing about from a Catholic point of view that reconciliation with progressive intellect which had been the hallmark of the liberal enterprise. In this cause inductive logic acquired from Mill, or the idea of the world as a theatre of God's self-revelation picked up from Hegel, or any version of the idea of progress, could be employed towards the construction of a theology of the Incarnation. As early as 1873 E. S. Talbot was saying that it was impossible to continue the work of the Tractarians, and that what was needed was a Catholic theology fixed in its central principles 'yet ever yielding up new meanings even from its central depths in the light of other knowledge and human development.'[1]

To young men whom the split in the party had compelled to re-examine their political and intellectual attitudes, the liberal Catholic group had a further attraction in two sterling father-figures, R. W. Church and in a lesser degree J. B. Mozley. Church had already perceived a Christian significance in culture, and what he called the gifts of civilisation were increased, not diminished in importance by man's eternal destiny. He was moreover an eminently fair-minded man, and one of the pillars of Gladstone's interest in the *Guardian*. To E. S. Talbot, Church was an unrivalled hero. Scott Holland revered him; Francis Paget was his disciple and married his daughter. J. B. Mozley also played his part, for he had proved his intellectual elasticity by concluding that there was something to be said for the Gorham judgement, that bitterest of all pills to the High Church party; and after Gladstone had brought him back to Oxford as Regius professor of divinity in 1871, he had most of the *Lux Mundi* group in his graduate class. Here, at any rate, was the encouragement which the young men needed on the intellectual side.

If, however, the intellectual and the political roots of liberal Catholicism are ascribed to the Oxford battles in the 1860s, does not the problem of Liddon become more insoluble than ever? If he had been living beside the principles of *Lux Mundi* not for five years but for twenty is it conceivable that he should have been surprised and shocked by its publication? Liddon and Pusey, it must be said, allowed their affection for Gladstone and their deep-rooted suspicion that conservatives regarded the Church as merely part of the constitution to bring them into some very strange company. So

[1] Gwendolen Stephenson, *Edward Stuart Talbot 1844-1934*, London 1936, 55.

far was Liddon from regarding the Oxford philosophy of the 'sixties as suitable for Christian thinkers, that in the winter of 1867-8 he engaged in a fruitless conspiracy to reform the Greats School either by removing infidel examiners or, still better, by removing the philosophy from the school altogether.[1] A decade later he engaged in a circuitous campaign to chain most men to compulsory Greek by allowing the minority to take a new degree in Natural Science without Greek.[2] This scheme was also a failure, and not unnaturally Liddon despaired of modern Oxford, talked of seceding, and did his best to get young Catholic intellectuals to leave as well. Scott Holland recognised before Pusey's death that a breach between Liddon and the younger men must come, and Liddon himself fought furiously on the governing body of Keble College to narrow Edward Talbot's conception of what Anglican influence in the new foundation ought to be.[3] What enabled Liddon to go on thinking that all was well was perhaps the very circumstance that enabled the younger men to look liberalism in the face without recoil, namely, that in various uncomfortable and untidy ways the Church movement from very early in its history had been associated with the liberalism against which it had protested. Moreover, during the whole of Liddon's active life Gladstone had been holding together the apparent incompatibles of liberalism and Catholicism, and Liddon clung fiercely to him. From the autumn of 1876, not only in the pulpit but in the *Guardian*, he added his own brand of demagogy to Gladstone's campaigns against the Turkish atrocities in Bulgaria. Surely Gladstone and the *Guardian* would still provide a rallying power sufficient to meet the strains which the party had always suffered.

This proved, however, not to be the case, and the difficulties of the inherently unstable association of liberalism and Catholicism became manifest among both the older and the younger men. Liddon buried himself in the early history of the movement in writing his *Life of Pusey* and was horrified at *Lux Mundi*. Church, who had been the mainstay of the younger generation, despaired of

[1] Liddon House MSS, Liddon Diary, 20 Dec. 1867; 11 Feb. 1868.

[2] See e.g. *Guardian*, 1877, 156, 148; 1879, 1441, 1677; 1880, 713; *The Times*, 23 May 1879, 9, 10; 27 May, 9; 31 May, 7 (and following numbers); 3 June, 9; 28 April 1880, 7; 16 April 1881, 9.

[3] Liddon House MSS, Liddon Diary, 6 March 1880; 1 Feb. 1881.

Gladstone, and also turned back in mind to the early days of the party which he recounted in his celebrated book, *The Oxford Movement*. He encouraged Gore to publish *Lux Mundi* but did not like the result when it came. And the younger men were also wobbling on the tightrope. Liberalism was now so largely made up of intractable sectional causes like disestablishment, teetotalism, and opposition to Church schools, that although the young men might make concessions to liberalism in theology, they had to be radicals in politics. And in a world where politics consisted of all those things which divided liberals from conservatives they were increasingly attracted by those issues of social reform which were still regarded not as party concerns but as technical crossbench matters. In this respect one might say that the unpolitical politics which the *Guardian* tried to see in Gladstone reappeared in the Christian Social Union. And even in theology, as Gore himself was to find as a bishop, his successors would fall off into popery on the one side or modernism on the other.

The Theology of Graduation: an Experiment in Training Colonial Clergy

PETER HINCHLIFF

Professor of Ecclesiastical History,
Rhodes University, Grahamstown, C.P., South Africa

NOWADAYS when 'Executive Officers' and 'Councils for Evangelical Strategy' plan a 'Younger Church' one of the things they worry about most is the training of an indigenous clergy. In the nineteenth century men were not so self-conscious about missions. You took the Gospel to the heathen. You relied upon clergy coming from 'home.' Even where there was a small population of white colonists, they did not often expect to have to produce their own clergymen. Of the fifty or sixty Anglican clergymen who served in South Africa between the second British occupation of the Cape and the appointment of the first bishop (1806-1848), only one was born in the colony—and he was a white man.

Before Robert Gray became first bishop of Cape Town, there was, indeed, very little that could be called an Anglican *Church* in the colony. What organisation there was has been described as 'Erastian Congregationalism'[1]—separate congregations of white Anglicans, each responsible for its own finances and buildings, each regarded as part of the established Church of England, each separately recognised by an ordinance of the colonial administration.[2] The governor acted as ordinary.[3] Clergymen were appointed

---

[1] A. T. Wirgman, *English Church and People in South Africa*, 1895, 123.

[2] For a fuller treatment of this system see P. Hinchliff, *The Anglican Church in South Africa*, 1963.

[3] See A. J. Hewitt, *Sketches of English Church History in South Africa*, Juta 1887, 12 ff.

by the Colonial Office, sometimes on the nomination of the S.P.G.[1]

All this was changed at one stroke by the arrival of Bishop Gray. He was appointed by letters patent from the Crown, so he was able to take over the governor's ordinary jurisdiction over the 'Erastian congregations.' But he had to do far more. For the first time there was someone responsible for general *episkope*, missions, new parochial development, and everything else, including the training of ordinands when he should be able to find them. The colony was still very undeveloped. There was very little in the way of any communications system. There were not even proper roads connecting Cape Town with the interior. Sixty-five days was considered a quick voyage from England. There were, of course, no universities in the Cape. A man might be sent to England, but then it might take as much as six years before he would get back to the colony. The bishop first tried to have prospective ordination candidates living in his own home, supervising their studies himself. It gradually became the practice to board them out with senior and scholarly priests, who were made responsible for their practical and academic training. But this did not solve the chief problem—that there was no examining body to maintain standards; no university to encourage learning.

In 1869, not long before Gray's death, the synod of South African bishops (there were now half-a-dozen bishops in the subcontinent) resolved that the minimum 'literary qualification' for ordination should be a second class in the public examination of the colony.[2] This examination had been established by the civil administration in 1850. The public service of the colony was labouring under the same handicap as the Church. There was a great need for some means of testing the literacy and intelligence of aspiring civil servants.

A letter written to Gray's successor illustrates what the new regulations required of ordinands. A lay reader, intending to be ordained, wrote to ask whether the bishop would be satisfied with a preliminary examination in 'English language, literature, history, composition, arithmetic and Latin.' 'I do not wish,' he said, 'to pass an examination that would be at all derogatory to the dignity and

[1] Bishopscourt Archives, Cape Town; Index of letters to S.P.G.; W. E. Gladstone, 8/5/1845, Earl Grey, 14/12/1846.

[2] Bishopscourt Archives; Minutes of Episcopal Synod.

sacredness of the office, but at the same time, as you know, I am engaged the whole day in a counting house so that my time will not allow me to study any subjects that may well be dispensed with.'[1] Modern theological colleges might well be surprised at being asked to teach any of the subjects mentioned.

In 1876 Bishop Webb of Bloemfontein (previously vice-principal of Cuddesdon under Bishop King) founded a theological college with money subscribed by friends in England as a memorial to Bishop Wilberforce.[2] The college only had a very small number of students, black and white. The bishop requested the Provincial Synod to provide some academic standard or examination for the college to aim at. But the college ceased to exist after a few years and before anything had been done.

In 1883, however, the Provincial Synod revived the matter, directing that a body be constituted 'to examine candidates in Theology.'[3] But the South African bishops failed to implement the resolution.

The Lambeth Conference of 1897 appointed a committee to investigate the possibilities of establishing an examining body for the whole Anglican Communion. The committee recommended that one of three courses might be adopted:

1. Certificates might be granted by those provinces where there were no universities teaching theology, but it would be better if this were done by a central board whose 'certificates or degrees would command universal respect';

2. Recognised universities might be asked to grant degrees in theology to 'colonists' without requiring them to come into residence in England; or

3. The archbishop of Canterbury might be asked to confer Lambeth degrees—a B.A. for those who passed the standard for ordination and a B.D. to encourage priests to continue with academic work after ordination.[4]

In the meantime a small group of South African clergymen, led by Dean Green, began to agitate for immediate action. Green had been dean of Colenso's cathedral church and the bishop's principal

[1] Bishopscourt Archives; Documents of the Archdeaconry of George; letter dated 11 November 1884.
[2] *Bloemfontein Quarterly Paper*, no. 40 (April 1878), 8.
[3] See *Constitution and Canons of the Church of the Province of South Africa*, 1950, 105.
[4] R. T. Davidson, *The Five Lambeth Conferences*, 1920, 285.

opponent in the long controversy which led to his famous trial and excommunication. Green was, like Colenso, primarily a mathematician, but he had also become something of an expert in canon law and medieval scholastic theology.[1] He set out his views on the training of ordinands in a paper 'On the Importance of the Universities admitting Students in the Colonies to Degrees.' [2] Green's argument was that a degree was not a certificate for a certain quantity of learning, but for a quality, 'soundness in the Faith, godliness of life, and studious habits.' These qualities had, he believed, been demanded by the medieval universities, who conferred their degrees in the name of the Trinity. 'A Degree is . . . a gift from God through His Church.' Green desired that the English universities should confer that gift on students living in hostels in the colonies. But it soon became plain that this scheme would receive very little support and Green began to prepare another paper for the Provincial Synod of 1898.[3]

Green now pressed for the creation of a provincial examining body. The Church, he said, is the proper authority to constitute a university, for the medieval universities derived their right to confer degrees from the Pope. 'The acts of the Board, performed by virtue of its spiritual authority . . . will convey grace: in short the degrees . . . will be the degrees of B.D. and D.D. of the Catholic Church.'

But even Green was willing to admit that besides being spiritual, the board must be academic. He wanted it to be modelled on the Faculty of Divinity at Cambridge, where the doctors formed a closed corporation and were all potential examiners. If the South African board were to be a similar corporation of academically qualified persons, it could maintain standards, and perpetuate itself at the same time, by admitting to membership those who passed its examinations.

Green's quasi-sacramental theology of graduation was never officially adopted by the Province. But nevertheless his influence on the way in which the Provincial Faculty of Divinity was constituted is unmistakable. In 1898, only one year after the Lambeth resolution suggesting the formation of a central board, the South

---

[1] For a full life of Green see A. T. Wirgman, *James Green*, 2 vols, 1909.

[2] See A. T. Wirgman, 'Dean Green' in *S.A. Church Quarterly Review* (a learned but short-lived journal, edited and almost entirely written by Wirgman), October 1906.

[3] Printed in Wirgman, *James Green*, II, 225 ff.

African bishops determined to found one of their own. They had delayed for fourteen years but would now wait no longer. They constituted a Faculty, consisting of themselves (for they were all, of course, in those days Lambeth doctors of divinity) and all other doctors and bachelors of divinity in the Province. They proposed to award diplomas, which they did not specifically call 'degrees,' but they provided a Latin form of graduation ceremony and a hood for each 'distinction.' No specific mention of the qualifying examination for ordinands was made. The chief overt purpose was, rather, to encourage scholarship amongst the clergy.[1]

The new corporation was simply called 'The South African Faculty of Divinity,' and in those days this was neither a proud, rash claim nor a misnomer. The only university in the country had been founded in 1873, but it had no Faculty of Divinity until 1903, ten years after the creation of the Provincial Faculty. But even after that there was no actual university in the country where theology was taught in the English language until fifteen years ago. There was some real justification for calling the board 'The South African Faculty of Divinity'. It modelled its diplomas on the Cambridge degrees, making the licentiate in theology take an examination in two parts, and offering the diploma of associate in divinity as a further 'distinction' corresponding to the Cambridge B.D. Even the shape of the hood was defined as similar to those of the Cambridge equivalent.

It is possible to be immensely thankful that the Province did not formally commit itself to Green's quaint theories. Yet there can be no doubt that the immediate practical results of the establishment of the Faculty were of enormous advantage to the Church. Once the Faculty had been constituted, theological colleges began to appear and they became permanent instead of ephemeral institutions. In 1907 and 1908 the bishops in synod resolved that they would accept the licentiate's certificate of the Faculty as a sufficient academic qualification for ordination and, in spite of the fact that several South African universities now offer degrees in theology, the normal training for ordinands has remained (for better or for worse) a period at a theological college during which time the candidates sit the licentiate's examination of the Provincial Faculty.

[1] *Handbook of the Faculty of Divinity*, Church of the Province of South Africa, 1950, 3.